Lecture Notes in Computer Science 7039

Commenced Publication in 1973
Founding and Former Series Editors:
Gerhard Goos, Juris Hartmanis, and Jan van Leeuwen

Editorial Board

David Hutchison
Lancaster University, UK

Takeo Kanade
Carnegie Mellon University, Pittsburgh, PA, USA

Josef Kittler
University of Surrey, Guildford, UK

Jon M. Kleinberg
Cornell University, Ithaca, NY, USA

Alfred Kobsa
University of California, Irvine, CA, USA

Friedemann Mattern
ETH Zurich, Switzerland

John C. Mitchell
Stanford University, CA, USA

Moni Naor
Weizmann Institute of Science, Rehovot, Israel

Oscar Nierstrasz
University of Bern, Switzerland

C. Pandu Rangan
Indian Institute of Technology, Madras, India

Bernhard Steffen
TU Dortmund University, Germany

Madhu Sudan
Microsoft Research, Cambridge, MA, USA

Demetri Terzopoulos
University of California, Los Angeles, CA, USA

Doug Tygar
University of California, Berkeley, CA, USA

Gerhard Weikum
Max Planck Institute for Informatics, Saarbruecken, Germany

Jan Camenisch   Dogan Kesdogan (Eds.)

Open Problems in Network Security

IFIP WG 11.4 International Workshop, iNetSec 2011
Lucerne, Switzerland, June 9, 2011
Revised Selected Papers

 Springer

Volume Editors

Jan Camenisch
IBM Research - Zurich
Säumerstrasse 4, 8803 Rüschlikon, Switzerland
E-mail: jca@zurich.ibm.com

Dogan Kesdogan
Universität Siegen
Institut für Wirtschaftsinformatik
Hölderlinstr. 3, 57068 Siegen, Germany
E-mail: kesdogan@fb5.uni-siegen.de

ISSN 0302-9743   e-ISSN 1611-3349
ISBN 978-3-642-27584-5   e-ISBN 978-3-642-27585-2
DOI 10.1007/978-3-642-27585-2
Springer Heidelberg Dordrecht London New York

Library of Congress Control Number: 2011944283

CR Subject Classification (1998): K.6.5, K.4, C.2, E.3, D.4.6, H.3.4-5

LNCS Sublibrary: SL 4 – Security and Cryptology

© IFIP International Federation for Information Processing 2012

This work is subject to copyright. All rights are reserved, whether the whole or part of the material is concerned, specifically the rights of translation, reprinting, re-use of illustrations, recitation, broadcasting, reproduction on microfilms or in any other way, and storage in data banks. Duplication of this publication or parts thereof is permitted only under the provisions of the German Copyright Law of September 9, 1965, in its current version, and permission for use must always be obtained from Springer. Violations are liable to prosecution under the German Copyright Law.
The use of general descriptive names, registered names, trademarks, etc. in this publication does not imply, even in the absence of a specific statement, that such names are exempt from the relevant protective laws and regulations and therefore free for general use.

Typesetting: Camera-ready by author, data conversion by Scientific Publishing Services, Chennai, India

Printed on acid-free paper

Springer is part of Springer Science+Business Media (www.springer.com)

Preface

The international workshop iNetSec 2011 – Open Problems in Network Security— is dedicated to open problem and research directions on all aspects related to network security. It is the main workshop of working group WG 11.4 of the IFIP. This year, iNetSec was co-located with IFIP SEC 2011 in Lucerne on June 9 and shared with it the keynote talk by the Kristian Beckman award-winner Ann Cavoukian.

Originally, iNetSec was run in the traditional format where research papers get submitted, peer-reviewed, and then presented at the workshop. Since 2009, the format was changed to discuss open research problems and directions in network security. To enable this open workshop style yet remain focused on particular topics, we called for two page abstracts in which the authors were asked to outline an open research problem or direction. This year, we received 28 short submissions. Each of them was independently reviewed by six Program Committee members with a focus on the relevance and suitability for discussion. After a round of discussion in the Program Committee, 12 papers were selected for presentation at the workshop. For these presentations almost the same time was given to discussions as for presentations. After the workshop, the authors submitted a full paper that also takes the discussion into account. These papers are in the proceedings you are now holding in your hands. We hope that they will serve as a source of inspiration for new research.

We thank the authors of all submissions for enabling the workshop and the presenters and all participants for making it a success with their lively contributions! We also thank the local organizers Carlos Rieder, Colette Hofer-Schürmann, and Fabia Bommes for making our stay in Lucerne such a pleasure.

September 2011

Jan Camenisch
Dogan Kesdogan

iNetSec 2011

Open Research Problems in Network Security

Lucerne University of Applied Sciences and Arts
June 9, 2011
Lucerne, Switzerland

Organized in cooperation with *IFIP WG 11.4*

Executive Committee

Program Chairs

Jan Camenisch	IBM Research – Zurich, Switzerland
Dogan Kesdogan	University of Siegen, Germany

Organizing Chair

Carlos Rieder	Lucerne University of Science & Arts, Switzerland

Program Committee

Endre Bangerter	Bern University of Applied Sciences, Switzerland
Jan Camenisch	IBM Research – Zurich, Switzerland
Hannes Federrath	University of Regensburg, Germany
Simone Fischer-Hübner	Karlstad University, Sweden
Virgil Gligor	Carnegie Mellon University, USA
Thomas Gross	IBM Research – Zurich, Switzerland
Dogan Kesdogan	University of Siegen, Germany
Engin Kirda	Northeastern University, Boston, USA
Albert Levi	Sabanci University, Turkey
Javier Lopez	University of Malaga, Spain
Ulrike Meyer	RWTH Aachen University, Germany
Refik Molva	Eurecom

Local Organizing Committee

Carlos Rieder	Lucerne University of Science and Arts
Colette Hofer-Schürmann	Lucerne University of Science and Arts
Fabia Bommes	Lucerne University of Science and Arts

Table of Contents

IV Policies

V Problems in the Cloud

Evoking Comprehensive Mental Models
of Anonymous Credentials

Erik Wästlund, Julio Angulo, and Simone Fischer-Hübner

Karlstad University,
Universitetsgatan 2, 651 88 Karlstad, Sweden
{erik.wastlund,julio.angulo,simone.fischer-huebner}@kau.se
http://www.kau.se

Abstract. Anonymous credentials are a fundamental technology for preserving end users' privacy by enforcing data minimization for online applications. However, the design of user-friendly interfaces that convey their privacy benefits to users is still a major challenge. Users are still unfamiliar with the new and rather complex concept of anonymous credentials, since no obvious real-world analogies exists that can help them create the correct mental models. In this paper we explore different ways in which suitable mental models of the data minimization property of anonymous credentials can be evoked on end users. To achieve this, we investigate three different approaches in the context of an e-shopping scenario: a *card-based* approach, an *attribute-based* approach and an *adapted card-based* approach. Results show that the adapted card-based approach is a good approach towards evoking the right mental models for anonymous credential applications. However, better design paradigms are still needed to make users understand that attributes can be used to satisfy conditions without revealing the value of the attributes themselves.

Keywords: Credential Selection, Anonymous Credentials, Mental Models, Usability.

1 Introduction

Data minimization is a fundamental privacy principle which requires that applications and services should use only the minimal amount of personal data necessary to carry out an online transaction. A key technology for enforcing the principle of data minimization for online applications are *anonymous credentials* [1], [2], [5]. In contrast to traditional electronic credentials, which require the disclosure of all attributes of the credential to a service provider when performing an online transaction, anonymous credentials let users reveal any possible subset of attributes of the credential, characteristics of these attributes, or prove possession of the credential without revealing the credential itself, thus providing users with the right of anonymity and the protection of their privacy.

Even though Microsoft's U-Prove and IBM's Idemix anonymous credential technologies are currently introduced into commercial and open source systems and products, the design of easily understandable interfaces for introducing these

J. Camenisch and D. Kesdogan (Eds.): iNetSec 2011, LNCS 7039, pp. 1–14, 2012.
© IFIP International Federation for Information Processing 2012

concepts to end users is a major challenge, since end users are not yet familiar with this rather new and complex technology and no obvious real-world analogies exist. Besides, users have grown accustomed to believe that their identity cannot remain anonymous when acting online and have learned from experience or word of mouth that unwanted consequences can come from distributing their information to some services providers on the Internet.

In other words, people do not yet posses the right *mental models* regarding how anonymous credentials work and how anonymous credentials can be used to, for example, protect their personal information.

In order to tackle the challenge of designing interfaces that convey the principle of data minimization with the use of anonymous credentials, we have, within the scope of the EU FP7 project PrimeLife[1] and the Swedish U-PrIM project[2], investigated the way mental models of average users work with regards to anonymous credentials and have tried to evoke their correct mental models with various experiments [10].

In this article, we first provide background information on the concepts of anonymous credentials and mental models and then present previous related work. Then, we describe the experiments that were carried out using three different approaches, and present the analyses and interpretations of the collected data. Finally, we provide conclusions in the last section.

2   Background

In this section we present a description of the concept of anonymous credentials and the definition of mental models.

2.1   Anonymous Credentials

A traditional credential (also called a certificate or attribute certificate) is a set of personal identifiable attributes which is signed by a certifying trust party and is bound to its owner by cryptographic means (e.g., by requiring the owner's secret key to use the credential). With a credential system, users can obtain a credential from the certifying party and demonstrate possession of these credentials at the moment of carrying out online transactions. In terms of privacy, the use of (traditional or anonymous) credentials is better than the direct request to the certifying party, as this prevents the certifying party from profiling the user. When using traditional credentials, all of the attributes contained in the credential are disclosed to the service provider when proving certain properties during online transactions. This contradicts the privacy principle of data minimization and can also lead to unwanted user profiling by the service provider.

---

[1] EU FP7 integrated project PrimeLife (Privacy and Identity Management for Life), http://www.primelife.eu/

[2] U-PrIM (Usable Privacy-enhancing Identity Management for smart applications) is funded by the Swedish Knowledge Foundation, KK-Styftelsen, http://www.kau.se/en/computer-science/research/research-projects/u-prim

Anonymous credentials (also called private certificates) were first introduced by Chaum [5] and later enhanced by Brands [1] and Camenisch & Lysyanskaya [2] and have stronger privacy properties than traditional credentials. Anonymous credentials implement the property of data minimization by allowing users to select a subset of the attributes of the credential or to prove the possession of a credential with specific properties without revealing the credential itself or any other additional information. For instance, a user who has a governmentally issued anonymous passport credential (with attributes that are typically stored in a passport, such as the date of birth) can prove either the fact that she is older than 18 without revealing her actual age, her date of birth or any other attribute of the credential, such as her name or personal identification number. In other words, anonymous credentials allow the selective disclosure of identity information encoded into the credential. However, also information about the certifier is revealed (if the user uses for instance a governmentally issued credential, information about the government of the user (i.e. his nationality) is also revealed as meta-information) - illustrating the disclosure of this type of meta-information to end users poses further HCI challenges.

In addition, the Idemix anonymous credential system has also the property that multiple uses of the same credential cannot be linked to each other. If, for instance, the user later wants to shop another video which is only permitted for adults at the same video online shop, she can use the same anonymous credential as proof that she is over 18 without the video shop being able to recognize that the two proofs are based on the same credential. This means that the two rental transactions cannot be linked to the same person. The main focus of our usability studies, which we present in this paper, has so far been on the comprehension of the selective data disclosure property.

2.2 Mental Models

Mental models are people's perceptions or understandings on how a system works. A mental model provides a deep understanding of people's motivations and thought processes [6], [7], [12]. One of the major obstacles when introducing new technology to the general public is presenting the technology in terms that the average user will comprehend without having to resort to the advice of an expert or complicated instruction manuals. For the users to adapt novel technologies, they have to comprehend their advantages, disadvantages, and the benefits that the technology can bring into their daily lives. The introduction of incremental innovations is often framed in the terms of previously existing systems or objects that users are already familiar with. For example, people can generate a mental picture of how fast, functional, aesthetic, and effective the new system is in comparison with its predecessors. Then, they are able to adjust their already existing mental models accordingly, without great effort. However, when it comes to radical changes or completely new innovations the adaptation of the mental model is not always an easy task. It is therefore that designing interfaces that support the relatively new anonymous credential technology is an excruciating challenge for user interface (UI) designers.

In this work, we explore different user interface approaches based on three different metaphors (*card-based*, *attribute-based* and *adapted card-base* approaches) that we have developed in order to get users to start thinking in the right direction when it comes to anonymous credentials and their private information on the Internet. In other words, our aim is to investigate which of these approaches works better at evoking a comprehensive mental model of anonymous credentials.

3   Related Work

Within the scope of the PRIME[3] project, our usability tests of PRIME prototypes revealed that users often did not trust privacy-enhancing technologies and their data minimization properties, as the possibility to use Internet services anonymously did not fit to their mental model of Internet technology [3], [9]. Camenisch et al. [4] discuss contextual, browser-integrated user interfaces for using anonymous credential systems. In user tests of anonymous credential selection mockups developed within the PRIME project, test subjects were asked to explain what information was actually given to a web site that demanded some proof of age when a passport was used to produce that proof (more precisely, the phrase `Proof of ''age > 18''` [built on ``Swedish Passport``] was used as a menu selection choice in the mockup). The test results showed that the test participants assumed that all data normally visible in the physical item referred to (i.e., a passport) was also disclosed to the web site [8]. Hence, previous HCI studies in the PRIME project showed already that designing user interfaces supporting the comprehension of anonymous credentials and their selective disclosure property is a challenging task. As far as we are aware of, no many other studies have considered the usability of anonymous credentials, neither the way people perceive this relatively new technology.

More than a decade ago, Whitten & Tygar [11] discussed the related problem that the standard model of user interface design is not sufficient to make computer security usable to people who are not already knowledgeable in that area. They conclude that a valid conceptual model of security has to be established and must be quickly and effectively communicated to the user.

4   Methodology

As part of the PrimeLife project, we have conducted a series of experiments based on interactive mockups for an e-shopping scenario that used anonymous credentials technology for proving that the user holds a credit card and another credential (passport or driving license) with the same name. During the experiments we used three different approaches to evoke different mental models of anonymous credentials and observed which of these would best fit the

---

[3] PRIME (Privacy and Identity Management for Europe)
   https://www.prime-project.eu/

representation of an actual anonymous credentials system. The different UIs were then tested at various instances with individuals coming from different age groups, backgrounds, and genders. Many of them were employees or students from diverse disciplines at Karlstad University (KAU) and many others were recruited at various locations, such as Karlstad's train station. The methodologies, test designs, and results from the first two approaches, i.e. the card-based and attribute-base approaches, have been reported in more detailed by Wästlund & Fischer-Hübner [10]. We present an overview of the results of those two previous approaches here. Then, we introduce the third concept of an adapted card-based approach, the description of its interface and the results from testing.

4.1   The Card-Based Approach

The first design concept was based on the idea that people are already acquainted with the way cards work in the non-digital world. A person can usually pay for a product at a store with a credit card and use an identification card to verify their identity, such as their driving license or password. For that reason, a card-based metaphor was used, in which test participants were introduced to the concept of electronic credentials as being images of the ordinary "cards" they are already familiar with. However, in the non-digital cards do not possess the property of data minimization, thus the challenge lied on how to convey the idea of selective disclosure to users through an interface.

A number of mockup iterations were implemented using this metaphor in order to test the different levels of understanding on the concept of anonymous

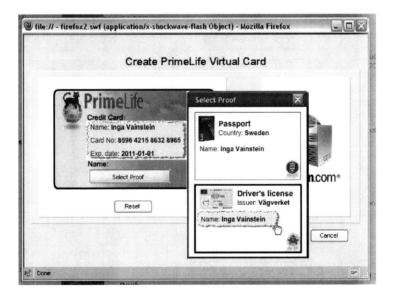

Fig. 1. Cutting out attributes to be revealed as part of a newly created virtual card

credentials. In the initial iterations, the property of data minimization was illustrated with an animation that "cut out" selected attributes from the card and transitioned them into a newly created *virtual card*, which was to be revealed to a service provider (Figure 1). The idea was to make users visually aware of the pieces of information that were being cut out and moved into the new virtual card, making it clearer that only the information on the virtual card was being sent to the service provider. In later iterations the attributes of the card which were not to be disclosed to the service provider were blacked out, leaving only the card attributes to be sent visible to the user (Figure 2).

Fig. 2. Card-based approach blacking out non-disclosed attributes

In total, a number of seventh design iterations were carried out with slight improvements at every iteration cycle and testing the alternatives with five test participants at a time. Results showed that using this approach, 86% of test participants (30 out of 35) believed that the anonymous credentials would work in the same fashion as the commonly used non-digital plastic credentials. In other words, they thought that more information from the source card (passport or driving license) was sent to the service provider than it really was sent. Only 14% participants understood up to a point the principle of data minimization, indicating that using a card-based metaphor is not an ideal approach to show this concept.

4.2   The Attribute-Based Approach

The second design concept was based on what we called the attribute-based approach (Figure 3), in which test participants were told that "attributes" of information were imported from different certifying authorities. Participants could select the authorities that certified certain attributes, and thereby choosing the attributes they would like to reveal to the service provider. After they had selected the attributes they were asked to confirm their decision at a second step, before the information was sent.

Fig. 3. One example of the attribute-based approach

A total of sixth iterations were made using this attribute-based approach with an average of 8.5 participants per iteration. This time only 33% of the test participants (16 out of 48) did not understand the data minimization property and thought that more information than the one needed was disclosed to the service provider. However, 67% understood the selective disclosure principle, showing an improvement over the card-based approach. Curiously enough, with the attribute-based approach, some of the test participants made the error of thinking that their personal identification number and address would be disclosed as well, even though these attributes were not part of the e-shopping scenario.

Moreover, post-test interviews also revealed that, some of the participants who used the attribute-based UI with the instructions to select a verifying authority believed that their data was being sent via the verifier who would then be able to trace all transactions they made. Hence, those participants got the wrong impression that the verifier (e.g., the police or the Swedish road authorities) could trace their online activities. An interesting finding in this approach regarded the use of the Swedish personal number. As this number is widely used in Sweden, users anticipated that this number should be present in the transaction portray in the scenario, despite the fact that it was neither asked for nor shown anywhere in the interface.

4.3   The Adapted Card-Based Approach

Our latest design concept is basically a hybrid version of the two previous approaches. The idea was to keep the notion of cards and card selection, since people already accept and comprehend that metaphor, but at the same time emphasizing the data minimization properties of the application. In order to accomplish this, the third approach was based on the idea of an adapted card-based metaphor, in which users were made aware of the fact that the information in their source cards would be adapted to fit the needs of the current online transaction (Figure 4). The idea was to show only the selected information inside the newly created adapted card, and to convey the notion that only the information in this card was sent to the service provider and nothing else.

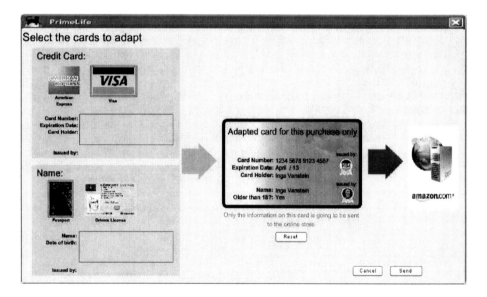

Fig. 4. The adapted card-based approach

Test Design. In order to test this approach, one more interactive mockup was created. The setup for this round of testing was made as consistent as possible to the setup for testing the two previous approaches, using the same e-shopping scenario and the same method for inputting answer to their questions (i.e., participants could freely write their beliefs about what information about them was being sent). This time we tested the users' understanding that a service provider does not need to know the exact value of an attribute in the credential, for example the exact age of the user, but instead the service provider would only need to know if an attribute satisfies a certain condition, for instance, that the user is over 18 years old.

During a test session participants were first asked to read a description of the test, which was written to fit the purposes of this metaphor and to introduce participants to the notion of selective disclosure. The test description read as follows:

> *You are going to test an Adaptable Electronic ID System - a new way of paying on the Internet. This new way is based on the idea that you have installed this security and privacy system in your computer that only you have access to. The system lets you buy online in a secure and privacy-friendly way - no one else than you can use your information.*
>
> *The system allows you to import all types of electronic IDs and use them online, such as your driving license and passport, and other personal information, such as your credit cards. The unique feature of this system is that it adapts your IDs to the current online payment situation and makes sure to send only the information that is necessary for this transaction.*
>
> *During this test, you will pretend that your name is Inga Vainstein and that you use this Adaptable Electronic ID System to be able to shop safely and privately on the Internet. You will buy and download an e-book (audio-book) from Amazon.com which is only available for adults over 18 years old, and you will pay it with your new Adaptable Electronic ID System.*

In order to create a realistic e-shopping experience, participants were then presented with an interactive Flash animation resembling a Firefox browser window showing the Amazon.com website. Participants were asked to carry out the task of buying an e-book using the presented animation, as instructed in the test description. At the moment of paying for the book, the Amazon.com website was dimmed in the background and the credential selection user interface popped-up. Using this interface, shown in Figure 4, participants were asked to select a payment method, either Visa or American Express, and a way to verify their name and the fact that they were over 18 by choosing either their driving license or their passport.

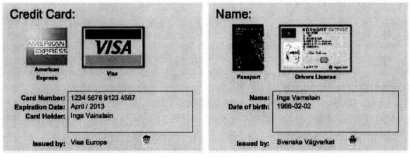

(a) Mouse over the Visa card   (b) Mouse over the driving license

Fig. 5. Examples of mouse-over states when selecting one of the credentials

A `mouse-over` state was added to each of the credentials, so that if participants would drag the mouse over a credential, they could get a preview of the information they were about to select, as shown in Figure 5. Once a credential (or "card") was selected, a green frame was place around it to indicate the selection.

When a credential was selected, the adapted information from that credential was also faded in with a smooth transition into the card in the middle with the title "*Adapted card for this purchase only*" (Figure 6). For example, if the participant chose a driving license a method for identification, the attribute *Name*, the condition *Over than 18?* and the issuer of the credential appeared in the adapted card with the corresponding values.

When participants were done selecting the credentials they press the "Send" button located in the bottom right corner and they were asked question "*What information do you believe you have sent to Amazon.com?*" (and the subheading "*Write what pieces of personal information you think will be sent to Amazon.com when you pressed the 'Send' button*").

Fig. 6. Example of the adapted card containing the selected information

In order to account for the users' understanding that the issuer of the credential is also send to the service provider, we included the multiple choice question "*Additionally, does "Amazon.com know some of the following?*" with the options to answer "*The fact that you hold a Swedish passport*", "*The fact that you hold a driving license*", "*None of the above*", and "*Other*".

Afterwards, participants were also inquired about their beliefs of other third parties being able to get a hold of their information for the transaction ("*When you transferred your information to Amazon.com (by clicking the 'Send' button), do you think anybody else will be able to get a hold of that information?*"). This question was asked since our experience with previous tests of the attribute-based approach showed that some participants believed that their information would also be sent to the issuer in the credential, which is the wrong mental model of information flow (for example, when identifying themselves with their passport credential, the police would also get their information, since the police is the issuer of the credential). In this test, we wanted to confirm that the interface did not mislead participants to create this incorrect mental model.

Finally, participants were asked to fill in some demographic information and other short questions about their experience paying for services or products online.

Data Collection and Results. A total of 29 participants were invited to do the test, 16 males and 13 females from different ages (18 to 57 years old) coming from a different cultural backgrounds (15 Swedish, 5 Germans, 3 Mexicans, 2 Iranians, 1 Italian, 1 Chinese, 1 Japanese, 1 Nepali). Some of them were recruited at KAU, and the majority were recruited outside the University premises. All of them had previous experience paying over the internet.

The tests were carried out with the use of laptop computers and smart tablet computers running the prototyped Flash animation. The data was gathered using a common survey online tool and analyzed in terms of the number of extra attributes that participants mistakenly believed were sent and the concealed attributes that they mistakenly believe were not sent to a service provider during the transaction portrayed in the e-shopping scenario. Also, to examine the participants' understanding on attributes satisfying conditions, we classified the data in two categories: the answers that stated that the service provider only knows the fact that they are over 18 years old, and the answers which mention either the age, date of birth or personal identification number (which in Sweden is an identification for age).

The results showed that 65% of the test participants (19 out of 29) understood the data minimizing properties of the adapted card approach which is approximately the same as in the attribute based approach (66%). However, of the ten remaining test participants that overestimated the amount of data being send, six added only the attribute of "address". Presumably, these participants were thinking that their address was being sent in order to be able receive the product by mail, and misunderstood the scenario in which an e-book was being downloaded into their computer and no postal address was necessary. Assuming that these six participants were thinking in terms of their own experiences when buying products online and having them delivered at home, we can deduce that a total of 86% of the test participants (25 out of 29) understood that not all data from the source was being send, but that only a subset of data was being selected and subsequently sent; thus understanding the property of data minimization.

Regarding the mental model of information flow, only 2 out of 29 participants mentioned that the issuer of the credential (i.e., the police) would be able to get a hold of their information. This is a great improvement from the attribute-based approach, in which many of participants seemed to think that their information would travel via the issuing authority. Besides, we believed that the two participants of this test who responded that the police would be able to get a hold of their information, were actually thinking in terms of the authority the police has to access their information at a certain point in the future, but not that their information was flowing through the police when sending it to the service provider.

With regards to the attributes being selected to satisfy a condition (i.e., proving if the user is over 18 years old), 35% of the participants (10 out of 29) understood that they had proved only the fact that they were over 18, three participants made no reference to age at all, and the remaining sixteen stated that they had revealed their age, birth date, or personal identification number (some as part of revealing the full source credential). This low proportion leaves further challenges for the design of user interfaces that convey the notion that attributes can satisfy conditions without their actual value being sent to service providers.

5   Conclusions

The results of our user studies show that users often lack adequate mental models to protect their privacy online. Our work with a credential selection mechanism for anonymous credentials highlights the difficulties in using metaphors when describing this novel technology. In our first rounds of testing the majority of users believed that anonymous credentials would work in the same fashion as the plastic credentials we compared them to, such as driving licenses or passports. However, in our latest tests we focused on the main difference between the two types of credentials (i.e. that they are adapted) and thus successfully changing the induced mental model of most test participants.

Taken together, the results from the three rounds of testing using the three different approaches clearly show how inducing adequate mental models is a key issue in the successful deployment of the novel technology of anonymous credentials. Our results also show that the adapted card-based approach is a right step towards evoking a comprehensive mental model for anonymous credential applications, and that using a traditional card-based approach (as presented in our first approach) is not recommended since it does not seem to fit the appropriate mental models of this technology. The adapted card-based approach also seems to be very efficient at making users understand that the issuer of a credential is not involved in the flow of the data during an online transaction. Moreover, the results also indicate that better user interface paradigm are needed for making users understand that attributes in a credential can be used to satisfy conditions, and that service providers would not have knowledge of the actual value of the attribute when it is not requested.

As a future suggestion for evoking correct mental models of anonymous credentials we suggest the exploration of a *form filling* approach, based on the idea that users are already accustomed to fill forms when carrying out online transactions. In this approach users would be presented with a common Internet form with its boxes already filled with values from a credential and some visual indication showing that these values are certified by the issuer of the credential. The data minimization property in this case can be illustrated by only filling the textboxes required by the service provider and indicating to the user that additional data is not needed for a particular transaction.

Moreover, the increased use of smart mobile devices brings the challenge of creating user-friendly interfaces that allow users to select anonymous credentials and are able to convey the property of data minimization.

All in all, it can be noted that, when it comes to privacy, the effects of incorrect mental models leads to difficulties in using a given application or not being able to take adequate steps in order to protect one's information. Even though our attempt to evoke the correct mental models of anonymous credentials has shown positive results throughout the different approaches, there is still room for improvement and future research in this area and in the usability of credential selection in general.

Acknowledgments. Parts of the research leading to these results have received funding from the Swedish Knowledge Foundation (KK-stiftelsen) for the U-PrIM project and from the EU 7th Framework programme (FP7/2007-2013) for the project PrimeLife. The information in this document is provided "as is", and no guarantee or warranty is given that the information is fit for any particular purpose. The PrimeLife consortium members shall have no liability for damages of any kind including without limitation direct, special, indirect, or consequential damages that may result from the use of these materials subject to any liability which is mandatory due to applicable law.

References

1. Brands, S.: Rethinking Public Key Infrastructure and Digital certificates - Building in Privacy. Ph.D. thesis, Eindhoven. Institute of Technology (1999)
2. Camenisch, J., Lysyanskaya, A.: An Efficient System for Non-Transferable Anonymous Credentials with Optional Anonymity Revocation. In: Pfitzmann, B. (ed.) EUROCRYPT 2001. LNCS, vol. 2045, pp. 93–118. Springer, Heidelberg (2001)
3. Camenisch, J., Crane, S., Fischer-Hübner, S., Leenes, R., Pearson, S., Pettersson, J.S., Sommer, D., Andersson, C.: Trust in PRIME. In: Proceedings of Fifth IEEE International Symposium on Signal Processing and Information Technology, pp. 552–559 (December 2005)
4. Camenisch, J., Shelat, A., Sommer, D., Zimmermann, R.: Securing user inputs for the web. In: Proceedings of the Second ACM Workshop on Digital Identity Management, DIM 2006, pp. 33–44. ACM, New York (2006)
5. Chaum, D.: Security without identification: Transaction systems to make big brother obsolete. Communications of the ACM 28(10), 1030–1044 (1985)
6. Johnson-Laird, P.N.: Mental models: towards a cognitive science of language, inference, and consciousness. Harvard University Press, Cambridge (1983)
7. Jonassen, D.H.: Operationalizing mental models: strategies for assessing mental models to support meaningful learning and design-supportive learning environments. In: The First International Conference on Computer Support for Collaborative Learning, CSCL 1995, pp. 182–186. L. Erlbaum Associates Inc., Hillsdale (1995)
8. Pettersson, J.S.: HCI Guidelines. PRIME deliverable D6.1.f (February 2008)
9. Pettersson, J.S., Fischer-Hübner, S., Danielsson, N., Nilsson, J., Bergmann, M., Clauss, S., Kriegelstein, T., Krasemann, H.: Making PRIME usable. In: Proceedings of the 2005 Symposium on Usable Privacy and Security, SOUPS 2005, pp. 53–64. ACM, New York (2005)

10. Wästlund, E., Fischer-Hübner, S.: The Users' Mental Models' Effect on their Comprehension of Anonymous Credentials. In: Privacy and Identity Management for Life, pp. 229–240. Springer, Heidelberg (2011)
11. Whitten, A., Tygar, J.D.: Why Johnny Can't Encrypt: A Usability Evaluation of PGP 5.0. In: Proceedings of the 8th USENIX Security Symposium (1999)
12. Young, I.: Mental Models: Aligning Design Strategy with Human Behavior. Rosenfeld media (2008)

Towards Usable Interfaces for Proof Based Access Rights on Mobile Devices

Marcel Heupel and Dogan Kesdogan

Chair for IT Security Management
University of Siegen, Germany
heupel@wiwi.uni-siegen.de, kesdogan@uni-siegen.de

Abstract. Access rights management is in the middle of many collaboration forms such as group formation or sharing of information in different kinds of scenarios. There are some strong mechanisms to achieve this, like anonymous credential systems. However in general their usage is not very intuitive for lay users. In this paper we show the potential of using proof-based credential systems like Idemix to enhance the usability of privacy-respecting social interaction in different collaborative settings. For instance transparently performing authorization without any user intervention at the level of the user interface becomes possible. In order to improve the usability, we complement this by introducing a mental model for intuitive management of digital identities. The approach should also empower users to define their own access restrictions when sharing data, by building custom proof specifications on the fly. We show this exemplary with a developed prototype application for supporting collaborative scenarios on a mobile device. We also present first evaluation results of an early prototype and address current as well as future work.

1   Introduction

For quite some time, a major trend in our information society is the increasing use and disclosure of personal information in private and in business life. The recent massive propagation of mobile devices and mobile applications gains strength from leveraging efficient, secure and privacy-respecting interaction as well as communication patterns between individuals and communities that are seamlessly supported with mobile devices in term of enjoyable user experience [4].

On the one hand security and privacy are one of the most-cited criticism for pervasive and ubiquitous computing [15]. On the other hand usability is a prerequisite for security and privacy. Therefore, it is part of a major effort to balance and improve security and privacy design of mobile applications by considering usability aspects especially due to the limitations and capabilities of mobile devices (e.g. screen size, limited memory, computation capabilities and ease of localization). One of the most disregarded and critical topics of computer security has been and still is, the understanding of the interplay between usability and security [9]. In social and collaborative interaction settings, advantages such as enhancing social contacts, personalizing services and products

J. Camenisch and D. Kesdogan (Eds.): iNetSec 2011, LNCS 7039, pp. 15–27, 2012.
© IFIP International Federation for Information Processing 2012

compromise with notable security and privacy risks arising from the user's loss of control over their personal data and digital footprints [10]. From the usability perspective, large amounts of scattered personal data lead to information overload, disorientation and loss of efficiency. This often results in not using security options offered by the application.

One of the means for enhancing privacy in communication to individuals and services is to allow for the usage of partial identities or digital faces, i.e. user data selected to be disclosed for a particular purpose and context. Privacy-enhancing technical systems and applications supporting collaborative users activities have to allow for user-controlled identity management (IdM). Furthermore, such an IdM system has to be deployable on mobile platforms by providing good performance in terms of response time as a quality of service factor for usability [20] and also as part of the security protection goal availability [5]. Poor response times lead to end-user frustration and negatively affect the usage of the applications especially when no adequate help or feedback is provided. With respect to the different capabilities and restrictions of modern mobile devices (e.g. smartphones and tablet PCs), addressing security and usability aspects becomes crucial. Experts from various research communities believe that there are inherent trade-offs between security and usability to be considered [6,9,21]. These general requirements are based on the objectives of the EU FP7 project di.me [10].

One of the most powerful and future promising IdM systems is IBM's "Identity Mixer" (Idemix) [7], which is also able to run on smart cards [2]. Due to the strong cryptographic algorithms, proving of powerful and complex statements (like e.g. inequality of attributes) needs quite some computation time [8,23] and thereby influences the performance of the whole application. This is especially true if only devices with relatively weak computation power, like mobile phones, are used. However, since the newest generation of smartphones and tablets come with really strong processors a new evaluation of the capability of those devices seems reasonable.

In a user controlled IdM the user needs to have the capability to define the access rights by himself. Therefore a good and usable interface is essential. Lab tests with some early prototypes showed, that many users had problems with defining complex proof based access rights. Therefore we aim to implement and evaluate a mental model for the representation of partial identities in the user interface (UI), which is strong oriented on real world observation, where the identity of the user stays the same and only the view of participating third parties can vary.

In this paper, we present our current work to enhance the usability of end-user controlled access rights management in privacy-respecting mobile collaborative settings.

The reminder of this paper is organized as follows. An overview on the state-of-the-art is given in Section 2. In section 3 we present the derived requirements primarily based on Di.Me. Next, section 4 presents our approach. Finally, we conclude with a presentation and discussion of our evaluation results in Section 5 and present our conclusions and outline ongoing and future work in Section 6.

2   State of the Art

Access control means in general controlling access to resources, which are e.g. made available through applications. It entails making a decision on whether a user is allowed to access a given resource or not. This is mostly done by many techniques like comparing the resources access attributes with the users granted authorities. For access control, the authentication of the *who* is the process of verifying a principals [1] identity whereas the authorization is the process of granting authorities to an authenticated user so that this user is allowed to access particular resources. Therefore, the authorization process is mostly be performed after the authentication process. Often, IdMs are responsible for authentication. There is a lot of work about Idm an access control in the literature. A good overview of the field of user centric identity management is given by Jøsang and Pope [16] and also by El Maliki and Seigneur [12].

With respect to the different capabilities and restrictions of modern mobile devices (e.g. smart-phones and tablet PCs), addressing authentication, authorization and usability aspects becomes crucial. Often, the complexity of authentication and authorization is reflected in UI which is critical for mobile applications deployed on mobile devices with limitations in the screen space. A contribution from the usability field to enhance authentication is e.g. the usage of graphical passwords. An example is the usage of pass-faces for graphical authentication in Android smart-phones to unlock the main screen. However also those approaches have been proven to be not secure enough e.g. due to the smudge traces that can emerge on the screen surface. A recent publication showed that is really easy to guess the right pattern and break such authentication system [1]. Biometrics also allows for enhancing authentication but are still "classified as unreliable because human beings are, by their very nature, variable" [9,17]. Related to authorization, most systems need the interaction of the end-users at least in form of confirmations. The challenges increase if (lay) users are asked to set access rights for others, delegate rights, or manage their own security and privacy preferences. In the context of this work, the EU Project PICOS (Privacy and Identity Management for Community Services) represents a good and current example. The *2010 First Community Prototype Lab and Field Test Report D7.2a* [19] cites that users had problems to use the PICOS privacy manager on mobile devices (Nokia MusicExpress 5800). Notifications and (automatic) advisory might lead to actions which the user finds intrusive or annoying in some cases (such as in the well-known case of Windows pop-ups or MSWord's paper-clip). Especially in collaborative applications as socio-technical systems, this will affect the psychological acceptance of the application which leads to not using security and privacy mechanisms. This mostly results in expensive change requirements affecting the technical realization of mobile applications [9,18]. Indeed, people involvement varies and the usage can range from occasional to frequent according to a given setting and circumstances.

---

[1]   A principal can be a user, a device, or a system, but most typically it means a user.

For both, authentication and authorization, cryptography is an established used mechanism for increasing confidentiality and integrity of exchanged data. However, a total security or privacy provision is an illusion [15] because current approaches are not able to avoid at least threats and attacks e.g. emerging from loosing devices or based on physical access to them [11]. Approaches mostly only focus on hindering such attacks or making them difficult.Trade-os between security and other (non-)functional requirements such as usability and cognitive mental models supporting interaction design are well-described in tremendous lot of classical literature in the corresponding research communities, e.g. Computer-Supported Collaborative Work (CSCW), Human-Computer Interaction (HCI), psychological, and sociological sciences etc. Nevertheless, the current state of the art leaves room for considerable improvement how such systems can support an usable and secure user experience. Security and usability research for developing usable (psychologically acceptable) security mechanisms and mental models is a young research field which depends on the context in which those mechanisms have to be used [9]. Researchers especially from the CSCW and HCI research fields generally agree on that security and privacy issues arise due to the way systems are designed, implemented, and deployed for a specific usage scenario [9, 6, 21]. Because of this and many facts cited above, we argue that security and privacy design by considering usability is specific to the project context. Thus we analyze user-controlled access rights management related requirements in this paper based on concrete Di.Me requirements by considering security and usability along with performance in our initial design and architecture. Furthermore, many related work is focusing on improving collaborative interaction related to access rights in general. For instance, the recently opened social networking platform Google plus [13] proposed a similar approach in some points. They also emphasized to focus on real world behaviors and introduced an promising approach with their circles concept, which is oriented on the real world circle of friends. However, the room for improvements still needs further work as we intend to reach with the work presented in this paper.

3   Requirements

Our approach is based on the usage of the proof-based anonymous credential system Idemix. The gathered requirements related to usability result from using Idemix for our first prototype of a mobile application for Android devices to support complex mobile collaborative scenarios. Further requirements were derived from the scenario are based on our work at the EU FP7 project digital.me. In contrast to related work, we used the latest reference implementation of the Idemix specification released on June 2011 and provided first performance evaluation for non-atomic Idemix operations.

3.1   Requirements Derived from the Scenario

In our scenario, Alice is attending on a business conference. Therefore she activates her business profile on her mobile device, selects some of the attributes she likes to reveal (like her last name, or her occupation) and broadcasts them. Other conference participants can now find her by browsing broadcasted contact information and can send her a contact request. Alice also adds some additional information about selected ongoing projects. This information can only be obtained by invitees, who are also sharing their profile and are working as engineer in the automotive sector. In our use case, Bob, another participant of the conference, is browsing the profile information. When he comes across Alices' profile, he likes to read the additional project papers. By requesting the information, Bobs device receives a challenge, stating that he has to prove that he fulfills certain conditions (e.g. that he is working as an engineer in the automotive sector). This is automatically carried out by the devices in the background. After Alice is convinced that Bob is actually working as an engineer and grants him access to the requested documents. The whole protocol is automatically carried out by the devices in the background without disturbing Alice. She can review at a later time, who requested her documents. If she likes, she could activate a notification about requests for her information and also manually grant or prohibit access. Figure 2 illustrates the main scenario as an interaction diagram.

Publishing Data with Individual Access Rights. The attendees of the conference should be enabled to create and publish individual profiles and publish them on the conference platform. Other attendees can log in to the conference server and browse the list of profiles. Because there are different kinds of profile attributes, like e.g. affiliation, interests, real name, and the users probably do not want to publish all of them to everyone. The users might want to publish selected attributes, like for example project papers or the real name only to selected individuals. This finer access rights are even more important for dynamic attributes like location, current activity or reachability.

Creation of Partial Identities. In order to publish different sets of information, maybe by also using different pseudonyms, we have the need for multiple partial identities. Together with the definition of fine grained access rights, this also gives the possibility to define multiple values for profile attributes. This would be very useful concerning the availability or reachability, because when in a meeting, the user might still want to be available for members of his family in case of emergency, while being not available for everyone else.

From the described scenario we could derive the following important requirements:

R1 The user can use partial identities
R2 The user can browse data published by others
R3 Fine grained access rights for published data can be defined
R4 Capability to prove attribute values (Idemix + Certificate Authority (CA))

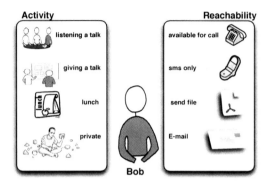

Fig. 1. Reachability management

3.2   Non-functional Requirements

Based on our experiences from the early evaluation of our first prototype and derived from requirements from the di.me project we defined several major non-functional requirements which will be explained in the following.

Minimization of User Interaction. The main goal is to balance and also improve the security and privacy in our scenario with the usability of the prototype. Therefor an important step, especially on mobile devices with limited screen size and interaction capabilities, is the minimization of user interaction in general. Besides this main non-functional requirement, we have further functional requirements derived from the scenario described above.

New Concept for Partial Identities. A central point of our approach should be to make the UI as intuitive as possible. Therefore we are trying to implement a new mental model for (partial) digital identities, which is strongly oriented on the real world observations. The point we are addressing in our approach is the fact, that it is not intuitive for human beings, to have multiple identities as it is common practice in the digital world. Most people definitely act different when they are interacting with different people, but this happens almost unconscious. People will not actively switch identities like embodying a different person, they will stay the same person. What we try to implement in our approach, is a new concept, where we have no names or avatars for digital faces, profiles, identities etc. in the UI. Instead the different partial identities of the user will be represented as a picture of the contacts this identity is used for. The identity of the user stays the same, only the view of others can vary. The mental model for the UI will visually represent the faces with pictures of the people this face is used to interact with.

Context Sensitivity. An important added value due to the use of modern smart-phones, is the availability of additional sensor data. This opens new

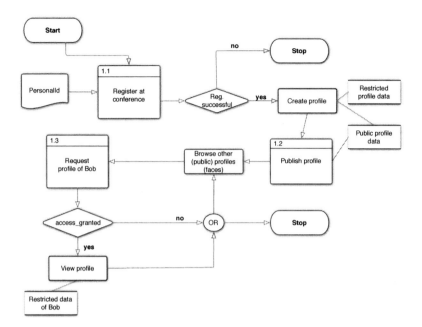

Fig. 2. Interaction flow of the scenario

possibilities for access and reachability management. The system can e.g. automatically mute the phone when attending a talk, or give access to information depending on the proximity to the requesting person.

NFR1 Minimization of user interaction
NFR2 Intuitive representation of partial identities
NFR3 Context sensitive access rights

4 Approach

To verify our prototype and evaluate the UI concepts in a running application we extended the Android-based prototype used in previous lab trials as well as the shared (collaborative) conference server. We provided various user interfaces (UIs) for creating digital faces and credentials as well as their attributes, formulating proofs, selecting attributes to be disclosed in a given context and certifying them with the help of an Idemix CA. Figure 7 illustrates the implemented architecture. Since the first prototype used XML-RPC, the mobile client application is now able to perform the main protocols of Idemix (e.g. *Get Credential* or *Show Proof*) also via XMPP. This Section should give a short overview about the implementation details and also present the developed interfaces.

4.1 Implementation of the Scenario (R2, R4)

We provided various user interfaces (UIs) for creating digital faces and credentials as well as their attributes, formulating proofs, selecting attributes to be
disclosed in a given context and certifying them with the help of an Idemix CA.
In contrary to our first prototype, which purpose was more to test the feasibility
and performance of Idemix on a modern smartphone [14], we did not integrate
an additional Tor client in our approach. This significantly increased the overall
response times and is only a small trade-off concerning privacy. Since we are
using a XMPP server for communication, the IP addresses are not that easily
traceable and moreover our scenario takes place in a more or less closed environment, the conference. Most people will be in the same network anyway. However,
if users still like to hide their IPs to the XMPP server, they can still easily install a separate Tor client like Orbot [22] on their smartphone and obfuscate the
network traffic. In order to publish data we build a server, where people can
upload their profiles and also request a list of profiles previously published by
other users.

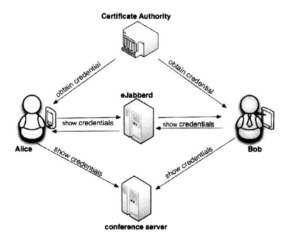

Fig. 3. Architecture of the implemented scenario

Automated Proof Generation in the Background (NFR1). Besides the
possibility to create customized proof statements, our approach also supports
automatic proof generation in the background, without the need for user interaction. Like stated in the scenario, users have the option to publish information
or documents with custom restrictions. When a user is trying to access that
restricted data, a challenge is sent by the data provider to the user, that certain
predicates need to be proven in order to gain access to the data. For instance
the user can be asked to prove that he is working in the automotive industry. If
the necessary credential is available, a proof containing the required predicate,
is computed automatically in the background and sent back to data provider.

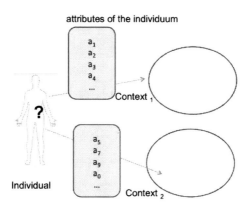

Fig. 4. Identity management becomes context management

4.2   The Interface (NFR1)

In order to ease the interaction by on the one hand make it very intuitive and on the other hand minimize the entering of data. Once the user has registered for the conference and received the initial credential from the conference CA, an initial root profile is created automatically. Profiles are called *digital faces* or just *faces* in our context. The default digital face contains the attributes that have been certified in the registration process. If the user wished to create a new digital face, he/she can use this default face as a starting point and add or remove attributes.

4.3   Context Dependent Identity Management (R1, NFR2, NFR3)

During the creation of a digital face it is possible to define the *context variables*, when this face is to be used. The context is defined mainly by the people the user is interacting with, but can be further extended by also taking the current activity or location into account. As an example, if Alice creates a face with her name, affiliation, and current activity and decides to use this in the context of *work*, she would set that this face is automatically used when interacting with persons from the group *colleagues*. Now she could also define exceptions, in which another face (e.g. *private*) is used, for example by setting an individual rule for her colleague Bob, or by making it also dependent on her current location (e.g. only show her phone number while in the office). Figure 4 shows an abstract illustration of the concept. for each different context, a different subset of all attributes is disclosed.

Definition of Fine-grained Acces Rights with Intuitive User Interfaces (R3). We build a UI that eases the complex process of proof generation with Idemix, even for lay users. In addition to the context dependent disclosure of digital faces, the user can define individual conditions that another person has

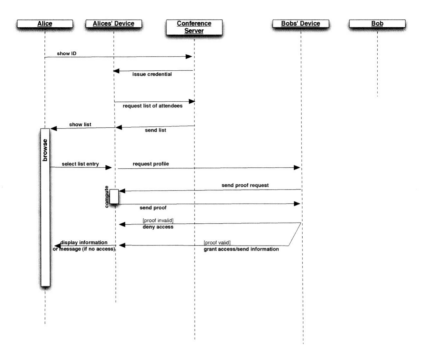

Fig. 5. Sequence diagram for accessing restricted information

to fulfill in order to access selected information of files. To to this, the user just clicks on the attribute of interest and a dialog will show up, where a statement like *affiliation = xyz*, or *age >30* can be defined with a few clicks, similar to the a building block concept.

5 Experiences and Discussion

According to our first experiences based on empirical evaluations of our prototype, end-users are able to use our approach. In the following, we describe how we carried out first lab testes and observed the users by the usage of our prototype.

To organize the development and evaluation process of the prototype, we followed the AFFINE methodology [3], which is an agile framework to enforce the consideration of non-functional requirements like e.g. usability and security. The lab tests were carried out periodically considering the provided feedback in each test iteration. For this, we followed as mentioned before an agile framework for integrating non-functional requirements earlier in the development process while considering end-users' as well as developers needs. Since the adopted AFFINE framework described in [3] is Scrum based, we provided continuously running prototypes granting so fast feedback loops. We split up the evaluation of the new

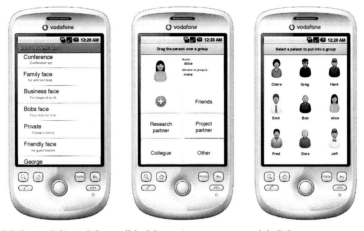

(a) List of digital faces (b) Managing groups (c) Select a person
                              of contacts

Fig. 6. Selected GUI masks of the prototype

user interface in two phases. In the first phase, we have conducted functional unit tests. For this, we extended the provided unit tests in the original Java Idemix implementation to check new functionalities related to R4. These functional tests concentrated on validating the intended interaction possibilities.

In the second phase, we evaluated the developed UIs of our system in different lab tests carrying out different tasks within the implemented "Conference Scenario". Different members from various departments in our university were invited to use the prototype in a simulated conference situation. The persons who contributed in our lab tests had different background in using collaborative systems and social software and had no knowledge about proof-based credential systems. Thus we provided an introduction to the essentials of Idemix from the usage perspective as we described it above in the corresponding Section. We observed that the positive resonance with respect to Idemix functionality generated some kind of curiosity which motivated the testers. Latter was very interested in knowing how they can generate attributes especially those one with vague assessments (e.g. "I m older than 18" etc.). However, this was a first indicator that the performance of the developed system has to fit the worst cases of a real usage scenario. The main issue thereby is that Idemix bases in its computation on data represented in the XML format which is expensive in terms of resources especially on mobile devices.

End-users enjoyed the transparent access rights management that was carried out in the background in general. However, many users wished to be able to view the access protocol and asked for new UIs in order to view detailed logs at a later time. Protocoling access at the level of the mobile device will surely represent a new performance challenge over the time.

The visualization of the digital faces by representatives of the persons that face is shown found good acceptance in the group of testers. However, some questions arose about how to decide which of the persons in a group should be the representative, or if a merged picture would be better. Some users also brought up the suggestion, to also include symbolic graphics chosen by the user, which can also be associated to a specific context. This could be especially useful when no pictures are available of the person or the group.

6   Conclusion and Future Work

With our approach we presented a way to represent a very strong and complex concept for fine grained access control to personal information with the anonymous credential system Idemix and an unconventional mental model for the representation of partial identities supported by context-dependent identity management. With the extended prototype we were able to perform first usability and performance tests which gave us promising results. We built and evaluated various prototypes for checking the feasibility of our approach. First evaluations showed this feasibility and beyond good initial acceptance we got valuable feedback for future improvements. Currently we are fine-tuning the prototype as a preparation for widespread user tests in order to get valuable data about user acceptance and behavior pattern when dealing with partial identities. It will be also targeted to look deeper into the behavior patterns of users dealing with partial identities and to evaluate them.

References

1. Aviv, A.J., Gibson, K., Mossop, E., Blaze, M., Smith, J.M.: Smudge attacks on smartphone touch screens (2010)
2. Bichsel, P., Camenisch, J., Gross, T., Shoup, V.: Anonymous credentials on a standard java card. In: CCS 2009: Proceedings of the the 16th ACM Conference on Computer and Communications Security, pp. 600–610. ACM, New York (2009)
3. Bourimi, M., Barth, T., Haake, J.M., Ueberschär, B., Kesdogan, D.: Affine for enforcing earlier consideration of nfrs and human factors when building sociotechnical systems following agile methodologies. In: Proceedings of the 3rd Human-Centered Software Engineering Conference, Reykjavik, Iceland (2010)
4. Bourimi, M., Haake, J.M., Heupel, M., Ueberschär, B., Barth, T., Kesdogan, D.: Enhancing privacy in mobile collaborative applications by enabling end-user tailoring of the distributed architecture. International Journal for Infonomics (IJI) 3(4), 563–572 (2011)
5. Bourimi, M., Ossowski, J., Abou-Tair, Berlik, S., Abu-Saymeh, D.: Towards Usable Client-Centric Privacy Advisory for Mobile Collaborative Applications Based on BDDs, pp. 1–6 (February 2011)
6. Boyle, M., Neustaedter, C., Greenberg, S.: Privacy factors in video-based media spaces. In: Harrision, S. (ed.) n Media Space: 20+ Years of Mediated Life, pp. 99–124. Springer, Heidelberg (2008)
7. Camenisch, J., Lysyanskaya, A.: An efficient system for non-transferable anonymous credentials with optional anonymity revocation (2001)

8. Camenisch, J., Van Herreweghen, E.: Design and implementation of the idemix anonymous credential system. In: CCS 2002: Proceedings the 9th ACM Conference on Computer and Communications Security, pp. 21–30. ACM, New York (2002)
9. Cranor, L., Garfinkel, S.: Security and Usability. O'Reilly Media, Inc. (2005)
10. T. di.me project. di.me - integrated digital.me userware (2011)
11. Dwivedi, H., Clark, C., Thiel, D.: Mobile Application Security. The McGraw-Hill Companies (2010)
12. El Maliki, T., Seigneur, J.-M.: A survey of user-centric identity management technologies. In: The International Conference on Emerging Security Information, Systems, and Technologies, SecureWare 2007, pp. 12–17 (October 2007)
13. Google Inc. The google+ project
14. Heupel, M.: Porting and evaluating the performance of idemix and tor anonymity on modern smartphones. Master's thesis, University of Siegen (December 2010)
15. Hong, J.I., Landay, J.A.: An architecture for privacy-sensitive ubiquitous computing. In: MobiSys 2004: Proceedings of the 2nd International Conference on Mobile Systems, Applications, and Services, pp. 177–189. ACM, New York (2004)
16. Jøsang, A., Pope, S.: User centric identity management. In: Proceedings of AusCERT (2005)
17. Kryszczuk, K., Drygajlo, A.: Credence estimation and error prediction in biometric identity verification. Signal Process. 88(4), 916–925 (2008)
18. Lee, V., Schneider, H., Schell, R.: Mobile Applications: Architecture, Design, and Development. Prentice Hall PTR, Upper Saddle River (2007)
19. PICOS TEAM. PICOS Public Deliverables Site (January 2010),
    http://picos-project.eu/Public-Deliverables.29.0.html
20. Shneiderman, B., Plaisant, C.: Designing the User Interface: Strategies for Effective Human-Computer Interaction, 4th edn. Pearson Addison Wesley (2005)
21. Shneiderman, B., Plaisant, C., Cohen, M., Jacobs, S.: Designing the User Interface: Strategies for Effective Human-Computer Interaction, 5th edn. Shneiderman (March 2009)
22. The Tor Project. Tor on android (2010),
    http://www.torproject.org/docs/android
23. Verslype, K., Lapon, J., Verhaeghe, P., Naessens, V., De Decker, B.: Petanon: A privacy-preserving e-petition system based on idemix. Report CW522 (October 2008)

Commercial Home Assistance (eHealth) Services

Milica Milutinovic[1], Koen Decroix[2], Vincent Naessens[2], and Bart De Decker[1]

[1] K.U.Leuven, Dept. of Computer Science, DistriNet/SecAnon
firstname.lastname@cs.kuleuven.be
http://www.cs.kuleuven.be/~distrinet/
[2] Katholieke Hogeschool Sint-Lieven
firstname.lastname@kahosl.be
http://www.msec.be/

Abstract. In this paper, we describe the software architecture of a commercially run home assistance system that allows patients or elderly people to stay longer at home. Since such systems often have to handle sensitive medical information, the protection of the privacy is a major concern. Also, legislation often restricts access to health information to qualified persons (i.e. medical personnel), who are not always available in a commercial company.

The home assistance system can offer several services, going from scheduling necessary tasks and following up their execution, to monitoring the patient's health status and responding promptly to requests for help or to emergency situations, and all this without the need to maintain personal medical data or identifying information in the home assistance center.

This paper focusses on how the commercial home assistance center will keep track of the anonymized patients' networks. A network consists of all the caregivers of a patient; each member of the network has been assigned a role, which is used in course-grained authorization decisions. The protocols involve anonymous credentials for the caregivers and smartcards for patients.

Keywords: eHealth, privacy, caregiver, commercial.

1 Introduction

The average life expectancy in the Western world has risen well above 80 years. Also, the limited birth rate has resulted in a greying population and caused the population pyramid to flip upside down or at least to become more cube-like. The progress of medicine has made many diseases and disorders curable or at least less life-threatening. However, the downside of this evolution is that the government's social security budget needs to expand year after year and may grow faster than the country's economic growth. One way to cut costs is to have elderly people stay at their homes much longer instead of moving them to nursing homes and dismiss patients sooner from hospitals. However, these elderly people or patients often need extra care or have to be followed-up from time to time or monitored continuously. Luckily, technology can fulfill these needs.

J. Camenisch and D. Kesdogan (Eds.): iNetSec 2011, LNCS 7039, pp. 28–42, 2012.
© IFIP International Federation for Information Processing 2012

There are many initiatives for designing and building such advanced home assistance centers. Often, hospitals are involved since they have skilled employees who are qualified to handle medical data and to make the correct assessments. However, hospitals are not the best players to run these home assistance centers. They often lack the technicians who are necessary to install and maintain the necessary equipment on a large scale. Moreover, these assistance centers should also offer support for non-medical services such as catering, cleaning, shopping, etc. These services are already provided by specialized organizations or companies. Hence, it is very likely that in the near future commercial businesses will start to operate home assistance centers. There is one important impediment for a commercial deployment, however. Many countries have legislations that limit the access to medical data to qualified personnel (e.g. doctors, paramedics, etc.). That means that if the home assistance centers (HACs) have to process medical data, they also have to employ medical personnel. Also, home assistance systems are by definition distributed systems (part of the system is deployed at the patient's home and part at the center) with many access points, which makes it much harder to restrict access to sensitive (medical or health) data. Therefore, the system should preferably be designed in such a way that HACs never see or process such data.

Protecting the privacy of the elderly person or patient is of utmost importance. Even when the patient's medical data is properly protected, information about the patient's health could be indirectly deduced if one knows which specialist is treating the patient (e.g. when the doctor in attendance is an oncologist, one can easily deduce that the patient suffers from cancer). Therefore, not only the medical data needs to be protected, but also the patient's social network should remain hidden as much as possible. We have seen in the past many cases of accidental or deliberate leakage of privacy sensitive information; often because of the loss or theft of storage media or laptops. Hence, the system should avoid to store as much as possible identifying information about patients, doctors, etc. On the other hand, in case of an alert or emergency situation, the appropriate caregiver needs to be notified as soon as possible.

In this paper we propose a novel system architecture aiming to fulfil the requirements mentioned above. We give an in-depth overview of the system and evaluate functional requirements. We also focus on organizing the network of patient's caregivers. The protocols that lead to improved privacy compared to existing systems are discussed in detail.

The rest of this paper is organized as follows. Sect. 2 describes the architecture of the system, the functional requirements and the patient's social network. In Sect. 3 the security and privacy requirements are listed and the attacker model is discussed. Sect. 4 gives an overview of the protocols used by the system to protect the patients' privacy. Sect. 5 evaluates the design and Sect. 6 gives an overview of related work. Concluding remarks and future work are given in Sect. 7.

2   Functional Description of the System

The home assistance system offers different services which patients can subscribe to. For a system providing pervasive care, services offered to the patient should include:

- **Monitoring the health status** of a patient. Depending on the patient's requirements, a network of different sensors can be deployed in his household. It has a task of monitoring different health parameters of the patient, such as blood pressure, heartbeat rate or pulse oximetry, detecting falls, or monitoring environmental parameters, such as temperature or humidity. In addition, each patient should have a hand-held control unit that would allow him to indicate emergencies, request for help/advice or cancel an alarm. The device can further be equipped with a speaker and a microphone in order to allow for a conversation between the patient and a caregiver and to provide the patient with an automatic reminder or advice.
- **Scheduling and following up on tasks** that need to be performed by the patient's caregivers. Those include both daily tasks, such as catering, cleaning or scheduled visits, but also help in emergency situations. Tasks that are assigned are dynamic and patients or their guardians can always enter new tasks, remove or modify the existing ones. For every task, minimal skills may be required (e.g. medical expertise), a time frame within which the task should be performed may be defined, and a set of preferences regarding caregivers may be suggested. The tasks are assigned via the home assistance center (HAC) that makes a schedule according to the caregivers' availability, skills and preferences. It also supports last-minute changes and immediate substitutes for caregivers not able to perform an assigned task in a timely manner.

  As explained in the introduction, this service is often performed by the patient's close relatives. However, since the number of single persons are growing, chances are that no family members are available to coordinate this service.
- **Choice of services** should be provided to the patients by the HAC. All organizations may publish their services through the system, so that patients can anonymously browse through the database in order to choose appropriate service providers. The payment for the services can be made directly to the organizations or through the home assistance system which would subsequently charge the patient.
- **Remote access to patient's health information** is a service provided to the caregivers. Authorized caregivers should be able to access the sensor readings remotely in order to assess them. Patient's policies would govern the access control for this service.
- **Privacy-protected social networks** are meant to organize self-help groups for the patients. They would allow exchange of information between patients with similar illnesses, but also medical personnel specialized in the particular field. This service would help the patients reducing their solitude

or providing information relevant to them. All users should be able to stay anaonymous, while strict access control needs to be imposed in order to make sure that only authorized individuals can communicate with their peers.

It is clear that the patient's caregivers are not only individuals, such as relatives or neighbours, but organizations can also be integrated into the system in order to offer a wider range of services to the patient. Examples are businesses providing catering or cleaning, but also medical institutions – hospitals or organizations offering nursing services.

2.1   The Patient's Social Network

The home assistance center handles scheduling of tasks to the patient's caregivers and mediates communication between them. Therefore, it needs to maintain all the patient-caregiver connections. The connections are represented by *patients' social networks.* These networks are patient-centric and all the caregivers belonging to a network are assigned a role, such as relative, neighbour, GP, specialist, etc. Roles are assigned by the patients and are used for coarse grained access control in the home assistance center. In order to prevent misuse, caregivers need to provide proof of their expertise in order to have certain roles assigned to them. Examples are roles of medically trained caregivers.

In order to preserve privacy in the system, all users, both patients and caregivers, need to be pseudonymous in the network. Therefore, all the information that is handled in the system can only be linked to the pseudonyms and no identifying information would be available to unauthorized parties.

2.2   System Architecture

The system functionalities are separated into several entities, as shown in Fig. 1.

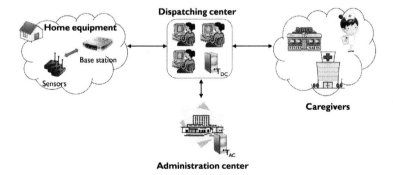

Fig. 1. The global architecture

32   M. Milutinovic et al.

In order to provide services to the patient, a *base station* is installed at the patient's home. It acts as a gateway towards the rest of the system and stores and controls access to patient's data. It also records the patient's dynamic privacy policies. All the recordings of the sensor network, including the signals from the fall detector and the hand-held control unit are sent to the base station, where they are assessed (Fig. 2). As a result of the assessment, the base station can request a caregiver's intervention or start an automatic task. The base station also controls a door system that allows authorized caregiver to enter the patient's house, thereby circumventing the need for distributing physical keys, which cannot be easily controlled or revoked. Authorization to enter the patient's home is represented by access tokens assigned to caregivers and can be provided or revoked dynamically. They are also characterized by a time slot in which they can be used.

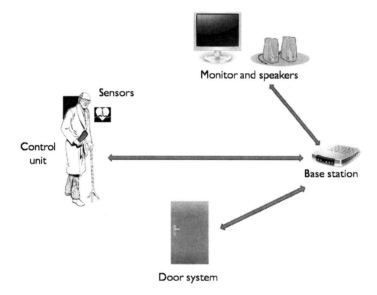

Fig. 2. Patient's home equipment

All the communication between the base system and the caregivers is mediated by a *dispatching center* (DC). The center is therefore responsible for maintaining the anonymized networks of patient's caregivers, assigning and/or scheduling tasks, monitoring the proper working of the base stations, notifying caregivers in case of alert or emergency situations and following up on their responses, providing authorized caregivers with access tokens for the door system, exercising (course-grained) access control to the resources controlled by the base stations, and collecting and archiving evidence of actions taken by the DC. Because it does not have access to medical data of the patient, it does not need to employ medically trained personnel.

Finally, a separate entity, namely the *administration center* (AC), handles all the administration tasks, such as registration of users, invoicing or receiving payments. This separation of functionality allows the system to be privacy-friendly and circumvents the need to keep identifying information about the users in the dispatching center and allows anonymization of patient's connections.

Trusted devices are also a part of the system architecture. They need to be deployed in the dispatching (T_{DC}) and the administration center (T_{AC}). They perform conversion of encrypted data into data encrypted with another key, or provide (part of) the encrypted plaintext under certain conditions. Examples are re-encrypting the patient's address information with a public key of an authorized caregiver who needs to assist the patient or decrypting the patient's identity in case of a misuse. However, before performing these actions, the trusted devices perform predefined checks in order to detect attacks and prevent unauthorized parties from obtaining patient's private information.

2.3 Functional Requirements

System's functional requirements can be defined according to the overview of the offered services presented above.

1. The system should provide the *scheduling of tasks*.
   - In order to create schedules for patient's caregivers, it should maintain all the connections between patients and their caregivers.
   - The system should keep a profile for each caregiver stating his qualifications, willingness to perform certain tasks and availability.
   - According to the available information, the system should be able to assign regular or one-time tasks to the members of the patient's social network and make up a schedule according to the caregivers' stated availability. In addition, some members, such as organizations, should be self-scheduling. They should be able to assign the received tasks to their personnel themselves.
   - Another very important property, is timely response to last-minute changes. An example is a caregiver that cannot keep an appointment, so that the system needs to assign the task to another caregiver, or – in the worst case – notify a close relative or neighbour.
2. The system should support *continuous monitoring* and *communication* with the patient.
   - The system should be able to interface with different sensors, such as a fall detector, heatbeat sensor or motion sensor. Some sensors may be sophisticated and able to detect anomalies (e.g. exceeding a threshold) and raise an alarm; others may merely measure body parameters and send these measurements to the base station at regular intervals, where they will be assessed by special tasks.
   - The assessments performed by the system should be dynamic. They can be pre-defined, or performed on-demand. Demanding computations could also be performed remotely, e.g. on hospital computers.

– According to the assessment results, the system should be able to raise alerts and report emergencies. Some actions could be pre-defined and automatically executed. Examples are playing a prerecorded advice to the patient or notifying caregivers.
– Communication means, such as a microphone and a speaker should be available (possibly incorporated in the control unit) so that verbal communication is possible.
– Video cameras installed in different rooms of the patient's house allow for assessing the situation when the patient does no longer respond to stimuli from the system. Access to the video stream requires strict access control.
– All the above communication means should be easy to handle and have a simple interface.
3. The system should provide *flexible access control.*
  – The patients should be able to define privacy policies that control the access to the sensor data. Authorized caregivers would be able to see and assess the sensor measurements. Some caregivers should also be allowed to specify automatic actions to be performed and conditions for their initiation. Examples are setting thresholds for sensor measurements and defining tasks to be performed in case of detected problems.
  – Flexible access control to the patient's home should also be provided by the system. Since different caregivers may need access to the patient's home, using physical keys is not desirable. Not only many copies of the same key are necessary, but they also give the bearer the possibility to enter the house at any time. Moreover, some services (such as nursing, catering, cleaning) are offered by organizations that may not always send the same caregiver to the patient. Therefore, virtual keys (or access tokens) are preferable. They provide more fine-grained access control, as the validity can be limited to a specific time interval and they can be dynamically provided or revoked.

3   Security and Privacy Requirements

As the system handles personal medical data, which is exceptionally privacy sensitive, the following requirements need to be fulfilled:

– Only authorized individuals, such as medical personnel or explicitly authorized caregivers of a patient, should be able to *access the personal medical data.* Even more so, since legislation in many countries imposes this rule. Therefore, strict access control must be provided.
– The patient's *network* should be *anonymized.* This requirement arizes from the fact that knowledge of some of the caregivers of a patient's network sometimes allows one to deduce the illness the patient suffers from. It will not be possible to hide everything, though. In general, one cannot hide that someone has health problems or needs permanent care, since passers-by may

notice and recognize caregivers who enter or leave the patient's house. However, the amount of deduced information should be limited. If someone gets hold of the database of the patients' networks, because of a deliberate leak by a disgruntled employee or a break-in into the system, he should not be able to learn privacy-sensitive information.

- Actions that are performed in the system should be *logged*, and treated as extremely *confidential*. Except to a trusted (external) party in case of disputes, these logs should not be accessible to anyone. If such logs are necessary to check the proper working of the system, then they should be anonymized previously.

3.1 Attacker's Model

There are three kinds of attackers the system should be secure against, differing in their roles in the system and authorizations:

The first kind of attacker is an **entity external to the system**. They do not have authorized access to any data handled by the system and can try to acquire information by passive observation, but can also illegally break into the system. Deducing any private information should not be possible for them.

Another kind of attacker is a **caregiver** who belongs to one or more patient's networks. A distinction needs to be made between medical professionals and other caregivers, since the former typically have access to the medical data of the patient. However, they are bound by a duty of professional confidentiality. On the other hand, non-medical caregivers without special authorization should never get access to the patient's medical data. Moreover, the system should only allow access to medical professionals that belong to the patient's social network.

Finally, another kind of attackers are **employees** of the home assistance center. Clearly, since they have to install the system at the patient's house and keep it running, they already have some background information that others do not have (e.g. they know which sensors are being used by which patient). However, the system should not provide them with more information than necessary, namely what they learned at the patient's house. Medical data –if kept at the home assistance center– should not be readable to employees. That requires its encryption with a key which employees cannot obtain. Also connections between patients and their caregivers should be anonymized. In order to limit the information that can be deduced by observing the available data about connections – the companies and individuals that belong to several patient's networks are represented by different pseudonym in each network. Hence, indiscretions about one network do not reveal anything about other networks. As a consequence of the listed requirements, disclosing the complete network database would not reveal more than a set of random numbers associated with general attributes, such as roles and rights.

It is, however, difficult to prevent the employees from learning some information by observing the system (e.g. the mobile phone number of the patient's GP), since the system may need to contact a caregiver and his phone number would need to be provided to a dialing device. Therefore, the design of the system should make it extremely difficult to link these phone numbers to pseudonyms of the networks.

In short, the employees should not be able to modify the data in the system or tamper with the software so that programmed checks are eliminated or that identifying data (such as phone numbers or email addresses), which may be temporarily kept in volatile memory is continuously recorded.

4   System Protocols

In this section we describe the protocols for user registration, the creation and extension of patients' social networks.

4.1   User Registration

All parties using this system initially need to register with the administration center. Depending on their role in the system, different procedures are followed.

Patients subscribe to a certain set of services offered by the home assistance center, and possibly sign a contract with a service provider. A Service Level Agreement (SLA), listing the subscribed services and the conditions, will be agreed upon. The users also prove their identity and contact information (possibly with their eID card), so that the administration center can personalize and issue a new *patient smart card* (SC_{PT}). The patient's identity, address information and SLA are stored on the card, which will generate a new pseudonym (Nym_{PT}) and two new key pairs (SK_{PT}^i, PK_{PT}^i), ($i = $ enc or sig), one to be used for encryption/decryption, the other for signing/verification. The administration center certifies the public keys PK_{PT}^i and the certificates are stored on the card during personalization. Every patient card will also have a public key of the trusted devices running in the dispatching and the administration center.

All issued cards will share a common authentication key pair (SK_{co}, PK_{co}) (cfr. also [15] for the rationale behind this privacy–friendly identity card). The card is necessary to authenticate the base station towards the dispatching center and the caregivers, and to sign or decrypt information. Hence, the base station will only run as long as the SC_{PT} is inserted in the card reader.

After patient registration, the administration center stores the patient's pseudonym, certificates, SLA and the encrypted patient's identity and address information (encryption is done with the public key of T_{AC}; see further). The home equipment can then be installed at the patient's home.

Individual caregivers, such as relatives, neighbours or self-employed doctors, often perform registration after being invited to join the network of a patient. As patients, caregivers need to provide proof of identity and address (contact) information. That can be done using their eID card. Also, medically trained caregivers would need to provide signed qualifications in order to be allowed to assume such roles in patient's networks. For verification of contact information, the administration center would send an authentication code to each address and expect for it to be returned within a limited time interval. The caregiver can then generate and send to the administration center a pseudonym (Nym_{CG}) and a commitment ($Comm_{CG}$) to a secret, random number ($Rand_{CG}$). In return, the caregiver is issued an anonymous credential ($Cred_{CG}^{anon}$) certifying the pseudonym, identity, qualifications, contact information and the committed random value.

After the registration, the administration center records the caregiver's pseudonym, along with all the identifying information encrypted with the public key of the trusted device.

Organizations offering paid services to the patients do not need to be anonymous in the system. They can register with the administration center disclosing their identity, contact information, certified public key (PK_O^{enc}) and list of offered services. If the registration is accepted, the organization can send a commitment ($Comm_O$) to a random value $Rand_O$. An anonymous credential is then issued to the organization certifying the exchanged information.

The administration center will record the identity of organization and related information, so that the patients can browse through the database and choose an appropriate organization.

4.2   Creation of the Patients' Network

When a base station has been installed at the patient's home, he can initiate connections with his caregivers and the creation of his social network. This is depicted in Fig. 3. Firstly, mutual authentication is performed between the patient and the dispatching center. Authentication of the patient is anonymous and is done using the patient's smart card (SC_{PT}) and the common authentication key pair (SK_{co}, PK_{co}). After a successful authentication, an end-to-end secure (SSL) channel is created between the base station and the dispatching center. The patient's pseudonym, public key certificate, SLA and a vault containing his pseudonym, identity and address information (encrypted with the T_{DC}'s public key) is sent over this channel. Since the patient's card is trusted, the contents of the vault is assumed to be correct.

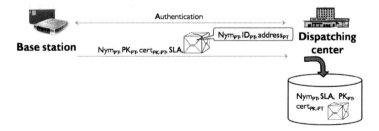

Fig. 3. Creation of the patient's network

In the dispatching center's database a new network is created, consisting of one node characterized by the patient's pseudonym, certificate (binding his pseudonym to his public encryption key PK_{PT}^{enc}), SLA and a vault with encrypted identity and address information.

4.3   Extension of the Patients' Networks

If a patient wishes for a specific caregiver to join his network, he needs to send him a specific request. All connections are initiated by patients and if a caregiver responds positively to the request, the patient is presented with his real identity, so he can verify that the connection was established with the intended individual. This is important to make sure that an unauthorized person cannot pose as a legitimate caregiver and endanger the patient's privacy. The protocol describing the extension of patient's network is depicted in Fig. 4.

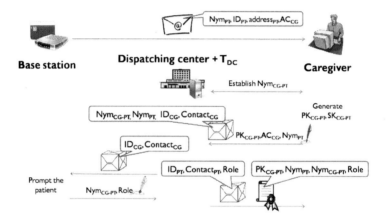

Fig. 4. Extending the patient's network

Initially, the patient will contact the dispatching center and request *access codes* in order to connect to his caregivers. Fresh access codes are generated and issued to the patient, but a fingerprint and validity period of every access code is recorded and linked with the patient's pseudonym.

After obtaining access codes, the patient can send a connection request to a desired caregiver. That request contains patient's identity, pseudonym, address, access code, and possibly additional information and can be sent to the caregiver via email. It is assumed that the patient does not hold caregiver's certified public key, and therefore, the information that he sends in the request is encrypted with a known public key of an applet used by the caregivers.

This applet is used at the caregiver's side, when he wants to respond by accepting the request for connection. When the caregiver starts the applet, it first loads the data received via email and the caregiver's anonyous credential. Note that if the caregiver is not yet registered with the administration center, he would need to perform that step in order to connect to the patient. In the next step, the applet establishes a new pseudonym Nym_{CG-PT} with the dispatching center, using the patient's pseudonym Nym_{PT} and the random number contained in the credential ($Rand_{CG}$). That allows the caregiver to subsequently prove possession of the pseudonym, by proving that it was properly generated using data contained in his credential. Next, the applet generates a new key pair (SK_{CG-PT}, PK_{CG-PT}) and verifiably encrypts the new pseudonum, the patient's pseudonym and the caregiver's identity and contact information with the public key of a trusted device T_{DC}. It also signs this information, together with the patient's pseudonym, the public key PK_{CG-PT}, and access code (AC_{CG}) with the caregiver's anonymous credential, thereby proving that the Nym_{CG-PT} was correctly generated and that the verifiably encrypted information contains the corresponding values from the credential (i.e. identity and contact information is correct). The dispatching center verifies the signature and the proofs mentioned above and checks the validity of the access code. If all the checks pass, the access code is marked invalid and the public key and the encrypted information are stored with the new pseudonym Nym_{CG-PT}.

In the next step, all the exchanged information is given to the trusted device T_{DC}, together with the certificate linking the patient's public key and his pseudonym. The trusted device performs the same checks in addition to which it checks whether the pseudonyms in the certificate and the encrypted vault are the same. If all the checks pass, the trusted device re-encrypts the caregiver's pseudonym, identity and contact information from the vault with the public key of the patient, PK_{PT}^{enc}. This vault is sent to the patient and decrypted by the SC_{PT}. The patient is then presented with the caregiver's identity, so he can confirm the connection and assign a role to the caregiver. This confirmation is sent to the dispatching center as a signature on the caregiver's pseudonym and the new role.

After receiving the confirmation, the dispatching center records the new caregiver's pseudonym as a permanent node in the patient's network and the trusted device will generate a certificate confirming membership (with a certain role) of the patient's network. It also prepares a vault with the patient's identity, which is sent to the caregiver (for verification).

In case the caregiver is a registered organization, the protocol slightly differs, as the user can obtain its certified public key and the initial request can be encrypted using that key.

5   Evaluation

In this section, we investigate the security and privacy properties of the system and protection against the different types of attackers described above.

The first requirement in this system is that unauthorized individuals should never have access to the medical data of a patient. Since neither the dispatching, nor the administration center store any medical data of patients, employees or attackers breaking into the system cannot see any private health information. In addition, any party accessing patient's data in the base station is authenticated and authorizations are checked. The patient or his guardian can specify policies defining the authorizations of different caregivers or roles.

However, indirect information can also lead to unintentional disclosure of private information. For instance, knowing a specialist who treats a patient can be used to deduce the illness of the patient. However, the patient's networks are anonymized and all identifying information is not readable at the dispatching or the administration center, in order to counter these risks. Moreover, caregivers belonging to different patient's networks are assigned different pseudonyms in each network, ensuring that indiscretions about one network do not reveal information about other networks.

It is also not possible for an attacker with access to the dispatching center data to try to infiltrate into a patient's network, since every patient is presented with the real identity of the caregiver before confirming the connection. An attacker that is not a patient's caregiver could try to plant his own public key to the trusted device in order to have some secret patient's data re-encrypted with this public key. However, the trusted device performs sufficient checks, as explained in Sec. 4, which prevents this attack.

Finally, actions that are performed in the system should be logged. It is required to keep all the logging information confidential. Indeed, the dispatching center will sometimes send text messages or emails to caregivers. Hence, phone numbers or address information used need to be kept confidential. This can be fulfilled by encrypting all logging information with the public key of an external trusted third party. Also, trusted devices log their actions for later auditing.

6   Related Work

There is a significant body of research focusing on eHealth systems for providing care in the patient's household. Most research initiatives in this area focus on the remote monitoring service that allows supervising the patient's health status. However, security and privacy problems in these systems are not fully tackled.

The research in this field typically assumes a three-tier system architecture. Patient monitoring can be bootstrapped using sensors that measure physiological parameters such as EEG, ECG or GSR, or environmental parameters such as temperature and humidity. Furthermore, system can incorporate sensors detecting user indicated alarms [12]. Video monitoring was also explored for deployment in these systems, as it allows communication with caregivers [5], but also fall detection [13] and movement, posture and gait analysis [10]. Sensors performing health monitoring can be deployed as a personal area network [7] or can be integrated in a single device [2]. Desirable types of monitoring sensors were investigated in [11].

Proposed systems also incorporate a personal server, used to gather data recorded by the sensors. The collected data is then sent to a remote care center for assessment [3] [8] [6]. Recorded data can also be forwarded to another predefined care provider. Although relaying the data to a central station assures greater resources for data analysis, if all the tasks are performed in the central station, the patient has no substantial control over the disclosed information and services that are deployed.

Other research initiatives consider interoperability in these systems. [4] proposes a novel architecture in order to tackle cross-context identity management in eHealth systems with the goal to improve interoperability between providers. Interoperability between relevant standards, namely HL7 and IEEE 1451 standard was explored in [9]. HL7 is a messaging standard for exchanging medical information and IEEE 1451 standard deals with various aspects of sensors, the format of data sheets and how to connect and disconnect the sensors from a system. This work is complementary with our proposal, as these standards can also be used for information exchange in our architecture.

Importance of security and privacy in these systems is widely recognized [1], [14], but research proposals do not solve those issues fully. Reliability is another important requirement, that needs to be tackled.

7   Conclusion and Future Work

In this paper we propose a novel architecture for a home assistance system, providing care for the elderly or stay-at-home patients. Offered services of this pervasive system include continuous monitoring of patients, scheduling of patient-requested tasks to their caregivers, follow-up on the responses, help in emergency situations and remote access to the patient's data to authorized caregivers. This approach allows the system to be run by a commercial organization without the need to employ medically trained personnel. It is designed in such a way that the home assistance center cannot access patients' medical data. Instead, it maintains patients' anonymous networks and only mediates communication between patients and their caregivers. Protocols employed in the system, that lead to improved privacy and patient's control over his data, are described in detail.

Another important feature of this approach is openness of the system. New users, caregivers and even services and service providers can easily and seamlessly be integrated into the system.

A possible extension of the system are anonymous self-help groups that would allow the patients to anonymously communicate with their peers with similar health conditions. Strict admission procedures would be employed.

Acknowledgement. This research is partially funded by the Interuniversity Attraction Poles Programme Belgian State, Belgian Science Policy, and by the IWT-SBO project (DiCoMas) "Distributed Collaboration using Multi-Agent System Architectures".

References

1. Health Insurance Portability and Accountability Act (HIPAA),
   http://www.hhs.gov/ocr/privacy/

2. Boulos, M.N.K., Rocha, A., Martins, A., Vicente, M.E., Bolz, A., Feld, R., Tchoudovski, I., Braecklein, M., Nelson, J., Laighin, G., Sdogati, C., Cesaroni, F., Antomarini, M., Jobes, A., Kinirons, M.: Caalyx: a new generation of location-based services in healthcare. International Journal of Health Geographics 6 (2007)
3. Chakravorty, R.: A programmable service architecture for mobile medical care. In: Proceedings of the 4th Annual IEEE International Conference on Pervasive Computing and Communications Workshops, PERCOMW 2006 (2006)
4. Deng, M., Cock, D.D., Preneel, B.: An interoperable cross-context architecture to manage distributed personal e-health information. In: Cunha, M.M., Simoes, R., Tavares, A. (eds.) Handbook of Research on Developments in e-Health and Telemedicine: Technological and Social Perspectives, ch. 27, pp. 576–602. IGI Global, Inc., Hershey (2009)
5. Johnston, B., Weeler, L., Deuser, J., Sousa, K.H.: Outcomes of the kaiser permanente telehome health research project. Arch. Fam. Med. 9(1), 40–45 (2000)
6. Jovanov, E., Milenkovic, A., Otto, C., de Groen, P.: A wireless body area network of intelligent motion sensors for computer assisted physical rehabilitation. Journal of NeuroEngineering and Rehabilitation 2(1), 6 (2005)
7. Jovanov, E., Raskovic, D., Price, J., Chapman, J., Moore, A., Krishnamurthy, A.: Patient monitoring using personal area networks of wireless intelligent sensors. Biomedical Sciences Instrumentation 37 (2001)
8. Kim, H., Jarochowski, B., Ryu, D.: A Proposal for a Home-Based Health Monitoring System for the Elderly or Disabled. In: Miesenberger, K., Klaus, J., Zagler, W.L., Karshmer, A.I. (eds.) ICCHP 2006. LNCS, vol. 4061, pp. 473–479. Springer, Heidelberg (2006)
9. Kim, W., Lim, S., Ahn, J., Nah, J., Kim, N.: Integration of ieee 1451 and hl7 exchanging information for patients sensor data. Journal of Medical Systems 34, 1033–1041 (2010), doi:10.1007/s10916-009-9322-5
10. Lo, B.P.L., Wang, J.L., Zhong Yang, G.: From imaging networks to behavior profiling: Ubiquitous sensing for managed homecare of the elderly. In: Adjunct Proceedings of the 3rd International Conference on Pervasive Computing (2005)
11. Lymberis, A.: Smart wearables for remote health monitoring, from prevention to rehabilitation: current R&D, future challenges. In: 4th International IEEE EMBS Special Topic Conference on Information Technology Applications in Biomedicine 2003, pp. 272–275 (2003)
12. Sarela, A., Korhonen, I., Lotjonen, J., Sola, M., Myllymaki, M.: Ist vivago ®- an intelligent social and remote wellness monitoring system for the elderly. In: 4th International IEEE EMBS Special Topic Conference on Information Technology Applications in Biomedicine, 2003, pp. 362–365 (April 2003)
13. Tabar, A.M., Keshavarz, A., Aghajan, H.: Smart home care network using sensor fusion and distributed vision-based reasoning. In: Proceedings of the 4th ACM International Workshop on Video Surveillance and Sensor Networks
14. Varshney, U.: Pervasive healthcare and wireless health monitoring. Mob. Netw. Appl. 12, 113–127 (2007)
15. Vossaert, J., Lapon, J., Verhaeghe, P., De Decker, B., Naessens, V.: A smart card based solution for user-centric identity management. In: PrimeLife/IFIP Summer School 2010, Helsingborg, August 2-6 (2010)

Detecting Computer Worms in the Cloud

Sebastian Biedermann and Stefan Katzenbeisser

Security Engineering Group
Department of Computer Science
Technische Universität Darmstadt
{biedermann,katzenbeisser}@seceng.informatik.tu-darmstadt.de

Abstract. Computer worms are very active and new sophisticated versions continuously appear. Signature-based detection methods work with a low false-positive rate, but previously knowledge about the threat is needed. Anomaly-based intrusion detection methods are able to detect new and unknown threats, but meaningful information for correct results is necessary. We propose an anomaly-based intrusion detection mechanism for the cloud which directly profits from the virtualization technologies in general. Our proposed anomaly detection system is isolated from spreading computer worm infections and it is able to detect unknown and new appearing computer worms. Using our approach, a spreading computer worm can be detected on the spreading behavior itself without accessing or directly influencing running virtual machines of the cloud.

Keywords: Computer Worms, Anomaly Detection, Cloud Computing.

1 Introduction

Cloud computing offers the utilization of IT resources such as computing power and storage as a service through a network on demand. It can save a company the purchase of own data centers or the employment of own IT specialists. This is made possible through virtualization technologies.

The cloud consists of a network of hardware nodes, where each node is able to run several virtualized operating systems in parallel using a virtual machine monitor called hypervisor. A centralized cloud manager summarizes and monitors the resources of all connected hardware nodes and determines which node offers enough free resources to start a new virtual machine if needed. These virtual machines contain an operating system as well as additional software components or requested data.

The virtual machines of the cloud can be easily accessed from outside and their available performance can be flexibly scaled. This architecture results in an internal network running many operating systems which are usually able to connect to each other.

Various different definitions of cloud computing are available. Most of the time, cloud computing is considered as a compilation of abstract remote services. Figure 1 shows the cloud from a technical point of view which we use in our work. The cloud network is separated in a back-end and a front-end.

J. Camenisch and D. Kesdogan (Eds.): iNetSec 2011, LNCS 7039, pp. 43–54, 2012.
© IFIP International Federation for Information Processing 2012

The cloud management software is installed on the front-end. It monitors the resources of the back-end and is also connected to an external network, for example the Internet. Users can make a request on the front-end, usually with a web interface, and define which kind of virtual machine they want to start in the back-end in combination with reserved performance. The requested virtual machine can contain a previously chosen operating system and additional requested software. The core component of the cloud is the back-end network.

It consists of several hardware nodes where each has installed hypervisor software. With the help of the hypervisor software, many virtual machines can be launched in parallel on a single hardware node. Finally, the management component links a connection from the outside user to the started virtual machine in the back-end.

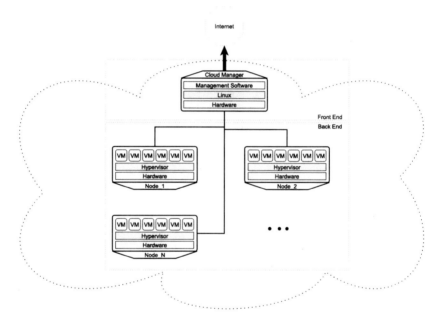

Fig. 1. Front-end and back-end of a cloud computing setup

Cloud computing networks that offer "Platform as a Service" ("PaaS") in homogeneous networks with Microsoft Windows operating systems are increasingly used in companies to save hardware resources. Especially in these private clouds, the network is often a homogeneous operating system environment. Employees have full control over these virtual machines which are connected to the internal company network through high-speed links and which can be remotely accessed and used like a normal workplace. The cloud manager can quickly balance and optimize the current needed resources.

To reach this goal, running virtual machines can be live-migrated from one hardware node to another hardware node in the back-end without notifying the logged-in remote cloud user.

Cloud computing offers many new opportunities like cost savings and high flexibility, but this new kind of network is still susceptible to the old open security problems which affect computer networks today.

In this paper, we address the problem of fast spreading malicious software (computer worms) in the cloud back-end network. These computer worms can have a devastating impact on the homogeneous and flexible cloud installation and can cause massive financial losses. The problem of computer worms exists since a long time and it does not seem as if the number of appearing computer worms would decrease. Further, the latest computer worms are becoming more sophisticated and complex and thus detection and containments get more challenging.

Traditional networks offer no means to inspect captures for malicious incidents, unless special intrusion detection systems (IDS) or special monitoring components are installed on the operating systems. On the contrary to this, the virtualized network of the cloud offers new opportunities to monitor internal events of virtual machines without the need of direct access or influence.

In this paper, we discuss the challenge of detecting spreading computer worms as fast as possible in a cloud back-end network. Even though the problem as such is old, we argue in this paper that it can be better addressed in virtualized networks like the cloud back-end.

To this end, we propose a new kind of computer worm detection system especially for the cloud back-end network. Our system is anomaly-based, very flexible and benefits directly from the virtualization technologies. The proposed detection system uses a centralized perspective on the entire back-end of the cloud network and interprets this network as a whole.

A particular advantage is that our proposed computer worm detection system can discover unknown computer worms and that it can not be manipulated by the computer worms because it runs isolated from the virtual machines on the hypervisor layer.

To be able to carry out various test-runs, we implemented a simulation framework which uses our IDS approach and which can run with a very large number of parallel simulated virtual machines. With the help of these simulations, a real spreading epidemic of a computer worm infection in a very large virtual back-end network can be investigated.

2   Open Problem and Approach

In the year 2003, the "Blaster" computer worm infected millions of Windows 2000, XP and Windows Server 2003 systems by remotely exploiting a RPC bug [1]. All infected systems were running a process called "msblast.exe" which started together with the operating system at boot time. The spreading behaviour of the "Blaster" computer worm became an annoying and tremendous costly epidemic.

In early November 2008, the "Conficker" computer worm infected up to 15 million Windows systems by exploiting a remote NetBIOS bug. It injects a randomly named dynamic link library (DLL) into the authentic "svchost.exe" Windows process and tries to hide its presence this way [2]. Version A of the "Conficker" computer worm was especially focused on the infection of other systems that were connected within an internal network which caused very fast spreading within organizations. Conficker B included a brute force attack mechanism to retrieve local passwords and version C even included a P2P protocol for its own distribution [3].

In the year 2010, the "Stuxnet" computer worm heralds the new era of spreading malicious software. This computer worm aims to manipulate industrial control systems, but it is also distributed on Windows systems from version 2000 to 7 using various exploiting technics [4]. The occurrence of the "Stuxnet" computer worm has once again shown that the dangers of spreading malicious software are far away from over.

These computer worms constitute only some examples of computer worms which caused huge economic damage in the last years.

The threat of spreading computer worms is not over: the past showed that continuously new worms arise, despite the deployment of new techniques for detection and abatement. Virus detection software or intrusion detection software can be installed on systems, but this software can also be manipulated by malicious processes or even deactivated from the users themselves by mistake. Until now, containment of fast spreading worms is an open problem to which no satisfying countermeasure is known.

Unlike traditional network subnets, on which one operating system was installed on each hardware node connected directly to the network, todays networking components are virtualized, i.e. multiple systems run in parallel on one hardware node, managed by a hypervisor software component from which the systems are completely isolated. In such virtual computing environments, worms can still spread through traditional methods. However, by utilizing the existing virtualization infrastructure, more useful information of each single running virtual machine can be obtained from the outside in a passive manner:

Virtual machine introspection (VMI) allows to get information on running virtual machines through the hypervisor layer without the need to directly access the machines. This information can contain a list of the current running processes of the operating system, current loaded modules or even an image of the whole random-access memory (RAM). There are flexible libraries available that provide virtual machine introspection without requiring changes to the hypervisor [5].

Based on this technology, intrusion detection systems (IDS) can be developed which monitor virtualized systems from the outside. This architecture has the benefit that this kind of intrusion detection systems can not be manipulated or even detected by malicious software running on the infected virtual machine, because the IDS code is out of reach and thus in a completely separated software environment [6].

The virtual infrastructure of the cloud network offers an elegant way to identify an infectious spread without auxiliary worm signatures. In a virtualized network, information can be obtained from each running virtual machine through VMI. A single centralized monitoring software component can receive all this information of all running virtual machines and interpret the current status of the network.

This way, an IDS can be built based on anomalies detected in the whole virtualized cloud computing network. To demonstrate the feasibility of this approach, we built a centralized anomaly detector which collects information using VMI of all running virtual machines in the cloud back-end. Our approach offers very fast detection of malicious spreading behaviour because of the centralized abstract view on the cloud network. Using our approach, spreading malicious processes can be detected based on their spreading behaviour in the back-end network itself, even without having previous knowledge about the threat like signatures.

After the detection of a computer worm, a signature can be generated and further used in an network traffic based IDS like "Snort" [7] to ban the threat at the gates of the network.

3   Technical Approach

To realize the proposed idea, we first have to define what we consider an anomaly in the cloud computing network. By our definition, an anomaly is a collection of more than one appearing single inconsistencies. In particular, we identify two different inconsistencies that can appear in an operating system in our virtual cloud computing network. An inconsistency arises if one or more of the following events are detected on a running virtual machine in the cloud using VMI or hypervisor information in general:

- A new process is started which is not in a list of known or usual processes.
- A new module is loaded which is not in a list of known or usual modules.

In this context, the execution of a "known" process or module is not uncommon and well known. In contrast, an "unknown" process or module can be a process or module which is not very popular or which execution is very unusual. Of course, one can define more complex event that cause inconsistencies, which may include, for example, unusual high outgoing traffic of a virtual machine or continuous high CPU performance. There are many ways to define triggers for inconsistencies in the cloud computing network. In this paper, we limit our inconsistency to the two listed events above.

Single inconsistencies are not conclusive; however, if a continuous distribution or increasing of exactly the same inconsistency in the cloud back-end network can be discovered, one can infer an anomaly. We define that an anomaly occurs when in successive scans of running virtual machines using VMI at predefined time intervals ΔT a continuous steady increase of an inconsistency in the cloud back-end network exceeds a predefined limit L.

These observations allow to detect computer worms indirectly through their spreading behaviour. These computer worms are unknown processes or modules even themselves or they use other unusual processes or modules during their malicious work on the operating system.

For example, the following steps identify an ongoing threat with the help of observed running processes on virtual machines in the cloud back-end network:

1. Retrieve a list of running processes of a randomly chosen virtual machine using VMI in the cloud back-end network.
2. Find processes which are not in a list of known or common processes and add these information temporarily to a list of unknown processes.
3. After a larger number of scans, identify a potential spreading process, characterized by the fact that this inconsistency occurs on an increasing number of virtual machines.
4. If the occurrence of this identified process exceeds the value of a predefined limit L, take corrective action (e.g. isolate infected virtual machines from the back-end network for further investigations).
5. In contrast, if the occurrence of this process decreases and reaches not the value of the predefined limit L, add its information to the list of known processes and continue. In this case, it is assumed that the process is not a computer worm, but an event occurring in parallel such as e.g. a simultaneously launched update on multiple virtual machines.

An algorithm following these steps is not only able to identify a spreading process in the cloud back-end network, it also improves itself by learning information about unknown harmless processes. This can be helpful to distinguish between the spread of malicious software and regular updates, which can have characteristics of a computer worm if they are installed on virtual machines simultaneously from the Internet.

Using these proposed steps, a computer worm can be identified only by its spreading behavior itself. In this way, no prior knowledge about the computer worm is necessary, such as a signature. This approach is benefiting from the virtualization technologies of the cloud in general by passively observing the running virtual machines with the help of VMI and it is also benefiting from an abstract centralized view on all network nodes of the entire cloud back-end network. New and unknown computer worms can be detected and the triggered anomaly may lead to further more active countermeasures.

4   Experimental Cloud Configuration

Our experimental implementation uses a simple setup. We focused only on monitoring running processes, accordingly we received a current process-list of running virtual machines on the back-end nodes. The implementation consists of a centralized cloud network management component including a "Spreading Process Monitor" component running on Linux. The cloud manager consists of scripts which are able to transfer virtual machine images to connected nodes, launch, stop and destroy them.

Each connected node uses the Xen hypervisor [8] and accordingly each connected node includes an administrative virtual machine which is called in Xen "Domain 0" ("dom0"). This administrative virtual machine can provide information about the CPU usage or the network traffic of the running virtual guest machines ("domU") on the same hardware node. For the implementation, the "dom0" virtual machine additionally uses the XenAccess[1] VMI library package to retrieve a list of the current running processes on each virtual guest machine on this hardware node.

This is done with the help of direct memory access technics and previously defined knowledge about the structure of the RAM dependent on the chosen operating system. Figure 2 illustrates the procedure of virtual machine introspection on a single hardware node in the cloud back-end network.

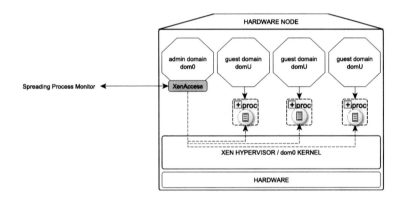

Fig. 2. Illustration of virtual machine introspection (VMI) on a single hardware node in the cloud back-end network

During the runtime, the "Spreading Process Monitor" collects the process-lists of randomly chosen virtual guest machines on different hardware nodes in the network. Continuously collecting and comparing these lists offers the opportunity to detect spreading inconsistencies which increase their appearance on other virtual guest machines in the cloud back-end network. This method is illustrated in Figure 3.

As countermeasures, isolating or freezing infected virtual machines are possible and this can be also controlled by the centralized cloud manager. The network traffic of all virtual guest machines is routed through a bridge which is configured in the administrative "dom0" virtual machine. The current network traffic of each guest machine can be easily scanned, analyzed and also blocked using host-based network filtering software in further steps after an anomaly.

---

[1] http://code.google.com/p/xenaccess/

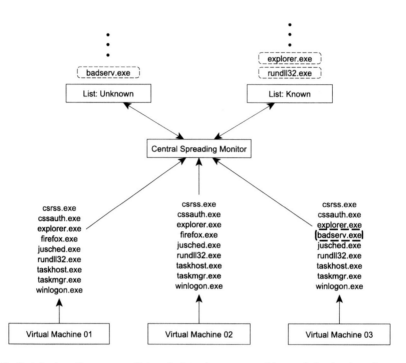

Fig. 3. Retrieving the process lists of virtual guest machines of the back-end network and subdivide this collected information in lists of known and unknown processes

This way, traffic of infected virtual machines can be isolated or filtered, so that infected virtual machines can be prevented from infecting other uninfected virtual machines inside the internal cloud back-end network. This is a simple but effective approach to get the ongoing spreading threat under control and to get more time for detailed investigations.

5 Simulation

To get a better view on the performance of the approach and practicality on the proposed technique, we developed a simulation framework. Our framework simulates many parallel running virtual machines, each infected one can also infect each other virtual machine with a malicious process. Once infected, the malicious process randomly scans for a new target virtual machine inside the simulated cloud back-end and infects this new victim. The simulation includes a centralized spreading process monitor to identify spreading behaviour on the simulated virtual machines.

Random virtual machines are continuously scanned by this centralized process spreading detector. In the real environment, this scan is done using virtual machine introspection. In such a simulation, time factors play a centralized role.

Figure 4 illustrates the amount of infected virtual machines for a simulated back-end network with 256, 512 and 1024 single virtual machines until detection of an anomaly in percent. The time interval for the scans of the centralized process spreading detector is set to $\Delta T = 500ms$ and the limit for the amount of inconsistencies until an anomaly L is set to 6. This simulation shows that the spreading time of the inconsistencies (the unknown process) is a very important factor using our approach. A fast detection can prevent major damage.

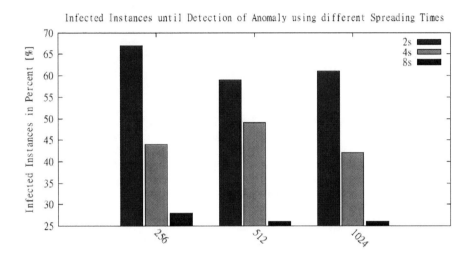

Fig. 4. Percentage amount of infected virtual machines until detection of the anomaly using different spreading times. Three test-runs with a cloud consisting of 256, 512, and 1024 single simulated machines. Average of eight runs.

A malicious process with a spreading time of two seconds easily infects more than 50% of the whole network until it is detected using the chosen parameters. However, the amount of infected virtual machines until detection decreases rapidly if the spreading time of the process is in the order of four or even eight seconds. Thus, feasible and matching selection of parameters ΔT and L is very important.

To defend the cloud back-end network from an entire infection causing a total black-out of the whole network, the spreading process can be disarmed by blocking identified ports which the malicious process uses for spreading, even the infected virtual machines can be completely isolated from the communication in the network.

Figure 5 shows the influence of a countermeasure approach which starts to isolate and remove the malicious process and make eight virtual machines per second immune from the infection after an ongoing anomaly has been detected. Here, we used a scanning interval $\Delta T = 125ms$. The Limit L is still 6 and the cloud back-end network consists of 512 running virtual machines.

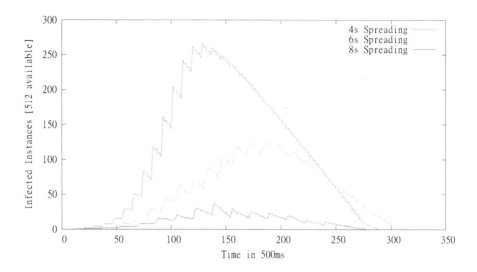

Fig. 5. Simulation of the detection of an anomaly and an immediate countermeasure. The spread is contained by the countermeasure. Different runs with spreading times of 4s, 6s and 8s and with 512 virtual machines. Average of eight runs.

It can be seen that after six seconds around 50% of the virtual machines are infected if the spreading time is four seconds. After the peak, the countermeasure works constantly because all other uninfected virtual machines have already been infected and are immune, which means the computer worm is defeated. The countermeasure works much better if the spreading time is six or eight seconds.

Here, this countermeasure is effective and keeps continuously the most virtual machines of the back-end network under control. The points in time a spreading process can be detected and a counteraction can be started are very important. Using these simple and very fast tactics, a black-out of the whole simulated cloud back-end caused by a total infection can be avoided.

6   Future Work

Our proposed solution benefits directly from the virtualization technologies in the cloud network. Our proposal observes passively the running virtual machines in the back-end and it is not vulnerable to attacks of the spreading computer worms, because our used software runs isolated in "dom0" administrative virtual machines which do not offer services to the network and which usually block unintended communication in general.

Though, there are some ways to improve this approach, with some of them we deal in actual work. Of course, it is not efficient enough to observe only the names of processes or loaded modules, recent computer worms hide mostly in other processes or change their names continuously. In actual work, we generate hashes of each process and module contained in the RAM image of the virtual guest machine and compare these collected integrity measurements.

At first glance, the monitoring of processes and modules do not appear sufficient to detect the new generations of sophisticated computer worms. But it can also be said that with this approach, for example the spreading computer worm "Stuxnet" should be detected as an anomaly. Because not the computer worm itself has to be detected, but the influence and the impact of the worm infection on the operating system in the virtual machine can be discovered. "Stuxnet" continuously loads correctly signed driver modules on each infected machine, because the creators have even stolen the signing keys from a hardware manufacturer. These modules would be added to the unknown list and the continuous spreading of them should be identified as an anomaly.

We propose a security system which uses anomaly detection and which should of course lead to further detailed investigations.

At last, the scanning and identifying progress can be greatly accelerated in future work with the help of parallelized scans and concurrent threads.

7   Conclusion

Cloud computing is changing the IT world and introduces enormous and great improvements. Still, cloud installations are vulnerable to classic open problems such as fast-spreading computer worms. Traditional detection methods, usually based on a signatures, are not able to bring this problem under control, because the amount of new occurring computer worms is steadily growing.

Anomaly detection approaches are more robust than signature based detection methods, but they need meaningful information from the network. The cloud offers new opportunities to monitor the network without directly influencing or accessing single virtual machines using virtual machine introspection. Therefore, this can be used to have an abstract view on the entire system and to interpret the state of the network with the help of a centralized detector to identify malicious spreading inconsistencies.

In this paper, we showed that it is possible to use features offered by virtual machine introspection to detect and to contain the spreading of computer worms. Our detection method is based on anomalies and works by observing the spreading behaviour of suspicious inconsistencies in the virtualized cloud back-end network. We optimized this detection method using a set of different simulations and we analyzed the influence of different parameters and a countermeasure.

References

1. Microsoft, "Buffer overrun in rpc interface could allow code execution (823980)"
2. Felix Leder, T.W.: Know your enemy: Containing conficker
3. Group, C.W.: Lessons learned june 2010 (2011)

4. Nicolas Falliere, L.O.M., Chien, E.: W32.stuxnet dossier. In: Symantec Security Response
5. Payne, B.D., Lee, W.: Secure and flexible monitoring of virtual machines. In: Annual Computer Security Applications Conference, pp. 385–397 (2007)
6. Garfinkel, T., Rosenblum, M.: A virtual machine introspection based architecture for intrusion detection. In: Network and Distributed System Security Symposium (2003)
7. Roesch, M.: Snort: Lightweight intrusion detection for networks. In: USENIX Systems Administration Conference, pp. 229–238 (1999)
8. Barham, P., Dragovic, B., Fraser, K., Hand, S., Harris, T.L., Ho, A., Neugebauer, R., Pratt, I., Warfield, A.: Xen and the art of virtualization. In: Symposium on Operating Systems Principles, pp. 164–177 (2003)

Efficient and Stealthy Instruction Tracing and Its Applications in Automated Malware Analysis: Open Problems and Challenges

Endre Bangerter[1], Stefan Bühlmann[2], and Engin Kirda[3]

[1] Bern University of Applied Sciences, Switzerland
endre.bangerter@jdiv.org
[2] Bern University of Applied Sciences and
Joe Security, Switzerland
stefan.buehlmann@bfh.ch
[3] Northeastern University, USA
ek@ccs.neu.edu

Abstract. Malware is substantial security threat today and most likely in the foreseeable future. The analysis of malware is a key activity in the fight against the threat. Since manual analysis is time consuming and given the extent of the malware threat, malware analysis needs to be automated. Malware analysis sandboxes offer such automation and play already an important role in practice. Yet, they only uncover certain aspects of malware behavior, and still require manual analysis in many cases. This is not a viable way to go, and thus the automation and quality of automated analysis needs to be pushed further. A promising technique towards this goal is instruction tracing combined with analyzes algorithms that uncover malware behavior from an instruction trace.

In this position paper, we shall argue that instruction tracing is still in its infancy and point out challenges and open problems of instruction tracing in general. In particular, we shall describe Helios, which is our new instruction tracer that offers a better balance of tracing speed and transparency than existing techniques.

1 Introduction

Malware is one of the major security issues threatening current networked devices and IT infrastructures. The root causes of the malware problem (i.e., software vulnerabilities, insufficiently secure operating systems, and human failures) are not likely to be solved anytime soon. Moreover, the proliferation of networked devices (e.g., smart phones, tablets, appliances, smart grids etc.) is ongoing. It is thus likely that the malware threat is going to increase further and stay with us for a long time to come. It thus seems that we need to learn to live with malware in the foreseeable future.

Currently, there are two main scenarios of how malware is deployed by miscreants. One are large scale attacks where the goal is to maximize the number

J. Camenisch and D. Kesdogan (Eds.): iNetSec 2011, LNCS 7039, pp. 55–64, 2012.
© IFIP International Federation for Information Processing 2012

of infections of a more or less arbitrary user base. The other are targeted attacks, where the goal is to compromise a small set of specific users within an organization. The first type of attack is used to commit fraud, steal money from e-banking systems, etc. The latter is used for intelligence gathering and espionage (industrial, and governmental) or selective attacks on the reputation of an institution.

The *analysis of (potential) malware is a key activity in dealing with the threat.* Analysis is required to update protection mechanisms (e.g., AV, IDS signatures, domain blacklists, etc.), to assess the effects and damages of an attack, to initiate recovery measures, etc. Important aspects of malware analysis are *quality* (i.e., to maximize the understanding of a piece of malware) and *speed* (i.e., to obtain the information as quickly as possible). These are clearly competing goals and we are thus in a trade-off situation.

While manual analysis delivers quality (if carried out by a qualified engineer), it lacks speed. Manual analysis does not scale, and given the shortage of qualified experts it is not a feasible way to handle the malware threat. Today, it is common for anti-malware organizations to receive thousands of new, unknown samples every day. As a result, *automated analysis techniques are indispensable tools in the fight against malware.*

Static analysis techniques potentially deliver the best analysis quality, and in particular, good code coverage. Unfortunately, static analysis techniques are easily defeated. In fact, it is often trivial for malware authors to automatically generate different versions of a specific malware component by using techniques such as encryption, code obfuscation, instruction substitution, self modifying code, etc. Thus a purely static analysis of modern malware is currently out of reach [MKK07].

Because of the limitations of static techniques, various dynamic techniques have been proposed that aim to automatically analyze a malware sample by executing it and by logging the behavior that it exhibits. Dynamic analysis is much harder to evade than static analysis, and it thus currently plays an important role in practical malware analysis.

So called malware analysis sandboxes, such as, Anubis [BKK06], Joebox [BK08], and CWSandbox [WHF07], have received considerable interest in the research community as well as by malware analysts in practice. Analysis sandboxes are one of the principal automated analysis technologies being used in practice. They are widely deployed and used by various CERTs, anti-virus companies, and governmental organizations. Technically, sandboxes mainly track the execution flow of a malware by instrumenting and recording API calls (user-space, and system calls), their arguments and related state information. Based on this information, the malware behavior is analyzed. Sandboxes are adequate for identifying the installation behavior of malware, infection strategies (e.g., code injections) and network communications. Some sandboxes track malware in nearly real-time, and there are systems in use that can process tens of thousands of samples per day.

Yet, since the tracking granularity of sandboxes is coarse grained (i.e., only API calls are recorded), sandboxes miss valuable information, which inherently limits their analysis quality. For instance, they are not adequate for detection of code similarity and vulnerabilities, data flow and execution flow - analysis. More generally, they give little information about purely algorithmic aspects of malware, like triggering logics, domain name generation, etc.

In summary, sandboxes excel through high analysis speed, but feature only a moderate analysis quality. They are thus appropriate for first cut and mass analysis. Yet, when it comes to understanding the details of a malware, which is typically required in targeted attacks, then sandboxes are of limited value only. In these cases one still needs to resort to manual analysis. This is a major bottleneck and challenge in current malware analysis. To be able to handle the malware threat, we need to push the boundary of automation further and develop novel techniques that improve the analysis quality.

2 Instruction Traces – Challenges and Open Problems

Instruction tracers (tracers, for short) record every single instruction and related state during execution of a piece of code. The resulting traces are then processed by a *trace analyzer* that extracts information on the behavior of the process being analyzed. By providing instruction level granularity, tracers clearly have the potential to offer better analysis quality than sandboxes. The major inherent short coming of instruction tracers, is that they only observe one code path at a time and thus lack code coverage. However, in practice, this is often not an issue since malware does show relevant behavior shortly after execution. It is thus not astonishing that instruction tracers and their applications have received considerable interest in the malware research community recently. Various tracers specifically geared towards malware analysis have been proposed. These are Ether [DRSL08], Cobra [VY06], TEMU [SBY+08], Pin [SDC+10] and MmmBop [Ban09]. Additionally, there are also hardware based tracers, such as ICE debuggers. Examples of applications of tracers are: Identification of keyloggers (by taint tracking keyboard inputs to a network interface) [EKK+07], detection of exploits [NS05] and self-modifying code [DRSL08], and automated protocol reverse engineering [LJXZ08, KKCW08, CYLS07].

Despite these promising results, tracers are still in their infancy and play little role in practice. In fact, there are substantial challenges that remain to be resolved:

- Current tracers are not ready for practical use, since they are either too inefficient or easy to detect and evade. Also, there are no viable solutions to improve the code coverage of tracers.

- The degree of automated analysis needs to be pushed further. To this end more advanced trace analyzers need to be explored, which can automatically uncover algorithmic aspects of malware, and "not just" interactions of malware with its run-time environment.

The first of the above challenges is more an engineering type of challenge, while the latter is a probably hard research challenge. In the following we describe these challenges, the underlying state of the art, and potential solutions in more detail (§3 discusses tracing technologies and §4 trace analysis).

3   Tracing

We believe that a practically viable tracer for malware analysis should be *efficient* (to facilitate live and ideally large scale analysis), *transparent* (to avoid detection and evasion by malware), and *complete* (i.e., record the instructions being traced, but also additional state information like register and memory values).

None of the current tracers achieves these goals simultaneously. In fact we have roughly the following situation: Emulation based tracers are detectable and rather slow. Those using dynamic binary instrumentation are fast but easily detectable. In fact, system emulation and dynamic binary instrumentation, are both easily detectable by malware [MPRB09]. Techniques using trap flags are transparent but rather slow. Finally, hardware based techniques, like branch tracing featured by certain Intel CPUs, are very promising, since they are fast and transparent. Yet, these techniques are not yet supported by virtual machines, which play an important role in malware analysis. Also, they do not feature completeness, since tracing is performed at basic block granularity. The completeness of such tracers operating at basic block granularity could be improved by reconstructing the state within the basic block in some cases. To our knowledge, this question has not yet been considered.

Let us briefly consider existing technologies. Ether [DRSL08] is highly transparent due to the fact that it is running in the hypervisor, it is quite slow since tracing is realized using single stepping. PIN [LCM⁺05] and the tracer proposed by Bania [Ban09]is fast, but both are detectable; PIN seems to have issues with self modifying code. On the other hand, TEMU [SBY⁺08, YS10] is very powerful but rather slow and detectable. Given these limitation, it is thus not astonishing that currently tracers play a little role in practical malware analysis.

3.1   Helios - Novel Techniques

To remedy the situation, we have developed a novel tracer termed *Helios*, which reaches the desirable properties mentioned above to a better overall level than existing ones. Helios essentially is a collection of optimization techniques designed to speed up malware tracing, e.g., by automatically skipping computationally costly, but non-relevant code parts like unpacking loops. While Helios improves over the state of the art, many challenges, like further improving performance and code coverage, remain.

The basic techniques underlying Helios are relatively straightforward: We interrupt the execution flow whenever a control transfer instruction (CTI) occurs, record the instructions between two such CTIs, and then continue to follow the execution from the destination address of the CTI. We implement this approach by using solely hardware breakpoints and the trap flag. Helios is currently implemented as kernel driver for the Windows OS, but it is likely to be portable to other operating systems running on Intel CPUs.

While the approach is simple on a high-level, there are series of challenges that need to be resolved. In fact, Helios combines novel and existing techniques to optimize performance and to achieve transparency. For instance, Helios is using a heuristic, that temporarily disables tracing in small code parts that make excessive use of loops, which are often found in packers; this technique alone yields a speed up of a factor of 40 when analyzing packed code. We also use techniques to be able to handle self-modifying code, which is quite common in malware. Finally, for achieving transparency, we use techniques to virtualize hardware debug registers.

Different experiments confirms the viability of Helios in practice. In fact, we were able to successfully trace code that was packed with a large number of commonly used packers used by malware. Since packer code typically contains detection and evasion techniques, these results hint that Helios is indeed reaches a high degree of transparency. In summary, Helios reaches transparency and efficiency in a more balanced way than existing tracers, and is thus a further step towards bringing tracing to practice. In the following we give an overview of the Helios design.

Helios Design Overview. To control the execution of a program our tracing algorithm uses hardware breakpoints and the trap flag (both debugging facilities of the CPU). Hardware breakpoints are controlled by the debug register on the x86 architecture. Four debug registers (Dr0-Dr3) and one control register (Dr7) exist. The four debug registers contain the breakpoint memory address and the control register defines the functionally of the breakpoints. Hardware breakpoints can be used for many different applications. Their main usage is detecting the execution at a memory address.

Figure 1 shows how Windows handles hardware breakpoints. If execution reaches a previously set breakpoint address (14B5A3) a debug interrupt (int1) is thrown by the CPU. If an interrupt is thrown, the CPU calls the appropriate interrupt service routine (ISR, TrapHandler) in kernelmode. It finds the correct trap handler by using the interrupt descriptor table (IDT). The Windows trap handler for interrupt 1 then calls KiDispatchException which is used to launch the exception handler in usermode (KiUserExceptionDispatcher) of the application which has caused the interrupt (program.exe).

The trap flag works in a similar way: if it is set the processor will execute only one instruction at time and then throw a debug interrupt.

Helios is implemented as a Windows kernel mode driver which intercepts the int1 trap handler and the thread creation system call. Figure 2 shows how the trap flag and hardware breakpoints are used to trace (control the execution flow) an application.

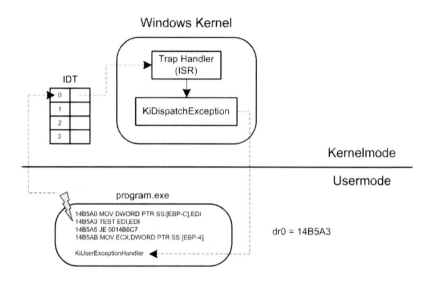

Fig. 1. Windows exception handling

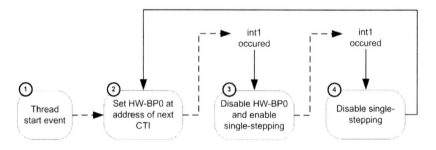

Fig. 2. Basic block tracing by using hardware breakpoints and the trap flag

The tracing algorithm is now explained in detail. If a new thread is detected by Helios ((1) in Figure 2) it will scan (disassemble) the binary code from the beginning of the thread start address until it finds a control transfer instruction (CTI) [Int10]. Then it finishes its first task by setting a hardware breakpoint (Dr0) at the address of the CTI (2). Next the applications thread begins its execution and reaches the address of the CTI where an interrupt is thrown (due to the hardware breakpoint). Helios will catch and handle this interrupt (3). Inside the interrupt handling routine of Helios the hardware breakpoint (Dr0) is cleared and the trap flag (single-stepping) is set. The interrupt handling routine finishes and finally calls the instruction IRETD. The IRETD instruction returns program control from the ISR to the program that was interrupted. Thus the Windows trap handler, KiDispatchException and KiUserException are not called, instead the application thread continues its execution where it has been interrupted before. The CTI is executed and right after the execution a next interrupt (due to the trap flag) is thrown. Again Helios catches and handles it (4). The trap flag is cleared and the next CTI is searched from the beginning of the current instruction pointer, which points to the address of the CTI target (where execution has been transferred to). Finally the algorithm jumps to its start and continues as described (1).

The algorithm described interrupts a program in a basic block granularity. A basic block is a sequence of instructions with a CTI at the end. Within the basic block, except at the end, no CTI is located. The start of a basic block begins with a target address of a CTI. Thus a basic block has exactly one entry and one exit point. Basic block tracing is much faster than single step tracing because the program is less frequently interrupted and thus the overhead introduced with the interruption and resumption process is smaller. However basic block tracing is not as precise as single step tracing. The CPU state can only be extracted when the program is interrupted and not for every instruction. However the granularity of basic block tracing is good enough for the application of instruction scanning, which is needed to find instructions which read sensitive memory locations.

The algorithm proposed above is portable because it uses hardware breakpoints and the trap flag which are available on all CPUs based on the x86 architecture. Furthermore, it is minimally invasive, meaning that beside debug registers no other register or memory contents are changed in the context of the application being traced. In addition our tests have shown that both mechanisms work inside virtual machines based on VMware and VirtualBox. These systems are mainly used in large scale malware analysis systems and thus it is necessary that the tracer works on them.

4   Advancing Trace Analysis

Current malware reverse engineering is performed essentially manually. That is, often a pseudo-code or C representation of relevant code parts is reconstructed from assembly. This decompilation step can also be automated by using tools such as Hex-Rays [HR]. From the resulting code the reverse engineer then recovers the semantic of the code under consideration. While this approach will certainly remain adequate and valuable for many years to come, we believe that research should focus on recovering code semantics directly and (semi-) automatically rather than "just" decompiling the code.

As mentioned above, so called sandboxes are a first step towards automating malware analysis and they are able to recover many aspects of the interaction of a malware with the operating system. While these are important malware features, there are many properties of malware which cannot yet be recovered automatically, and thus require manual analysis. These are typically purely algorithmic properties, running in user mode. On important example of such properties are domain name generation algorithms, which compute domain names for rendez-vous points of malware and command control servers [LW09, PSY09]. Another example is the use of cryptographic techniques used by malware, e.g., for authenticating and hiding the communication of malware with a command and control server.

Recovering algorithmic aspects is clearly a challenging goal, and hard in general. However, it might be somewhat easier in the malware domain, because many possible malware behaviors and techniques are known in advance, and can be specifically sought after. Ideally, these techniques would be realized using static analysis. Yet, static analysis is easily defeated by obfuscation, which is thus another formidable challenge to be overcome. Trace based analysis is considerably more resilient to obfuscation and also features state information, which makes analysis much easier. In fact, there has been some interesting initial work on automated analysis using traces.

One direction of research is concerned with recovering protocol specifications from code [Lut08, ZWCW08, CYLS07, CPSK09]. Other research has considered the identification of crypto code in malware using traces [GWH11]. These tools are for instance able to identify reliably certain crypto primitives like AES and RSA. Yet, they cannot handle the composition and higher-level use of cryptography. Recovering crypto code from traces is an example of the case mentioned above, i.e., of recovering a priori known constructs from code. Finally, VERA is an interesting piece of work on trace visualization [QL09, QLN09]. The goal of VERA is to visualize malware behavior, allowing the reverse engineer to identify malware features without resorting to code analysis.

Yet, we believe that the potential of traced based analysis is currently far form being fully utilized, and that there is substantial potential to push automation further. Additionally, there are further little explored related fields like the combination of dynamic analysis with static techniques.

References

[Ban09]   Bania, P.: Generic unpacking of self-modifying, aggressive, packed binary programs (2009)

[BK08]   Buehlmann, S., Kropp, M.: Extending joebox - a scriptable malware analysis system. In: University of Applied Science Northwestern of Switzerland, Bachelor Thesis (2008)

[BKK06]   Bayer, U., Kruegel, C., Kirda, E.: Ttanalyze: A tool for analyzing malware. In: 15th European Institute for Computer Antivirus Research, EICAR 2006 (2006)

[CPSK09]   Caballero, J., Poosankam, P., Song, D., Kreibich, C.: Dispatcher: Enabling active botnet infiltration using automatic protocol reverse-engineering. In: The 16th ACM Conference on Computer and Communications Security, CCS 2009, pp. 621–634. ACM (2009)

[CYLS07]   Caballero, J., Yin, H., Liang, Z., Song, D.: Polyglot: Automatic extraction of protocol message format using dynamic binary analysis. In: Proceedings of ACM Conference on Computer and Communication Security (2007)

[DRSL08]   Dinaburg, A., Royal, P., Sharif, M.I., Lee, W.: Ether: malware analysis via hardware virtualization extensions. In: ACM Conference on Computer and Communications Security (2008)

[EKK+07] Egele, M., Kruegel, C., Kirda, E., Yin, H., Song, D.: Dynamic spyware analysis. In: Proceedings of USENIX Annual Technical Conference (2007)

[GWH11] Groebert, F., Willems, C., Holz, T.: Automated identification of cryptographic primitives in binary programs. In: The 14th International Symposium on Recent Advances in Intrusion Detection, RAID (2011)

[HR] Hex-Rays. Hex-rays decompiler,
http://www.hex-rays.com/decompiler.shtml

[Int10] Intel. Intel 64 and ia-32 architectures software developer's manual. Basic architecture, ch. 5, 5.1.7, vol. 1, pp. 142–143, (2010)

[KKCW08] Kruegel, C., Kirda, E., Comparetti, P.M., Wondracek, G.: Automatic network protocol analysis. In: 15th Annual Network and Distributed System Security Symposium, NDSS 2008 (2008)

[LCM+05] Luk, C.-K., Cohn, R., Muth, R., Patil, H., Klauser, A., Lowney, G., Wallace, S., Reddi, V.J., Hazelwood, K.: Pin: building customized program analysis tools with dynamic instrumentation. In: Proceedings of the 2005 ACM SIGPLAN Conference on Programming Language Design and Implementation, PLDI 2005, pp. 190–200. ACM, New York (2005),
http://doi.acm.org/10.1145/1065010.1065034

[LJXZ08] Lin, Z., Jiang, X., Xu, D., Zhang, X.: Automatic protocol format reverse engineering through conectect-aware monitored execution. In: 15th Symposium on Network and Distributed System Security, NDSS (2008)

[Lut08] Lutz, N.: Towards revealing attackers intent by automatically decrypting network traffic. Master's thesis, ETH Zuerich (2008)

[LW09] Leder, F., Werner, T.: Know your enemy: Containing conficker - to tame a malware. In: Know Your Enemy Series of the Honeynet Project (2009)

[MKK07] Moser, A., Kruegel, C., Kirda, E.: Limits of static analysis for malware detection. In: 23rd Annual Computer Security Applications Conference, ACSAC (2007)

[MPRB09] Martignoni, L., Paleari, R., Roglia, G.F., Bruschi, D.: Testing cpu emulators. In: ISSTA (2009)

[NS05] Newsome, J., Song, D.: Dynamic taint analysis: Automatic detection, analysis, and signature generation of exploit attacks on commodity software. In: Proceedings of the Network and Distributed Systems Security Symposium (2005)

[PSY09] Porras, P., Saidi, H., Yegneswaran, V.: A foray into conficker's logic and rendezvous points. In: Proceedings of the 2nd USENIX Conference on Large-Scale Exploits and Emergent Threats, LEET 2009 (2009)

[QL09] Quist, D.A., Liebrock, L.M.: Visualizing compiled executables for malware analysis. In: 6th International Workshop on Visualization for Cyber Security, VizSec 2009 (2009)

[QLN09] Quist, D., Liebrock, L., Neil, J.: Visualizing compiled executables for malware analysis. Journal in Computer Virology (2009)

[SBY+08] Song, D., Brumley, D., Yin, H., Caballero, J., Jager, I., Kang, M.G., Liang, Z., Newsome, J., Poosankam, P., Saxena, P.: BitBlaze: A New Approach to Computer Security via Binary Analysis. In: Sekar, R., Pujari, A.K. (eds.) ICISS 2008. LNCS, vol. 5352, pp. 1–25. Springer, Heidelberg (2008)

[SDC+10] Skaletsky, A., Devor, T., Chachmon, N., Cohn, R.S., Hazelwood, K.M., Vladimirov, V., Bach, M.: Dynamic program analysis of microsoft windows applications. In: ISPASS (2010)

64   E. Bangerter, S. Bühlmann, and E. Kirda

[VY06]   Vasudevan, A., Yerraballi, R.: Cobra: Fine-grained malware analysis us-
            ing stealth localized-executions. In: IEEE Symposium on Security and
            Privacy (2006)
[WHF07]   Willems, C., Holz, T., Freiling, F.: Toward automated dynamic malware
            analysis using cwsandbox (2007)
[YS10]   Yin, H., Song, D.: Temu: Binary code analysis via whole-system layered
            annotative execution (2010)
[ZWCW08]   Jiang, X., Wang, Z., Cui, W., Wang, X.: Reformat: Automatic reverse
            engineering of encrypted messages. In: Technical report, NC State Uni-
            versity (2008)

Challenges for Dynamic Analysis
of iOS Applications

Martin Szydlowski[1], Manuel Egele[2], Christopher Kruegel[2],
and Giovanni Vigna[2]

[1] Secure Systems Lab, Vienna University of Technology, Austria
`msz@seclab.tuwien.ac.at`
[2] University of California, Santa Barbara
`{maeg,chris,vigna}@cs.ucsb.edu`

Abstract. Recent research indicates that mobile platforms, such as Android and Apple's iOS increasingly face the threat of malware. These threats range from spyware that steals privacy sensitive information, such as location data or address book contents to malware that tries to collect ransom from users by locking the device and therefore rendering the device useless. Therefore, powerful analysis techniques and tools are necessary to quickly provide an analyst with the necessary information about an application to assess whether this application contains potentially malicious functionality.

In this work, we focus on the challenges and open problems that have to be overcome to create dynamic analysis solutions for iOS applications. Additionally, we present two proof-of-concept implementations tackling two of these challenges. First, we present a basic dynamic analysis approach for iOS applications demonstrating the feasibility of dynamic analysis on iOS. Second, addressing the challenge that iOS applications are almost always user interface driven, we also present an approach to automatically exercise an application's user interface. The necessity of exercising application user interfaces is demonstrated by the difference in code coverage that we achieve with (69%) and without (16%) such techniques. Therefore, this work is a first step towards comprehensive dynamic analysis for iOS applications.

1 Introduction

Mobile devices and especially smart phones have become ubiquitous in recent years. They evolved from simple organizers and phones to full featured entertainment devices, capable of browsing the web, storing the user's address book, and provide turn-by-turn navigation through built in GPS receivers. Furthermore, most mobile platforms offer the possibility to extend the functionality of the supported devices by means of third party applications. Google's Android system, for example, has the official Android Market [1], and a series of unofficial descendants that provide third party applications to users. Similarly, Apple initially created the AppStore for third party applications for their iPhones. Nowadays, all devices running iOS (i.e., iPhone, iPod Touch, and iPad) can access and

J. Camenisch and D. Kesdogan (Eds.): iNetSec 2011, LNCS 7039, pp. 65–77, 2012.
© IFIP International Federation for Information Processing 2012

download applications from the AppStore. To ensure the quality and weed out
potentially malicious applications, Apple scrutinizes each submitted application
before it is distributed through the AppStore. This vetting process is designed
to ascertain that only applications conforming to the iPhone Developer Program
License Agreement [3] are available on the AppStore. However, anecdotal evidence has shown that this vetting process is not always effective. More precisely,
multiple incidents have become public where applications distributed through
the AppStore blatantly violate the user's privacy [6, 16], or provide functionality that was prohibited by the license agreement [26]. After Apple removed the
offending applications from the AppStore no new victims could download these
apps. However, users that installed and used these apps prior to Apple noticing
the offending behavior had to assume that their privacy had been breached.

Recent research [9, 13] indicates that AppStore applications regularly access
and transmit privacy sensitive information to the Internet. Therefore, it is obvious that the current vetting process as employed by Apple requires improvement.
With static analysis tools available to investigate the functionality of malicious
applications, one has to assume that attackers become more aware of the risk
of getting their malicious applications identified and rejected from the App-
Store. Thus, we assume attackers become more sophisticated in hiding malicious
functionality in their applications. Therefore, we think it is necessary to complement existing static analysis techniques for iOS applications with their dynamic
counterparts to keep the platform's users protected. We are convinced that the
combination of static and dynamic analysis techniques make a strong ensemble
capable of identifying malicious applications. To this end, this paper makes the
following contributions:

- We highlight the challenges that are imposed on dynamic analysis techniques
  when targeting a mobile platform such as iOS.
- We implement and evaluate a dynamic analysis approach that are suitable
  for the iOS platform.
- We create an automated system that exercises different aspects of the application under analysis by interacting with the application's user interface.

2   Dynamic Analysis

Dynamic analysis refers to a set of techniques that monitor the behavior of a
program while it is executed. These techniques can monitor different aspects of
program execution. For example, systems have been developed to record different
classes of function calls, such as API calls to the Windows API [25], or system
calls for Windows [8] or Linux [20]. Systems performing function call monitoring
can be implemented at different layers of abstraction within the operating system. For example, the JavaScript interpreter of a browser can be instrumented to
record function and method calls within JavaScript code [17]. Dynamic binary
rewriting [18] can be leveraged to monitor the invocation of functions implemented by an application or dynamically linked libraries. Similarly, debugging

mechanisms can be employed to gather such information [22, 23, 24]. Furthermore, the operating system used to perform the analysis might provide a useful
hooking infrastructure. Windows, for example, provides such hooks for keyboard
and mouse events. The dtrace [2] infrastructure available on Solaris, FreeBSD,
and Mac OS X can also be used to monitor system calls.

An orthogonal approach to function call monitoring is information flow analysis. That is, instead of focusing on the sequence of function calls during program
execution, the focus is on monitoring how the program operates on interesting
input data [7]. This data could, for example, be the packets that are received
from the network, or privacy relevant information that is stored on the device.
By tracking how this data is propagated through the system, information flow
monitoring tools can raise an alert if such sensitive data is about to be transmitted to the network [10, 27]. In the case of incoming network packets the same
technique can be applied to detect attacks that divert the control flow of an
application in order to exploit a security vulnerability [21].

3   Challenges for Dynamic Analysis on the iOS Platform

State of the art. Existing dynamic analysis techniques are geared towards applications and systems that execute on commodity PCs and operating systems.
Therefore, a plethora of such systems are available to analyze x86 binaries executing on Linux or Windows. While the x86 architecture is most widely deployed for
desktop and server computers, the landscape for the mobile device market has a
different shape. In the mobile segment, the ARM architecture is most prevalent.
The rise of malicious applications [15] for mobile platforms demands for powerful analysis techniques to be developed for these systems to fight such threats.
However, existing dynamic analysis techniques available for the x86 architecture
are not immediately applicable to mobile devices executing binaries compiled
for the ARM architecture. For example, many dynamic analysis approaches rely
on full system emulation or vitalization to perform their task. For most mobile
platforms, however, no such full system emulators are available. While Apple, for
example, includes an emulator with their XCode development environment, this
emulator executes x86 instructions, and therefore requires that the application
to emulate is recompiled. Thus, only applications that are available in source
code can be executed in this emulator. However, the AppStore only distributes
binary applications, which cannot be executed in the emulator. Furthermore,
the emulator's source code is not publicly available, and therefore, cannot be
extended to perform additional analysis tasks. OS X contains the comprehensive dtrace[1] instrumentation infrastructure. Although the iOS kernels and OS
X kernels are quite similar iOS does not provide this functionality.

Graphical user interfaces (GUI). An additional challenge results from the very
nature of iOS applications. That is, most iOS applications are making heavy use
of event driven graphical user interfaces. Therefore, launching an application and

---

[1] http://developers.sun.com/solaris/docs/o-s-dtrace-htg.pdf

executing the sample for a given amount of time might not be sufficient to collect enough information to assess whether the analyzed application poses a threat to the user or not. That is, without GUI interaction only a minimal amount of execution paths will be covered during analysis. Therefore, to cover a wide range of execution paths, any dynamic analysis system targeting iOS applications has to be able to automatically operate an applications' GUI.

Source vs. binary analysis. Combined static and dynamic analysis approaches, such as Avgerinos et al. [4], can derive a semantically rich representation of an application by analyzing its source code. However, applications distributed through the AppStore are available in binary form only. Therefore, any analysis system that targets iOS applications can only operate on compiled binaries.

Analyzing Objective-C. The most prevalent programming language to create iOS applications is Objective-C. Although Objective-C is a strict superset of the C programming language it features a powerful runtime environment that provides functionality for the object-oriented capabilities of the language. With regard to analyzing a binary created from Objective-C it is especially noteworthy that member functions (i.e., methods) of objects are not called directly. Instead, the runtime provides a dynamic dispatch mechanism that accepts a pointer to an object and the name of a method to call. The dispatch function is responsible for traversing the object's class hierarchy and identifying the implementation of the corresponding method.

The above mentioned problems combined with the constraint hardware resources of mobile devices pose significant challenges that need to be addressed before a dynamic analysis system for the iOS platform becomes viable.

4   Strategies to Overcome these Challenges

To tackle the above mentioned challenges, this work makes two major contributions. First, we implement and evaluate a dynamic analysis approach that is suitable for the iOS platform and provides a trace of method calls as observed during program execution. Second, we create an automated system that exercises different functionality of the application under analysis by interacting with the application's user interface.

4.1   Dynamic Analysis Approaches

As mentioned above not all dynamic analysis techniques available on the x86 architecture are feasible on iOS devices executing ARM instructions. Although there are many different approaches to dynamic analysis, we think that function call traces are a viable first step in providing detailed insights into an application's behavior. Therefore, in this section we elaborate on the lessons we learned while implementing a system that allows us to monitor the invocation of function calls of iOS applications.

Objective-C is the most prevalent programming language used to create applications for the iOS platform. However, as opposed to C++ where methods (i.e., class member functions) are invoked via the use of *vtable* pointers, in Objective-C methods are invoked fundamentally different. More precisely, methods are not called but instead a so-called *message* is sent to a receiver object. These messages are handled by the dynamic dispatch routine called objc_msgSend. This dispatch routine is responsible for identifying and invoking the implementation for the method that corresponds to a message. The first argument to this dispatch routine is always a pointer to the so-called *receiver* object. That is, the object on which the method should get invoked (e.g., an instance of the class NSMutableString). The second argument is a so-called *selector*. This selector is a string representation of the name of the method that should get invoked (e.g., appendString). All remaining arguments are of no immediate concern to the dispatch function. That is, these arguments get passed to the target method once it is resolved. To perform this resolution, the obj_msgSend function traverses the class hierarchy starting at the receiver and searches for a method whose name corresponds to the selector. Should no match be found in the receiver class, its superclasses are searched recursively. Once the corresponding method is identified, the dispatch routine invokes this method and passes along the necessary arguments. Due to the prevalence of Objective-C to create iOS applications we chose to implement a dynamic analysis approach that monitors the invocation of Objective-C methods instead of classic C functions.

Monitoring the dispatcher. One approach of monitoring all method invocations through the dynamic dispatch routine would be to hook the dispatch function itself. This could be achieved by following an approach similar to Detours [18]. That is, one would copy the initial instructions of the dynamic dispatcher before replacing them in memory with an unconditional jump to divert the control flow to a dedicated hook function. This hook function could then perform the necessary analysis, such as resolving parameter values, and logging the method invocation to the analysis report. Once the hook function finished executing, control would be transferred back to the dispatch function and regular execution could continue. Of course, the backed up initial instructions that got overwritten in the dispatcher need to be executed too before control is transferred back to the dispatch function. Although such an approach seems straight forward, the comprehensive libraries available to iOS applications also make extensive use of the Objective-C runtime. Therefore, such a generic approach would collect function call traces not only on the code the application developer created but also on all code that is executed within dynamically linked libraries. Often, however, function call traces collected from libraries are repetitive. Thus, we chose to implement our approach to only trace method invocations that are performed by the code the developer wrote.

Identifying method call sites. As a first step in monitoring Objective-C method calls we leverage our previous work PiOS [9] to generate a list of call sites to the dynamic dispatch function. Furthermore, PiOS is often capable of determining the number and types of arguments that are passed to the invoked method. This information is recorded along with the above mentioned call sites. Subsequently, this information is post processed to generate gdb[2] script files that log the corresponding information to the analysis report. More precisely, for each call site to the dynamic dispatch function, the script will contain a breakpoint. Furthermore, for each breakpoint hit the type (i.e., class) of the receiver as well as the name of the invoked method (i.e., the selector) get logged. Additionally, if PiOS successfully determined the number of arguments and their types, this information will also be logged.

4.2   Automated GUI Interaction

Most iOS applications feature a rich graphical user interface. Furthermore, most functionality within those applications gets executed in response to user interface events or interactions. This means that unless an application's user interface is exercised, most of the functionality contained in such applications lies dormant. As dynamic analysis only observes the behavior of code that is executing, large parts of functionality in such applications would be missed unless the GUI gets exercised.

Therefore, one of the challenges we address in this work is the automated interaction with graphical user interfaces. Such interaction with an application's GUI can be achieved on different levels. Desktop operating systems commonly support tools to get identifiers or handles for currently displayed GUI elements (e.g., UI explorer on Mac OS X). However, no such system is readily available for iOS.

Therefore, we turned our attention to alternative solutions to exercise an application's user interface. A straight forward approach could, for example, randomly click on the screen area. This method proved effective in detecting click-jacking attacks [5] on the World Wide Web. A more elaborate technique could read the contents from the device's frame buffer and try to identify interactive elements, such as buttons, check-boxes, or text fields by applying image processing techniques. Once such elements are identified, virtual keystrokes or mouse clicks could be triggered in the system to interact with these elements. We combined these two approaches into a proof-of-concept prototype that allows us to automatically exercise graphical user interfaces of iOS applications.

To interact with the device and get access to the device's frame buffer we leverage the open source Veency[3] VNC server. To communicate with the VNC server, and perform the detection and manipulation of UI elements, we have modified the python-vnc-viewer[4], an open source VNC client implementation in Python.

The basic idea behind this approach is to sample the screen and *tap* (i.e., click) locations on the screen that are determined by a regular grid pattern.

---

[2] http://www.gnu.org/s/gdb/

[3] http://cydia.saurik.com/info/veency/

[4] http://code.google.com/p/python-vnc-viewer/

Additionally, to identify interactive user interface elements, we perform the following steps in a loop: We capture the contents of the screen buffer and compare it to the previous screenshot (if present). If a sufficiently large fraction of pixels has changed between the images, we assume an interactive element has been hit. To tell input fields from other interactive elements apart, the current screenshot is compared to a reference image where the on-screen keyboard is displayed. This comparison is based on a heuristic that allows slight variations in the keyboard's appearance (e.g., different language settings). If we can determine that a keyboard is displayed, we send tap events to the first four keys in the middle row (i.e., ASDF on a US layout) and the return/done key to dismiss the keyboard again. When no keyboard is detected, we advance the cursor to the next location and send a tap event. In either case, we wait a brief amount of time before repeating the procedure, to give the UI time to respond and complete animations. We empirically determined a wait time of 3 seconds to be sufficient.

To avoid hitting the same UI elements repeatedly, we keep a greyscale image with dimensions identical to the frame buffer in memory. We call this greyscale image a *clickmap*. For each tap event, we perform a fuzzy flood-fill algorithm on the screenshot, originating from the tap coordinates, to determine the extents of the element we have tapped. That approach works well for monochrome or slightly shaded elements, like the default widgets offered by the interface builder for iOS applications. We mark these extents in the clickmap to keep track of the elements we have already accessed. That is, before a tap event is actually sent, the clickmap is consulted. If the current coordinates belong an element we already clicked, no tap event will be sent. Therefore, we avoid hitting the same element repeatedly, especially when the element in question is the background. Whenever we have a new screenshot containing changes, we clear the changed area in the clickmap so that new UI elements that might have appeared will be exercised too.

5   Evaluation

In this section we present the results we obtained during the evaluation of our prototype implementation. For the purpose of this evaluation we created a sample application that contains different user interface components such as buttons, text fields, and on/off switches. A screenshot of the application is depicted in Figure 1. The rationale for creating such a sample application is that by creating the application, we got intimately familiar with its functionality and operation. Furthermore, our experience with the static analysis of iOS applications allowed us to build corner cases into the application where we know static analysis can only provide limited results. For example, the test application would dynamically generate a new text field, once a specific button is clicked.

5.1   Method Call Coverage

PiOS identified a total of 52 calls to the dynamic dispatch function. Once our test application is launched, no further method calls are made unless the different user

Fig. 1. A screenshot of the sample application. The lower text field is dynamically created upon the first click to the *Reset* button.

interface elements are exercised. This is common behavior for iOS applications that are heavily user interface driven. During application startup only 8 of the 52 method calls (i.e., 16%) are executed. This underlines that dynamic analysis approaches that do not take the GUI of an iOS application into account, can only provide limited information about the application's functionality. Moreover, the methods that can be observed during program startup are generically added by Apple's build system and are almost identical for all applications targeting the iOS platform. Therefore, the valuable insights into application behavior that can be derived solely from the program startup phase are limited at best.

By executing our prototype to exercise the user interface of our test application, we could observe 36 methods being called. That corresponds to 69% of all methods being covered. Most importantly, we were able to exercise most of the functionality that is not part of the initial startup procedures for the applications. Our system did not observe the remaining 16 methods being invoked. One method would only be called if the user interface was in a very specific state.[5] However, our technique to exercise the user interface did not put the application in that state. All remaining 15 calls were part of the shutdown procedures (e.g., destructors) for the application. However, these methods are only invoked if the application terminates voluntarily. If the user presses the home button on the device, the application is terminated and no cleanup code is executed. As there

---

[5] If the switch has been switched from the default *on* setting to *off* and the *Reset* button is clicked afterwards, a message is sent to animate the switch back to its default *on* setting.

is not generic way to determine whether a certain user interface element will exit an application, our analysis terminates the application by tapping the home button. Thus, we did not observe these shutdown procedures being executed.

5.2   Comparison with Static Analysis

There are different possibilities on how to compare the static and dynamic analysis results. For example, static analysis covers all possible and thus also infeasible execution paths. Dynamic analysis can only observe the code paths that are executed while the program is analyzed. Therefore, we first evaluate how many and which methods get invoked during dynamic analysis. To compare the dynamic and static analysis results we first analyzed our test application with PiOS.

Static analysis results. PiOS detected 52 calls to the `objc_msgSend` dynamic dispatch function. In 49 cases (i.e., 94%) PiOS was able to statically determine the class of the receiver object and the value of the selector. Furthermore, PiOS validates these results by looking up the class of the receiver in the class hierarchy. A method call is successfully resolved if the class exists in the class hierarchy and this class or one of its superclasses implements a method whose name corresponds to the value of the selector.

The remaining three method calls that PiOS was unable to resolve are part of the function that dynamically creates and initializes the new text field. In our sample application this action is performed the first time the *Reset* button is clicked.

Comparison. We compared the receiver and selector for the 36 method calls present in the static and dynamic analysis reports. In all but 3 instances the results were identical. In two of these three instances PiOS identified the receiver type as `NSString`, whereas the dynamic analysis indicates that the actual type is `CFConstantStringClassReference`. However, according to Apple's documentation[6] these two types can be used interchangeably. In the third instance PiOS identified the receiver as `NSString` and dynamic analysis indicates the correct type to be `NSPlaceHolderString`. The difference is that for `NSPlaceHolderString` the initialization is not complete yet. This inconsistency is plausible as the only time this happened is in a call to `initStringWithFormat` to finish initialization.

5.3   Method Call Arguments

For 12 calls PiOS was able to determine the types of the arguments that get passed to the invoked methods. Thus, in these cases the dynamic analysis script is also logging information pertaining to these arguments. More precisely, for arguments of type `NSString` or any of its related types, a string representation of the argument is printed in the log file. For all other types, the address of the corresponding argument is printed instead.

---

[6]   http://developer.apple.com/library/mac/#documentation/CoreFoundation/
    Reference/CFStringRef/Reference/reference.html

5.4 Improvements for Static Analysis

As mentioned previously, static analysis is sometimes unable to compute the target method of an `objc_msgSend` call. More precisely, if PiOS is unable to statically determine the type of the receiver object or the value of the selector, PiOS cannot resolve the target method. This was the case for 3 method calls in our sample application. All 3 instances were part of the function that dynamically creates the additional text field. However, the dynamic analysis exercised this functionality and the analysis report contains the type of the receiver object and the value of the selector. Thus, the results from dynamic analysis can be leveraged to increase precision of our static analysis system.

6 Limitations and Future Work

Our proof-of-concept implementation relies on `gdb` to collect information about the program during execution. Thus, it is easily detectable by applications that try to detect whether they are analyzed. Therefore, we plan to evaluate stealthier ways of performing the necessary monitoring tasks in the future. Furthermore, our current implementation does not take system calls into account. However, for example Cydia's *mobile substrate* framework could be a good starting point to investigate system call monitoring on iOS devices.

Although our method of exercising the user interface resulted in high code coverage when compared to the functionality of program startup alone, we see room for improvement in this area too. That is, our current approach does not handle highly non-uniform colored (i.e., custom designed) user interface elements correctly. More precisely, our system does not detect the boundaries of such elements reliably and therefore might tap the same element multiple times. Furthermore, we only consider tap events and omit all interactions that use swipe or multi touch gestures. Therefore, to improve the automatic user interface interaction, one could try to extract the information about UI elements from the application's memory during runtime. This would entail getting a reference to the current `UIView` element and find a way to enumerate all UI elements contained in that view. We plan to investigate such techniques in future work.

7 Related Work

The wide range of related work in dynamic analysis mainly focuses on desktop operating systems. Due to the challenges mentioned above these techniques are not readily applicable to mobile platforms. For brevity, we refer the reader for such techniques to [11] and focus this section on related work that performs analysis for mobile platforms. TaintDroid [12] is the first dynamic analysis system for Android applications. However, it is limited to applications that execute in the Dalvik virtual machine. Thus, by modifying the open source code of the virtual machine, the necessary analysis steps can be readily implemented. However, the authors state that "Native code is unmonitored in TaintDroid".

Therefore, systems like TaintDroid are not applicable to the iOS platform as iOS applications execute on the hardware directly. That is there is no middle-layer that can be instrumented to perform analysis tasks.

Mulliner et al. [19] use labeling of processes to prevent cross-service attacks on mobile devices. However, this approach relies on a modified Linux kernel to check and verify which application is accessing which class of devices. Such checks only reveal the communication interfaces that are used by an application. Applications on the AppStore, however, are prevented from accessing the GSM modem, and thus can only access the network or Bluetooth components. Thus, such a system is too coarse grained to effectively protect iOS users. Furthermore, the source code for iOS is not available, and thus the necessary modifications to the operating systems' kernel cannot be made easily.

In previous work we presented PiOS [9] as an approach to detect privacy leaks in iOS applications using static analysis. This work demonstrated that it is indeed common for applications available in the AppStore to transmit privacy sensitive data to the network – usually without the users consent or knowledge. Furthermore, Enck et al. [14] presented Kirin a system that statically assesses, whether the permissions requested by an Android application collide with the user's privacy assumptions.

8 Conclusion

The popularity of Apple's iOS and the AppStore attracted developers with malicious intents. Recent events have shown that malicious applications available from the AppStore are capable of breaching the user's privacy by stealing privacy sensitive information, such as phone numbers, address book contents, or GPS location data from the device. Although static analysis techniques have shown that they are capable of detecting such fraudulent applications, we are convinced that attackers will employ obfuscation techniques to thwart static analysis. Therefore, this paper discusses the challenges and open problems that have to be overcome to provide comprehensive dynamic analysis tools for iOS applications. We tackled two of these challenges by providing prototype implementations of techniques that are able to generate method call traces for iOS applications, as well as exercising application user interfaces. Our evaluation highlights the necessity for taking user interfaces into account when performing dynamic analysis for iOS applications.

Acknowledgements. This work was partially supported by the ONR under grant N000140911042 and by the National Science Foundation (NSF) under grants CNS-0845559, CNS-0905537, and CNS-0716095. We would also like to thank Yan Shoshitaishvili for his help with the evaluation device.

References

1. Apps - Android Market, https://market.android.com/
2. BigAdmin: D'Trace,
   http://www.oracle.com/technetwork/systems/dtrace/index.html

3. iPhone Developer Program License Agreement,
   `http://www.eff.org/files/20100302_iphone_dev_agr.pdf`
4. Avgerinos, T., Cha, S.K., Hao, B.L.T., Brumley, D.: Aeg: Automatic exploit generation. In: 17th Annual Network and Distributed System Security Symposium, NDSS 2011 (2011)
5. Balduzzi, M., Egele, M., Kirda, E., Balzarotti, D., Kruegel, C.: A solution for the automated detection of clickjacking attacks. In: ASIACCS 2010: Proceedings of the 5th ACM Symposium on Information, Computer and Communications Security, pp. 135–144. ACM, New York (2010)
6. Beschizza, R.: iPhone game dev accused of stealing players' phone numbers, `http://www.boingboing.net/2009/11/05/iphone-game-dev-accu.html`
7. Chow, J., Pfaff, B., Garfinkel, T., Christopher, K., Rosenblum, M.: Understanding data lifetime via whole system simulation. In: Proceedings of the 13th USENIX Security Symposium (August 2004)
8. Dinaburg, A., Royal, P., Sharif, M.I., Lee, W.: Ether: malware analysis via hardware virtualization extensions. In: ACM Conference on Computer and Communications Security (CCS), pp. 51–62 (2008)
9. Egele, M., Kruegel, C., Kirda, E., Vigna, G.: PiOS: Detecting Privacy Leaks in iOS Applications. In: 17th Annual Network and Distributed System Security Symposium, NDSS 2011 (2011)
10. Egele, M., Kruegel, C., Kirda, E., Yin, H., Song, D.X.: Dynamic spyware analysis. In: Proceedings of the 2007 USENIX Annual Technical Conference, pp. 233–246 (2007)
11. Egele, M., Scholte, T., Kirda, E., Kruegel, C.: A survey on automated dynamic malware analysis techniques and tools. ACM Computing Surveys (to appear)
12. Enck, W., Gilbert, P., Chun, B.-G., Cox, L.P., Jung, J., McDaniel, P., Sheth, A.N.: TaintDroid: an information-flow tracking system for realtime privacy monitoring on smartphones. In: Proceedings of OSDI 2010 (October 2010)
13. Enck, W., Octeau, D., McDaniel, P., Chaudhuri, S.: A Study of Android Application Security. In: Proceedings of the 20th USENIX Security Symposium (August 2011)
14. Enck, W., Ongtang, M., McDaniel, P.: Understanding android security. IEEE Security and Privacy 7(1), 50–57 (2009)
15. Felt, A.P., Finifter, M., Chin, E., Hanna, S., Wagner, D.: A Survey of Mobile Malware in the Wild. In: ACM Workshop on Security and Privacy in Mobile Devices (SPSM), Chicago, IL, USA (October 2011)
16. B.R. for The Register. iphone app grabs your mobile number, `http://www.theregister.co.uk/2009/09/30/iphone_security/`
17. Hallaraker, O., Vigna, G.: Detecting malicious javascript code in mozilla. In: 10th International Conference on Engineering of Complex Computer Systems (ICECCS 2005), pp. 85–94 (2005)
18. Hunt, G., Brubacher, D.: Detours: binary interception of Win32 functions. In: 3rd USENIX Windows NT Symposium, pp. 135–143. USENIX Association, Berkeley (1999)
19. Mulliner, C., Vigna, G., Dagon, D., Lee, W.: Using Labeling to Prevent Cross-Service Attacks Against Smart Phones. In: Büschkes, R., Laskov, P. (eds.) DIMVA 2006. LNCS, vol. 4064, pp. 91–108. Springer, Heidelberg (2006)
20. Mutz, D., Valeur, F., Vigna, G., Krügel, C.: Anomalous system call detection. ACM Trans. Inf. Syst. Secur. 9(1), 61–93 (2006)

21. Portokalidis, G., Slowinska, A., Bos, H.: Argos: an emulator for fingerprinting zero-day attacks for advertised honeypots with automatic signature generation. In: Proceedings of the 2006 EuroSys Conference, pp. 15–27 (2006)
22. Vasudevan, A., Yerraballi, R.: Stealth breakpoints. In: 21st Annual Computer Security Applications Conference (ACSAC), pp. 381–392 (2005)
23. Vasudevan, A., Yerraballi, R.: Cobra: Fine-grained malware analysis using stealth localized-executions. In: IEEE Symposium on Security and Privacy, pp. 264–279 (2006)
24. Vasudevan, A., Yerraballi, R.: Spike: engineering malware analysis tools using unobtrusive binary-instrumentation. In: Proceedings of the 29th Australasian Computer Science Conference, pp. 311–320 (2006)
25. Willems, C., Holz, T., Freiling, F.: Toward automated dynamic malware analysis using CWSandbox. IEEE Security and Privacy 5(2), 32–39 (2007)
26. Wired. Apple Approves, Pulls Flashlight App with Hidden Tethering Mode, http://www.wired.com/gadgetlab/2010/07/apple-approves-pulls-flashlight%2dapp-with-hidden-tethering-mode/
27. Yin, H., Song, D.X., Egele, M., Kruegel, C., Kirda, E.: Panorama: capturing system-wide information flow for malware detection and analysis. In: ACM Conference on Computer and Communications Security (CCS), pp. 116–127 (2007)

Energy-Efficient Cryptographic Engineering Paradigm

Marine Minier[1] and Raphael C.-W. Phan[2]

[1] Université de Lyon, INRIA
INSA-Lyon, CITI, F-69621, Villeurbanne, France
Marine.Minier@insa-lyon.fr
[2] Loughborough University
Electronic, Electrical & Systems Engineering
LE11 3TU, Leicestershire, UK
R.Phan@lboro.ac.uk

Abstract. We motivate the notion of green cryptographic engineering, wherein we discuss several approaches to energy minimization or energy efficient cryptographic processes. We propose the amortization of computations paradigm in the design of cryptographic schemes; this paradigm can be used in line with existing approaches. We describe an example structure that exemplifies this paradigm and at the end of the paper we ask further research questions for this direction.

1 Motivation: The Future is Green

As worldwide demand for energy increases, our present world realizes that energy resources are valuable assets, and researchers simultaneously aim to develop techniques to generate energy from renewable resources and to ensure efficient usage of energy so that energy derived notably from non-renewable energy resources is not unnecessarily wasted.

The ICT sector in 2008 contributed to 2% of global carbon emissions [5] i.e. 830 MtCO$_2$e, and expected to increase to 1.43 GtCO$_2$e by 2020. In addition to making devices more energy-efficient thus reducing the carbon footprint, ICT stakeholders aim to utilize ICT to enable energy efficiency across the board in other non-ICT areas, in order to achieve energy savings of 15% (7.8 GtCO$_2$e) of global emissions by 2020. Thus, not only will ICT substantially influence global energy consumption, ICT mechanisms and networking will feature prominently in other non-ICT areas for better utilization of energy.

In the networking context, telecoms providers are moving to energy-efficient equipment and networks, and it is expected that by 2013 such equipment will be 46% of global network infrastructure [16]. For many years now, networking researchers have investigated ways to design and implement energy-efficient devices, networks and mechanisms ranging from lightweight resource-constrained devices like RFIDs and wireless sensor nodes to energy-aware routing algorithms.

Within network security, researchers have investigated impacts on energy due to authentication and key exchange protocols [6, 7], notably for wireless sensor

J. Camenisch and D. Kesdogan (Eds.): iNetSec 2011, LNCS 7039, pp. 78–88, 2012.
© IFIP International Federation for Information Processing 2012

networks (WSNs) where prolonging battery life is of utmost importance. Researchers have also compared the energy consumption of different cryptographic mechanisms e.g. RSA and ElGamal implemented in WSNs [14], pairing based cryptography notably key exchange [22]; and shown that public-key cryptography has non-negligible impact on sensor lifetime [4].

Most of these work consider energy efficiency of *implementation* on specific hardware, or compare energy consumption of cryptographic primitives on certain platforms. Few have treated how to *design* a cryptographic scheme whose structure is well suited for energy efficiency. Indeed, cryptographic schemes are central to security protocols in different layers of the network protocol stack, e.g. SSL/TLS at the transport layer, IPsec at the network layer, so if one aims to design energy-efficient security protocols for these layers, it makes sense to ensure that the underlying cryptographic schemes used by these energy-efficient protocols are also designed with energy efficiency in mind. To the best of our knowledge, a couple of such results exist, as to be discussed next.

Indeed, the solution to the energy efficiency problem should be a holistic one e.g. considering all levels of abstraction, with no obvious weak link in the green sense.

Related Work. Kaps et al. [13] made recommendations for cryptographic design suited for ultra low-power settings:

* scalability: able to efficiently scale between bit serial and high parallelism so that implementers can trade off speed for power
* regularity: only a few different primitives should be used
* multihashing and multiencryption: sequentially calling a simpler and seemingly less secure hash function or encryption multiple times to achieve higher security. This approach is similar to the iterated structure of constructing hash functions based on compression functions and ciphers based on round functions
* precomputation/offline: the bulk of the processing is performed offline, before going online to process the incoming input so there is less latency, thus less energy wasted during the wait.

[13] also contrasted different alternatives to implementing basic functions e.g. algebraic representation versus table lookup, polynomial arithmetic for hardware implementation, constant shifts/rotations vs data-dependent ones, logic functions vs arithmetic ones. These are more in terms of choosing the proper basic functions to minimize energy consumption.

Meanwhile, Troutman and Rijmen [23] advocate a green approach to the design process, i.e. recycling primitives since long established ones garner more trust. They illustrated the concept with a discussion on AES' pedigree and how AES-type primitives were subsequently recycled in some manner in many SHA-3 candidates.

Rogaway and Steinberger [18,19] show how to reuse block ciphers to construct hash compression functions, essentially emphasizing on the minimalist approach while at the same time attaining assurance (given that the reused primitive has been in existence for some time and therefore seen considerable public analysis). The minimalist approach gives rise to less hardware or smaller memory footprint. More interestingly, in [19], they consider the approach of fixing the underlying block cipher's key input so that the corresponding block cipher key schedule can be computed offline instead of in online streaming mode, thus achieving better efficiency.

Essentially, the approach to recycle primitives advocated by [13, 23] is aimed to optimize the efforts (and energy) of designers that had already been spent on designing a primitive, and to optimize the code size of the primitive's implementation. Indeed, recycling a primitive means less energy needs to be spent to design a new one, and less code size is taken up by having multiple different primitives since the same primitive code can be called multiple times instead of different codes for different primitives.

The approach in [13] to perform the bulk precomputation minimizes online time (i.e. time when actual input data is incoming and needs to be processed). This approach is similar to concepts in cryptography relating to remotely keyed encryption [24] and online/offline signatures [20] for the application of real-time streaming. Less online time means less time is dependent on receiving the transmitted input which may cause latency and therefore unnecessary usage of energy during then.

Minimal Energy Consumption and Lightweightness vs Energy Efficiency. It should be noted that minimizing energy consumption or emphasis on lightweight design do not necessarily imply energy efficiency, and vice versa. By definition, energy efficiency refers to efficient use of energy, without unnecessary wastage. A lightweight cryptographic scheme is designed to use low-power computations, have small code size or require small memory space, yet it may involve multiple different low-power operations; so from the viewpoint of recycling primitives, this approach is not energy efficient. In contrast, a design that efficiently reuses primitives, may have higher power requirements than a lightweight scheme if the primitive itself involves complex operations that have high power consumption.

This Paper. Here, we first discuss the notion for green cryptographic engineering wherein are approaches for energy-minimizing and/or energy-efficient cryptographic processing. We also propose an approach such that the energy consumed in performing any substantial computation, is optimized by amortizing the output of the computation over different states of the scheme: we denote this as *amortization of computations*. We describe the relevance of this notion against recent cryptographic schemes proposed in literature. We conclude by posing further questions to be answered, some of which we are currently investigating.

2   Green Cryptographic Engineering Paradigm

Being green means being energy efficient, and we will use these terms interchangeably. Efficient refers to being fit for purpose and not being wasteful: both in the sense that no energy is drawn unnecessarily and that energy once drawn should be put to good use. Energy here is in the sense of any kind of resources. To appreciate this *resources* term, it is worth being explicit here what kinds of resources one may be interested in not wasting:

* ⋆ human effort:
  within a cryptographic engineering paradigm, we can think of making efficient use of the effort (and time spent is therefore also implied) of cryptographic designers, cryptanalysts, implementers and users of cryptographic schemes.
* ⋆ computational effort:
  efficient use of this resource can be in the sense of minimizing the amount of computation required (and therefore the cost of access to such computational power), or making full use of the output of any computation.
* ⋆ space:
  space refers to the capacity required to store or execute the scheme's implementations. This includes, e.g. ROM or RAM size especially for embedded computing platforms.
* ⋆ energy supply:
  computational machines require electrical power to run, so being green here could mean minimizing the amount of electrical power required by such computations.
* ⋆ time:
  the issue of interest here is to minimize the amount of time required to perform cryptographic operations. Towards that aim, researchers could investigate parallelizable structures that reduce the time-per-output ratio.

Cryptographic engineering, i.e. the process life cycle for design, analysis, implementation and use of cryptographic schemes and cryptographic based security systems, can be approached with a green strategy, bearing in mind the aim to optimize usage of the above listed resources.

Each stage of the process can be green in the following directions:

* minimized energy consumption:
  there is considerable research in this regard, notably the work on designing lightweight cryptographic schemes for resource-constrained devices such as RFID and wireless sensor networks; lightweight in the sense of energy consumption, code size and/or memory requirements.
  Applying this approach to cryptographic scheme design, lightweight and/or low-energy operations can be selected for use as basic building blocks within the cryptographic scheme, such as logical operations, and addition/rotation/XOR (ARX) constructions rather than multiplications.

- amortization of primitives:
  this approach is essentially in terms of recycling primitives that have already been designed or implemented [13]. This efficient usage of primitives leads to efficient code size, since the size remains the same irrespective of how many times the primitive is run. The regularity and multihashing/encryption suggestions of [13] are of this type of approach.
  This approach is implicit in typical cryptographic designs for efficiency and simplicity, e.g. iterative block cipher structures, feedback shift register based stream ciphers, Merkle-Damgård hash function structures, modular design paradigms i.e. constructions based on fundamental building blocks, and modes of operation that transform existing primitives into other primitives e.g. stream cipher, hash function's compression function or message authentication code from block cipher.
  This approach is also implicit in the cryptanalytic community, where the effort invested in discovering new cryptanalytic techniques is amortized via its application (at times via some adaptation or generalization) to multiple schemes of the same type or of different types, e.g. differential cryptanalysis and the notion of distinguishers initially invented for block ciphers, later applied to stream ciphers and hash functions.
  Towards a longer term aim, one can design fundamental operations that can form generic structures for use as building blocks within different types of cryptographic schemes, e.g. the inversion based Sbox of AES used to construct the AES round function, the LEX stream cipher and the AES-inspired SHA-3 candidates. Or design common primitives used for a multi-type cryptographic scheme, e.g. in the case of ARMADILLO [2].

- input-independent bulk (pre)computation:
  the approach here it to partition the computation effort into input-dependent and input-independent functions, and where the bulk of computations are designed into the input-independent functions so that most computations can be done in offline mode or so that this scales well even for inputs of large sizes or that are time-consuming, thus drawing less energy.
  This approach is exemplified in hash function designs e.g. Fugue [12]; where the security of such designs relies on heavy-weight finalization functions such that the iterated message block-dependent compression functions can be designed to be less computationally intensive.

- amortization of computations:
  the approach here is to reuse the effort put into a computation, more specifically, reflected in its output, multiple times at that state of output and in subsequent states in feedforward fashion. Doing so allows subsequent states to be more directly influenced by the current state 'for free', i.e. without extra computations to produce that state; and the net effect of this is that we then require less number of iterations overall in order to retain similar level of security.

This approach is exemplified in the structure we propose later in this paper. Our structure is a generic one that subsumes feedforward-based constructions in literature, e.g. block cipher based hash compression functions like Davies-Meyer and Miyaguchi-Preneel are special cases when the state is only reused once, as well as more recent schemes that we will discuss in more detail in section 4.

During the conference, we hope to engage attendees in a discussion of other possible green approaches to the cryptographic engineering process, or whether there are any other instantiations of the above-listed approaches in existing cryptographic schemes.

3   A Computation-Amortizing Structure

One energy-efficient cryptographic structure that instantiates the amortization of computations approach is as follows. As with conventional design strategy, the structure is iterative, based on a round function $F(s_i, s_{i_-}^*)$ where s_i denotes the conventional type of input state to the function and where $s_{i_-}^*$ denotes one or more previous states for $i_- < i$.

Within $F()$, we have the following steps in sequence:

1. $s_i \leftarrow \mathsf{heavy}(s_i)$
2. $s_{i+1} \leftarrow \mathsf{light}(s_i, s_{i_-}^*)$

where $\mathsf{heavy}()$ is a computationally-intensive operation e.g. multiplication, while $\mathsf{light}()$ is a lightweight operation e.g. logical functions.

This way, from the computational viewpoint, the input vector $s_{i_-}^*$ does not substantially add to computational requirements (and thus energy) of F, and yet from a cryptographic viewpoint, adds substantially to the mixing process within F.

The basic idea here is that an intermediate state s_i after computation function F, is reused several times at the same state location (i.e. spatial amortization) and also fedforward in time (i.e. temporal amortization) to be reused in subsequent states s_j ($j > i$), and aside from the first time that the state is used, subsequent uses of that state will involve non-computationally intensive functions to mix that state back in. The gist is to fully utilize (and reuse) any state including the outputs of any function, as many times as possible; essentially using the 'copy' and 'feedforward' (these are computationally non-intensive) operations.

Amortization then comes from the fact that the light inputs are actually the reusing of states from other parts of the structure (so we kind of have them for free without having to do extra computations to get them), and the way that they should influence the F function should be in a non-computationally intensive manner e.g. XOR, logical operations.

In this way, it is intuitive that the required number of rounds can be less than conventional structures of F that process only the current state s_i, while maintaining the security level.

In analyzing this kind of construction, a new measure so-called *points of influence* (POI) can be considered. This notion measures how many other state points are immediately and directly affected by a change in a state at one point within a cryptographic scheme. Indeed, the probability of a differential distinguisher should be reduced given a higher points of influence, because the probability is a function of the number of active points affected by a difference in a state.

A preliminary step concerning diffusion when looking at F as a round function could be to consider that the injection of the $s_{i_-}^*$ state looks like a subkey addition in the block cipher context or a message reinjection in the hash compression function context. Indeed, it turns out that block cipher key addition and hash function message injection operations are typically designed to be light, thus fitting nicely with this convention. Thus, a first insight concerning diffusion could be to look at diffusion properties of the key into the cipher. A parallel could be made to evaluate the diffusion when considering $s_{i_-}^*$ taking into account the points of influence. Concerning hash functions, the theory of goal would be to readapt security proofs to the case of several intermediate message dependencies.

From this notion of diffusion which is among the most important when talking about cryptography (the other one is of course the confusion), we could derive the probability of success when looking at an adversary within the context of the differential or the linear distinguishers.

4   Computation Amortization in Practice

Our computation-amortizing structure in section 3 can in fact fit different kinds of cryptographic schemes in literature, including hash functions, message authentication codes (MACs) and stream ciphers.

For hash function structures, the feedforward strategy, i.e. to feed a state (output from some function) forward to be combined with a future state, is well established. For instance, the PGV [17] structure for constructing hash compression functions from block ciphers is a popular example of this strategy in practice.

This strategy is also exemplified in recent hash function structures constructed from compression functions where the feedforward enters two (instead of just one) future states. These include the 3C and 3C+ [9] constructions, where up to two copies of each state are fedforward to the final state for combination; and the ESS [15] and its predecessor [21], where one of the states is forwarded for combination with two different states.

More interestingly, related compression function constructions appear in independent work due to Rogaway and Steinberger in [18,19]. For some input x, the function of [18] is defined as:

$$\text{for } i \leftarrow 1 \text{ to } k \text{ do}$$
$$s_i \leftarrow f_i(x, s_1, \ldots, s_{i-1})$$
$$y_i \leftarrow \pi_i(s_i)$$
$$\text{endfor}$$
$$\text{return } g(x, s_1, \ldots, s_k)$$

where f_i denotes some function and π_i denotes some permutation. If we let the f_i and g functions be lightweight functions, and indeed, the particular compression function construction in [19] is one where such f_i and g are linear functions, i.e.

$$f_i = a_0 x + \sum_{j=1}^{i-1} a_j s_j,$$

where a_j (for $j \in \{0, \ldots, i-1\}$) is some constant and we let $g = f_{k+1}$; then the resultant construction of [19] can be seen as an instance of our computation-amortizing structure of section 3, where our heavy() function is instantiated with a permutation π_i.

In terms of MAC structures, the SS-NMAC scheme of [8] builds on the structure of [21] and retains the feedforward strategy. More specifically, for about half of its internal functions, the output state is fedforward onto two other states for combination.

For stream ciphers which are traditionally represented by first an updating function f that updates the content of an internal state s_i and then a filtering function g that filters the content of s_i, the model proposed for computation-amortizing structure leads to intrinsically modify the stream cipher in the following way:

▽ If the updating function f takes the role of the computation-amortizing F function described in section 3 to act on s_i and on $s_{i_-}^*$, then this means that the internal state becomes bigger. By this way maybe the f function could be lightened due to its bigger internal state. An example of a stream cipher that has a memory state is given in [3] for software cases. The case where g the filtering function takes the role of the F function must be carefully studied because at this time, it is not so clear that adding a light() part could be so directly derived to discard classical attacks because the resistance of a stream cipher against traditional distinguishers mainly depends on the clever choice of g.

Another way to build stream ciphers is to use a block cipher in the so-called counter mode (CTR) of operation where the keystream is generated by encrypting successive values of a counter, and then each plaintext block is XORed with each keystream block. As it is not possible to directly modify a block cipher using the computation-amortizing structure proposed in section 3 (due to the required invertibility property for conventional block cipher structures), we could try to modify the counter mode itself reinjecting previous values. For example, we could derive those possible modes from MILENAGE, the one-block-to-many mode used in 3GPP [1] which was proved to be secure in [10].

5   Open Research Questions

While it may be that no matter how energy *inefficient* the cryptography is and still it is unlikely to be the most inefficient component of a system, yet the right strategy should be to approach this analogous to security's celebrated weakest link property, i.e. viewing a system to be only as energy-efficient as its most energy-inefficient component. Thus, as researchers work hard to design and implement network security systems and protocols that are energy-efficient, the cryptographic schemes that underlie these network security protocols should also be designed with explicit energy efficiency.

The green cryptographic engineering paradigm discussed in section 2 is a good start towards approaching this aim, so that the process of engineering cryptographic schemes (design, analysis, and/or implementation) can be performed while maintaining energy efficiency.

The motivation is clear. Security is already largely seen frequently as an impediment to performance, yet needs to be there in view of constant threats of attacks. In a future where energy resources are increasingly becoming a scarcity, security will become all the more undesirable if in addition to trading off performance, they are also energy *in*efficient.

We conclude for now with some further research questions for this particular direction:

† Can we design cryptographic structures that are provably secure and provably energy efficient?

† Can we transform provably secure cryptographic structures into ones that are energy efficient, while still retaining provable security?

† How do we model energy efficiency in the provable sense?
To this aim, we have started to formalize faulty and/or loss of energy models where the designer or the user is not malicious in the security sense but does not take any care towards the energy efficiency goal (because he could be lazy, ignorant or indifferent to energy efficiency). Then provable energy efficiency for a scheme is to show that energy loss only occurs with negligible probability.

† What provably energy efficient notions can be defined?

† What metrics can be used to measure energy efficiency of cryptographic schemes?
Along the lines of the green cryptographic engineering paradigm approaches discussed in section 2, we suggest investigating metrics such as *primitive multiplicity* (the number of times a primitive is recycled), *state multiplicity* (the number of times a state is used elsewhere), *points of influence* (how many other state points are immediately affected when a change is made in one state).

References

1. 3rd Generation Partnership Project, "Specification of the MILENAGE Algorithm Set: An Example Algorithm Set for the 3GPP Authentication and Key Generation Functions f1, f1*, f2, f3, f4, f5 and f5* - Document 2 (TS 35.206): Algorithm Specification; Document 5 (TR 35.909): Summary and Results of Design and Evaluation", http://www.3gpp.org

2. Badel, S., Dağtekin, N., Nakahara, J., Ouafi, K., Reffé, N., Sepehrdad, P., Sušil, P., Vaudenay, S.: ARMADILLO: A Multi-purpose Cryptographic Primitive Dedicated to Hardware. In: Mangard, S., Standaert, F.-X. (eds.) CHES 2010. LNCS, vol. 6225, pp. 398–412. Springer, Heidelberg (2010)
3. Berger, T.P., Minier, M., Pousse, B.: Software Oriented Stream Ciphers Based upon FCSRs in Diversified Mode. In: Roy, B., Sendrier, N. (eds.) INDOCRYPT 2009. LNCS, vol. 5922, pp. 119–135. Springer, Heidelberg (2009)
4. Bicakci, K., Gultekin, H., Tavli, B.: The Impact of One-Time Energy Costs on Network Lifetime in Wireless Sensor Networks. IEEE Communications Letters 13(12), 905–907 (2009)
5. The Climate Group, "SMART 2020: Enabling the Low Carbon Economy in the Information Age" Global e-Sustainability Initiative, GeSI (2008)
6. de Meulenaer, G., Gosset, F., Standaert, F.-X., Pereira, O.: On the Energy Cost of Communication and Cryptography in Wireless Sensor Networks. In: Proc. WiMob 2008, pp. 580–585. IEEE (2008)
7. Delgado-Mohatar, O., Sierra, J.M., Brankovic, L., Fúster-Sabater, A.: An Energy-Efficient Symmetric Cryptography Based Authentication Scheme for Wireless Sensor Networks. In: Samarati, P., Tunstall, M., Posegga, J., Markantonakis, K., Sauveron, D. (eds.) WISTP 2010. LNCS, vol. 6033, pp. 332–339. Springer, Heidelberg (2010)
8. Dodis, Y., Steinberger, J.: Message Authentication Codes from Unpredictable Block Ciphers. In: Halevi, S. (ed.) CRYPTO 2009. LNCS, vol. 5677, pp. 267–285. Springer, Heidelberg (2009)
9. Gauravaram, P., Millan, W.L., Dawson, E., Viswanathan, K.: Constructing Secure Hash Functions by Enhancing Merkle-Damgård Construction. In: Batten, L.M., Safavi-Naini, R. (eds.) ACISP 2006. LNCS, vol. 4058, pp. 407–420. Springer, Heidelberg (2006)
10. Gilbert, H.: The Security of "One-Block-to-Many" Modes of Operation. In: Johansson, T. (ed.) FSE 2003. LNCS, vol. 2887, pp. 376–395. Springer, Heidelberg (2003)
11. Greenemeier, L.: Can the World's Telecoms Slash their Energy Consumption 1000-Fold? Scientific American (January 11, 2010)
12. Halevi, S., Hall, W.E., Jutla, C.S.: The Hash Function "Fugue". SHA-3 Candidate Submission (September 15, 2009)
13. Kaps, J.-P., Gaubatz, G., Sunar, B.: Cryptography on a Speck of Dust. IEEE Computers 40(2), 38–44 (2007)
14. Kayalvizhi, R., Vijayalakshmi, M., Vaidehi, V.: Energy Analysis of RSA and EL-GAMAL Algorithms for Wireless Sensor Networks. In: Meghanathan, N., Boumerdassi, S., Chaki, N., Nagamalai, D. (eds.) CNSA 2010. CCIS, vol. 89, pp. 172–180. Springer, Heidelberg (2010)
15. Lehmann, A., Tessaro, S.: A Modular Design for Hash Functions: Towards Making the Mix-Compress-Mix Approach Practical. In: Matsui, M. (ed.) ASIACRYPT 2009. LNCS, vol. 5912, pp. 364–381. Springer, Heidelberg (2009)
16. Pike Research, "'Green' Telecom Equipment will Represent 46% of Network Capital Expenditures by 2013" Pike Research (June 9, 2009)
17. Preneel, B., Govaerts, R., Vandewalle, J.: Hash Functions Based on Block Ciphers: A Synthetic Approach. In: Stinson, D.R. (ed.) CRYPTO 1993. LNCS, vol. 773, pp. 368–378. Springer, Heidelberg (1994)
18. Rogaway, P., Steinberger, J.: Security/Efficiency Tradeoffs for Permutation-Based Hashing. In: Smart, N.P. (ed.) EUROCRYPT 2008. LNCS, vol. 4965, pp. 220–236. Springer, Heidelberg (2008)

19. Rogaway, P., Steinberger, J.: Constructing Cryptographic Hash Functions from Fixed-Key Blockciphers. In: Wagner, D. (ed.) CRYPTO 2008. LNCS, vol. 5157, pp. 433–450. Springer, Heidelberg (2008)
20. Shamir, A., Tauman, Y.: Improved Online/Offline Signature Schemes. In: Kilian, J. (ed.) CRYPTO 2001. LNCS, vol. 2139, pp. 355–367. Springer, Heidelberg (2001)
21. Shrimpton, T., Stam, M.: Building a Collision-Resistant Compression Function from Non-Compressing Primitives. In: Aceto, L., Damgård, I., Goldberg, L.A., Halldórsson, M.M., Ingólfsdóttir, A., Walukiewicz, I. (eds.) ICALP 2008, Part II. LNCS, vol. 5126, pp. 643–654. Springer, Heidelberg (2008)
22. Szczechowiak, P., Kargi, A., Scott, M., Collier, M.: On the Application of Pairing based Cryptography to Wireless Sensor Networks. In: Proc. WiSec 2009, pp. 1–12. ACM (2009)
23. Troutman, J., Rijmen, V.: Green Cryptography: Cleaner Engineering through Recycling. IEEE Security and Privacy 7(4), 71–73 (2009)
24. Weis, R., Effelsberg, W., Lucks, S.: Remotely Keyed Encryption with Java Cards: a Secure and Efficient Method to Encrypt Multimedia Streams. In: Proc. ICME 2000, pp. 537–540. IEEE (2000)

Towards a Similarity Metric for Comparing Machine-Readable Privacy Policies

Inger Anne Tøndel and Åsmund Ahlmann Nyre

SINTEF ICT, Trondheim, Norway
{inger.a.tondel,asmund.a.nyre}@sintef.no

Abstract. Current approaches to privacy policy comparison use strict evaluation criteria (e.g. user preferences) and are unable to state how close a given policy is to fulfil these criteria. More flexible approaches for policy comparison is a prerequisite for a number of more advanced privacy services, e.g. improved privacy-enhanced search engines and automatic learning of privacy preferences. This paper describes the challenges related to policy comparison, and outlines what solutions are needed in order to meet these challenges in the context of preference learning privacy agents.

1 Introduction

Internet users commonly encounter situations where they have to decide whether or not to share personal information with service providers. Ideally, users should make such decisions based on the content of the providers' privacy policy. In practice, however, these policies are difficult to read and understand, and are rarely used at all by users [1]. Several technological solutions have been developed to provide privacy advice to users [2–5]. A common approach is to have users specify their privacy preferences and compare these to privacy policies of sites they visit. As an example, the privacy agent AT&T Privacy Bird [2] displays icons to the user based on such a comparison, indicating whether the preferences are met or not. In general, these types of solutions provides a Yes/No answer to whether or not to accept a privacy policy. There is no information on how much the policy differs from the preferences. A policy that is able to fulfil all preferences except for a small deviation on one of the criterion, will result in the same recommendation to the user as a policy that fails to meet all the user's requirements. The user is in most cases informed about the reason for the mismatch, and can judge for himself whether the mismatch is important or not. Still, there are situations where such user involvement is inefficient or impossible, and the similarity assessment must be made automatically.

Automatic comparison of privacy policies is important to be able to give situational *privacy recommendations* to users on the web. The Privacy Finder [3] search engine ranks search results based on their associated privacy practices. Policies are classified according to a predefined set of requirements and grouped into four categories. Thus, sites that are not able to fulfil one of the basic criteria,

J. Camenisch and D. Kesdogan (Eds.): iNetSec 2011, LNCS 7039, pp. 89–103, 2012.
© IFIP International Federation for Information Processing 2012

but offer high privacy protection on other areas will be given a low score. In order to provide more granularity and fair comparisons, a more flexible and accurate similarity metric is needed. Another application area of a similarity metric is for *preference learning in user agents* [6]. This is the application area that we focus on in this paper. To avoid having users manually specify their preferences, machine learning techniques can be utilised to *deduce* users' preferences based on previous decisions and experiences [7]. Thus, having accepted a similar policy before may suggest that the user is inclined to accept this one as well. Evidently, this approach requires a more precise mechanism to determine what constitutes a *similar* policy.

Automatic comparison of privacy policies is particularly complicated due to the subjective nature of privacy [8]. What parts of a policy are most important is dependent on the user attitude and context, and will influence how the similarity metric is to be calculated. In this paper we investigate the difficulties of defining a similarity metric for privacy policy comparison in the context of automatic preference learning. Several privacy policy languages are available, examples being P3P [9], PPL [10] or XACML [11]. Throughout this paper we use P3P in the examples to illustrate challenges as well as potential solutions, but our work is not restricted to P3P. The focus lies on the high-level concepts that need to be solved rather than the particular language dependent problems. The remainder of this paper is organised as follows. Section 2 gives an introduction to Case-Based Reasoning (CBR) and how it can be used to enable user agents to learn users' privacy preferences. Section 3 provides an overview of existing similarity or distance metrics that can be used for comparing policies. Section 4 describes the challenges of policy comparison in more detail, and takes some steps towards a solution. Then Section 5 discusses the implications of our suggestions, before Section 6 concludes the paper.

2   Case-Based Reasoning for Privacy

Anna visits a website she has not visited before. Anna's privacy agent tries to retrieve various information on the website, including its machine-readable privacy policy. Then the agent compares its knowledge of the website with its knowledge of Anna's previous user behaviour. In this case, the agent warns Anna that the privacy policy of the website allows wider sharing than what Anna has been known to accept in the past. Anna explains to the agent that she will accept the policy since the service offered is very important to her. The agent subsequently records the decision and explanation to be used for future reference.

Case Based Reasoning (CBR) [12, 13] resembles a form of human reasoning where previously experienced situations (cases) are used to solve new ones. The key idea is to find a stored case that closely resembles the problem at hand, and then adapt the solution of that problem. Figure 1 gives an overview of the main CBR cycle. First, the reasoner retrieves cases that are relevant for the new situation. Then the reasoner selects one or a few cases (a ballpark solution) to use as a starting point for solving the new situation. Then this ballpark solution

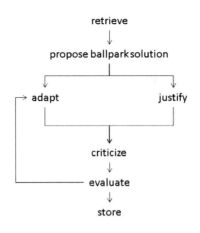

Fig. 1. CBR cycle [12]

is either adapted so that it fits the new situation better, or is used as evidence for or against some solution. The solution or conclusion reached is then criticised before it is evaluated (i.e. tried out) in the real world. It is the feedback that can be gained in the evaluation step that allows the reasoner to learn. In the end, the new case is stored to be used as a basis for future decisions. Central to the CBR approach is the retrieval of *relevant* cases to use as a basis for making decisions. The prevailing retrieval algorithm is *K-Nearest Neighbour* (KNN) [14], which requires a definition of what is consider the *nearest* case. In a privacy policy setting this translates to finding the *most similar* privacy policies, which is the main focus of this paper.

3   Existing Distance Metrics

There are several existing metrics for computing the difference (or distance) between text strings, vectors, objects and sets and these are often referred to as *distance metrics*. We have so far talked about *similarity metrics* which are really just the inverse of the distance metrics. That is, as the distance increases, the corresponding similarity decreases. However, in order to refer to the different metrics in their original form, we will use the term *distance metric* throughout this section.

Before we survey existing metrics, it is important to clarify what a distance metric actually is. A distance metric is a function d on a set M such that $d : M \times M \to \mathbb{R}$. Where $\mathbb{R}$ is the set of real numbers. Further, the function d must satisfy the following criteria for all $x, y \in M$ [15]:

$$d(x, y) = d(y, x) \qquad \text{(symmetry)} \qquad (1)$$

$$d(x, y) > 0 \iff x \neq y \qquad \text{(non-negative)} \qquad (2)$$

$$d(x, x,) = 0 \qquad \text{(identity)} \qquad (3)$$

$$d(x, y) \leq d(x, z) + d(z, y) \qquad \text{(triangle inequality)} \qquad (4)$$

The symmetry requirement seems obvious, as we normally do not consider the ordering of the objects to compare (whether x or y comes first). As a consequence of this, the second requirement states that there can be no negative distances, since this would indicate a direction and hence the order of comparison would matter. Further it seems obvious that the distance between an object and itself must be zero. The final requirement simply says that the distance between any two objects must always be less than or equal to the distance between the same objects if a detour (via object z) is added. This requirement corresponds to the statement that *"the shortest path between two points is the straight line"*. In the following we introduce three main types of distance metrics; for comparing sets, for comparing vectors or strings, and for comparing objects that are defined through an ontology.

For comparing *sets of objects*, the *Jaccard distance* ($\mathcal{J}_d$) is one alternative metric. It defines the distance between two sets s_1 and s_2 as:

$$\mathcal{J}_d(s_1, s_2) = 1 - \frac{|s_1 \cap s_2|}{|s_1 \cup s_2|} \tag{5}$$

The metric counts the number of occurrences in the set intersection and divides it by the number of occurrences in the set union. Then it is normalised to return a number in the range $[0, 1]$. All occurrences are treated equally, hence the metric does not cater for situations in which some set members are more important than others.

Distance metrics for comparing *vectors or strings* are commonly used to construct error detecting and correcting codes [16]. The predominant such metric is the *Hamming distance*[1], which is defined as *the number of positions in which a source and target vector disagree*. When used in binary representations the Hamming distance can be computed as the

$$d_H(s, t) = wt(s \oplus t) \tag{6}$$

where the function $wt(v)$ is defined as the number of times the digit 1 occurs in the vector v [16]. However when used in for instance string comparison, the textual definition above must be used. In order to compare vectors or strings of unequal size, the *Levenshtein distance* introduces insertion and deletion as operations to be counted in addition Hamming distance discrepancy count . More formally, it is defined as *the number of operations required to transform a source vector s to a target vector t, where the allowed operations are insertion, deletion and substitution*. Consequently, for equal size vectors, the Levenshtein distance and Hamming distance are identical.

Ontology distances utilise the inherent relationships among objects either explicitly or implicitly defined through an ontology [18]. The approach is used to compute the semantic similarity of objects rather than their textual representation. For example, the distance between *Apple* and *Orange* is shorter than the

---

[1] Note that the Hamming distance has also been defined for sets ($\mathcal{H}_d$) [17] can be considered a variation of the Jaccard distance, the main difference being that the Hamming distance is not normalised.

distance between *Apple* and *House*. In order to determine the distance from one object to another, we can simply count the number of connections in the defining ontology from a source object to a target object via their most recent common ancestor[18].

4   Towards a Similarity Metric for Privacy Policies

In this section we start by explaining the various ways in which similarity may be interpreted related to the different parts of privacy policies, and also give an overview of the main parts of the solution needed. Then we make suggestions and present alternatives for creating similarity metrics for comparing individual statements of policies, and also for aggregation of the similarity of statements. Finally we explain how the similarity metrics can be used together with expert knowledge and user interaction in the context of a preference learning user agent.

4.1   What Makes Privacy Policies Similar?

In order to be able to automatically determine whether two privacy policies are similar, it is necessary to answer a few basic questions:

- *What makes policies similar?* Can policies offer roughly the same level of protection without having identical practices? And if so, how to determine the level of protection offered?
- *What type of policy content is more important for privacy decisions?* Which policy changes are likely to influence users' privacy decisions? And is it possible to draw conclusions in this respect without consulting the user?

There are surveys available that are able to give some insights into what aspects of privacy are more important to users. As an example, studies performed by Anton et al. in 2002 and 2008 [19] show that Internet users are most concerned about privacy issues related to information transfer, notice/awareness and information storage. However, in order to address the above questions in a satisfactory way in this context, more detailed knowledge is needed.

In this section we start our discussion of similarity by investigating possible interpretations of similarity in the context of P3P policies. Then we outline main issues that need to be addressed in order to arrive at a solution.

Similarity in the context of P3P. P3P policies provide, among other things, information on the data handling practices; including the data collected, the purpose of the data collection, the potential recipients of the data and the retention practices. Figure 2 shows the alternatives for describing purpose, recipients and retention using P3P, and also gives an overview of the data types defined in the P3P Base Data Schema [9].

Consider the case where a user wants to compare whether two policies describe collection of similar types of data. Similar could in this context mean that they

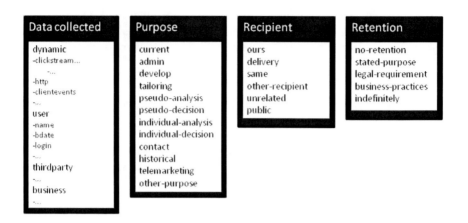

Fig. 2. Alternatives when describing data, purpose, recptients and retention in P3P

collect the same data, that they collect a similar number of data items, that they describe data practices that are at the same level in the hierarchy (as an example, `clickstream` and `bdate` is at the same level) or that they collect information that is semantically similar (e.g. part of the same subtree). It could also be possible to add sensitivity levels to data and consider policies to be similar if they collect information of similar sensitivity. For purpose, similarity can mean identical purposes, the same number of purposes or purposes with similar privacy implications. Which similarity interpretation to use it not obvious.

Comparing data handling practices based on their privacy implications is particularly complicated as there is in general no common understanding of the implications of the various practices. Thus, the similarity of for instance the purposes `individual-decision` and `contact` is a matter of opinion - one user may consider `individual-decicion` to be far worse than `contact`, while a second may argue that `contact` is far worse, and a third may consider them to be similar. For recipient and retention it is a bit different, as the alternatives in general can be ordered based on their privacy implications; e.g. `no-retention` is always better than `stated-purpose`, which is again better than `business-practices`, etc. Thus, `stated-purpose` is considered closer to `no-retention` than to `business-practices` The categories are however broad, and e.g. who is included in the recipient group `ours` or `unrelated` will probably vary between policies. The practices of two policies that both share data with `other-recipient` may thus not be considered similar by users.

Comparing full policies further complicates matters. Some users may for instance be most concerned with the amount of information collected, while others are more concerned about the retention practices. When considering the similarity of two policies, it is thus necessary to take into account this variation of importance.

Listing 1.1. Excerpt from a P3P privacy policy

```
<STATEMENT>
    <PURPOSE><admin/><develop/></PURPOSE>
    <RECIPIENT><ours/></RECIPIENT>
    <RETENTION><stated-purpose/></RETENTION>
    <DATA-GROUP>
        <DATA ref="#dynamic.clickstream"/>
        <DATA ref="#dynamic.http"/>
    </DATA-GROUP>
</STATEMENT>
```

What Is Needed. In order to compare privacy policies and use them in a CBR system we need *similarity metrics* for individual parts of the policy, as well as for entire policies. Such metrics need to be able to handle missing statements, and should also support *similarity weights* to be able to express the criticality or importance of individual statements. Central to the success of the metrics is the ability to understand what similarity means in a given context. Expert knowledge can provide necessary input to the similarity calculations, but as the end-users are experts on their own privacy preferences, it is also important to allow them to influence the similarity calculations.

In CBR, the similarity metric and weight function is normally what is required to compute the k-Nearest Neighbours (i.e. the k most similar policies). Thus, even if there are no policies that would be denoted similar, the algorithm will always return k policies. To cater for this, we require the notion of a similarity threshold such that the algorithm will return only policies that are within the threshold value and that are thus considered to be *similar enough* so that one can be used as a basis to give advice on whether to accept the other.

When using policies to provide advice to users on what to accept or not, it is important to have some understanding of not only the similarity of policies, but also which policy is better or worse. Thus, in addition to a similarity metric, we need a direction vector that can provide this information. This is in part discussed in Section 5, but is considered outside the scope of this paper.

4.2 Divide and Conquer

In our work, we make the assumption that the end-users' preferences when it comes to handling of their personal data is highly dependent on the type of data in question. Thus, we suggest comparing policies with a basis in what data is collected. To illustrate how this can be done we again look to P3P. P3P policies contain one or more statements that explain the handling of particular types of data. Listing 1.1 provides an example of such a statement considering the handling of clickstream data and http data. Due to our data centred approach, we translate such P3P statements into cases (case description) by adding one case per **DATA** item in a statement. As an example, Listing 1.1 contains two **DATA** elements and therefore results in two case descriptions; as given in Listing 1.2.

Listing 1.2. Case descriptions

```
datatype=dynamic.clickstream         datatype = dynamic.http,
recipients=['ours']              recipients = ['ours'],
purpose=['admin', 'develop']         purpose = ['admin',
'develop'], retention = ['stated-purpose']        retention =
['stated-purpose']
```

Table 1. Overview of local similarity metrics

Attribute	Similarity interpretation	Metric	Input
Data type	Semantic similarity	Ontology	Data schema (+ costs)
Purpose	Equality	Set	(Costs)
Recipients	Privacy implications	Vector/string	(Costs)
Retention	Privacy implications	Vector/string	(Costs)

4.3 Local Similarity: Attributes

In common CBR terminology, the term *local* similarity is used when considering the similarity of individual attributes. As already pointed out, similarity may be interpreted in different ways, and in the following we suggest how similarity can be calculated for the attributes data type, purpose, recipients and retention. Table 1 gives an overview of our suggestions. The suggestions have been made taking into account the possible interpretations of similarity and issues related to attribute representation.

The *data type* field is, at least in P3P, based on a data schema that defines a relatively clear semantic relationship between the possible values. Hence it is natural to use an ontology representation and the corresponding *ontology metric* to compute the similarities between these objects. This implies an understanding of similarity as the closeness of the concept. The metric will take into account the distance between the objects as defined in the ontology, resulting in e.g. `family name` being more similar to `given name` than, say, `birthyear`.

For purposes, retention and recipients there is no such data schema available that describes how close the alternatives are to each other. If such a schema is made, this can of course be used in similarity calculations. For *retention and recipient*, however, the alternatives can be said to be ordered, describing practices on a scale from low to high level of privacy-invasiveness. This ordering can be preserved if representing the values as vectors. To illustrate, if we use the ordering, from top to bottom, given in Figure 2 as our basis, we can represent the recipient attribute as a five-dimensional binary vector $v = (v_0, v_1, v_2, v_3, v_4)$ where $v_i = 1$ indicates that the i-th recipient type is present in the attribute. Following this reasoning, the vector representation of the retention attributes given in Listing 1.2 would be $v = (0, 1, 0, 0, 0)$ corresponding to the set representation [`'stated-purpose'`]. The recipient attribute may have a similar representation, however then using a six-dimensional binary vector corresponding to the six possible values it may take.

For *purposes* it is difficult, not to say impossible, to find an implicit ordering of the possible values. It is for instance difficult to say whether `admin` purpose is far away from `development` purpose, other than the fact that they are different. As a consequence, we believe that the set representation and the corresponding *Jaccard* distance metric are suitable. This implies looking at what purposes are identical.

All of the distance metrics introduced in Section 3 treat all instances equally, and do not take into account that a set or vector member may be more important than another, or that some of the connections in an ontology may be more costly than others. For all the attributes, it is possible to extend the original distance metrics to take into account the cost associated with a difference. This way, a high cost purpose will be more different from a low cost purpose than another high cost purpose, and a jump from e.g. `public` recipient to `unrelated` be rated different than a jump from `delivery` to `ours`.

4.4   Global Similarity: Cases

The term *global* similarity is used when aggregating the local similarity values from attribute comparisons to say something about the similarity the entire case descriptions. As our case descriptions are on the level of privacy statements, the global similarity will state the degree to which two statements are similar. Usually, the global similarity is computed by a function that combines the local similarity values.

The most basic of such functions are the average or sum of attribute similarity values. However, since such metrics give equal importance to all attributes, it is more common to use some sort of weighted sum, or weighted average. That way, some attributes may be given more importance (greater relative weight) than others, and therefore will contribute a greater part to the overall similarity assessment. Further, the weight or relative importance of the attributes may be specified by the user or updated on the basis of user feedback, so that these values are also learned by the CBR system.

This may then further be combined with threshold values, such that the global similarity will only be computed if the local similarities are within a predefined threshold. This is to ensure that policies are similar enough to make comparison meaningful and also provide value to the subsequent recommendation made by the CBR system.

4.5   Similarity of Policies

Calculating the similarity of cases is not the same as considering the *similarity of policies*, but like for cases, similarity of policies can be computed based on a weighted sum where the weightings taking into account the importance of various data items. But for preference learning user agents, we are not really that interested in comparing full policies. The reason for this is illustrated in Figure 3. As can be seen in this figure, for each individual cases of a policy there is a search for similar historical cases, and the cases that are a result of these

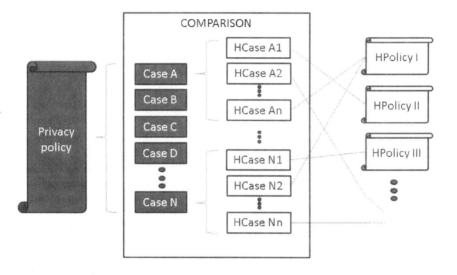

Fig. 3. The cases that belong to one policy may be found to be similar to a number of different historical cases belonging to different historical policies

searches may belong to a number of different policies, originally. Comparing all these historical policies to the current privacy policy is not necessarily useful. Instead it is important to determine, based on these similar cases, what advice to provide to the user. Thus it is more important to consider whether or not the user has accepted this kind of practice (as described by the case) in the past. For each case of a policy it should be possible to reach a conclusion about whether or not the user is likely or not to accept this practice (e.g. either yes, no or indeterminate). Then, to reach a conclusion about the policy, the total likelihood of acceptance could be computed based on a weighted sum taking into account the importance of each case (based on the type of data it concerns).

4.6 Applying Similarity Metrics in Preference Learning User Agent

Figure 4 gives an overview of the type of solution we envision for policy comparison in the context of a privacy agent. When the user visits a website, the machine-readable policy of this website is used as a basis for providing the user with recommendations as to whether or not to share personal information with this site. During policy evaluation the new policy is divided into a number of cases, based on the data collected, and each of these cases are evaluated towards the historical cases. The historical cases that are most similar to the current situation are used to come to a conclusion on what recommendation to give the user.

In order to be able to retrieve similar cases, the similarity metric is used together with the similarity weight function and the similarity threshold. The

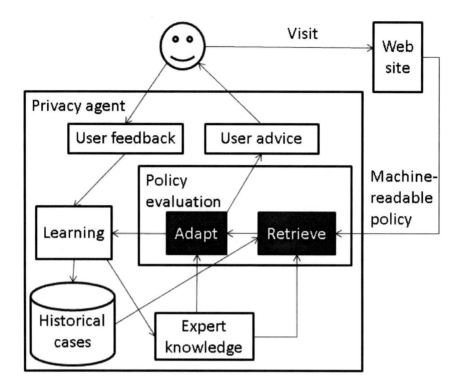

Fig. 4. Applying similarity metrics in preference learning user agents

necessary input to the similarity calculations, such as costs and weights, are included as expert knowledge. Expert knowledge also provide information on what alternatives are better or worse in terms of privacy protection. Privacy experts will be in the best position to provide this type of information, and let users benefit from their expertise. However, what is considered to be the most important privacy concepts will likely vary between user groups, and also individuals. It can also be dependent on the legal jurisdiction [20]. Expert knowledge can be specified in a way that takes into account some of these likely variations. However, it is also possible to make solutions that allow users to influence the expert knowledge that is used as a basis for making recommendations. We will come back to this shortly.

When the most similar cases have been retrieved, these are combined and adapted in order to come to a conclusion regarding the current situations. As already explained, this can be done by by simply taking a weighted majority-vote based on the set of cases selected. However, as the agent should be able to explain its reasoning to the user, there is also a need to build an argument that can be used to explain the agent's decision. In this process, expert knowledge also has a role to play by e.g. explaining why something is important.

The conclusion reached is presented to the user through for example a warning to the user of problems with the policy, or no warning if the policy is likely to be accepted by the user. The user, in the same way, may or may not provide feedback on this decision, e.g. by stating that he disagrees with the reasoning behind the warning. Either way, the acceptance or correction of the recommendation given is important and makes the agent able to learn and thereby improve its reasoning. A correction of the agent's reasoning may trigger a re-evaluation of the policy, and result in updates to the current cases that are stored in the case repository. But the correction can also, at least in some cases, be used to improve the expert knowledge used in the policy evaluation. After all, users are experts on their own privacy preferences, and can make corrections of type "I do not care who gets my email address", or "I will never allow telemarketing, no matter the benefits"

5   Discussion

In this paper we have shown how privacy policies can be divided into a number of cases that can then be compared to other cases individually. We have also proposed what type of similarity metric to use to compare attributes of cases, and shown how the results of these individual comparisons can be used to say something about the similarity of cases and policies at a higher level. In this section we discuss important parts of our suggestions, focusing mainly on areas where further research is needed.

5.1   The Role of the Expert

Existing distance metrics can be modified to take into account costs, but for this to work we need a way to determine these varying costs. As has already been pointed out previously in this paper, deciding what is better or worse when it comes to privacy, and how much better or worse it is, is very much a matter of opinion rather than facts. Privacy experts are the ones most capable of making such statements when it comes to cost, but further research may be needed in order to agree on useful cost values. The same goes for weights that are used for computing global similarity values, and for making recommendations to users.

5.2   Involving the End-User

In our suggestions for applying similarity metrics for preference learning user agents, we have emphasised the need to include user input and use this input to improve the similarity measures. For this to work, there is a need for good user interfaces and also a need to understand what users will be able to understand and communicate related to their preferences. A key dilemma is to find the right level of user involvement. It is important to involve users in the learning process, but if users receive a lot of requests for feedback on similarity calculations, this may be considered to be annoying interruptions and will likely result in users refraining from using the agent. It is also important to find ways to weigh the opinions of the users against the expert knowledge.

5.3   Differences between Policy Languages

In this paper we have used P3P as an example language, and the metrics suggested have been discussed based on the way policies are represented in P3P. The metrics selected may be different if policies are presented using other languages. As an example, the PPL specifications [10] show examples where retention is specified using days rather than the type of practice. This will result in the use of a different type of metric, e.g. the Euclidean distance. However, how would you compare a retention of 30 days with, say, `business-practices`? Here, again, experts are the ones that can contribute with knowledge on how to solve this, but to gain such explicit knowledge and agree on the necessary parameters will likely require further research.

5.4   Aggregation of Similarity Values

Though this paper provides some suggestions as to how the similarity of cases and policies can be computed, more work is needed on this topic. The examples we use only consider parts of the P3P policies. In addition, there will in many cases be a need to take into account the direction of the difference (better/worse). This direction cannot be included directly in the similarity metric, as this would violate the symmetry criteria in the very definition of a distance metric. Still the distance is important when making choices based on the result of a metric.

For preference learning privacy agents, the policy will only be one of several factors to consider when making recommendations to users. Additional factors include context information and community input [6]. This complicates the similarity calculations.

5.5   CBR vs. Policy Comparison in General

Up till now we have mainly discussed the problems related to policy comparison in a situation where historical decisions on policies are used to determine what recommendations to give to users in new situations. However, in the introduction we pointed at other types of applications where automatic policy comparison can be useful, e.g. in privacy-aware search engines. So, how do our suggestions relate to such other uses?

We have considered situations in which privacy policies are compared with policies the user has accepted or rejected previously, but this is not that different from comparing a policy to those of similar types of sites to e.g. find how a web shop's privacy practices are compared to other web shops. In both cases there is no strict pre-specified matching criteria to use. Expert knowledge will be important in both cases, to assess what aspects of a policy are better or worse, and how much better or worse. But where we have been mainly concerned with identifying similar cases, other uses may be more interested in identifying policies that offer better protection, and say something about how much better this protection is. Case retrieval will be different in such settings, as it is important to consider all cases belonging to one policy together. There is also a need to calculate the similarity of policies, and not only cases.

6   Conclusion and Further Work

In order to develop new and improved privacy services that can compare privacy policies in a more flexible manner than today, there is a need to develop a similarity metric that can be used to calculate how much better or worse one policy is compared to another. This paper provides some steps towards such a similarity metric for privacy policies. It proposes similarity metrics for individual parts of policies, and also addresses how these local similarity metrics can be used to compute more global similarity values. Expert knowledge serves as important inputs to the metrics.

In our future work we plan on implementing measures for policy comparison in the context of preference learning user agents. The similarity metrics will be evaluated by comparing the similarity values that are automatically computed with the values stated by users, when asked. The input received will also be used to improve the expert knowledge that the calculations rely on.

Acknowledgments. We want to thank our colleague Karin Bernsmed for useful input in the discussions leading up to this paper.

References

1. Jensen, C., Potts, C., Jensen, C.: Privacy practices of internet users: Self-reports versus observed behavior. International Journal of Human-Computer Studies 63(1-2), 203–227 (2005)
2. Cranor, L.F., Guduru, P., Arjula, M.: User interfaces for privacy agents. ACM Trans. Comput.-Hum. Interact. 13(2), 135–178 (2006)
3. Privacy Finder, http://www.privacyfinder.org
4. Camenisch, J., Shelat, A., Sommer, D., Fischer-Hübner, S., Hansen, M., Krasemann, H., Lacoste, G., Leenes, R., Tseng, J.: Privacy and identity management for everyone. In: Proceedings of the 2005 Workshop on Digital Identity Management, DIM 2005, pp. 20–27 (2005)
5. Levy, S.E., Gutwin, C.: Improving understanding of website privacy policies with fine-grained policy anchors. In: Proceedings of the 14th International Conference on World Wide Web, WWW 2005, pp. 480–488 (2005)
6. Tøndel, I.A., Nyre, Å.A., Bernsmed, K.: Learning privacy preferences. In: Proceedings of the Sixth International Conference on Availability, Reliability and Security, ARES 2011 (2011)
7. Berendt, B., Günther, O., Spiekermann, S.: Privacy in e-commerce: stated preferences vs. actual behavior. Commun. ACM 48(4), 101–106 (2005)
8. Bagüés, S.A., Surutusa, L.A.R., Arias, M., Fernández-Valdivelso, C., Matías, I.R.: Personal privacy management for common users. International Journal of Smart Home 3(2), 89–106 (2009)
9. W3C. Platform for Privacy Preferences, http://www.w3.org/P3P/
10. Trabelsi, S.: Second release of the policy engine. Prime Life, Tech. Rep. D5.3.2 (2010)
11. OASIS eXtensible Access Control Markup Language (XACML), http://www.oasis-open.org/committees/xacml

12. Kolodner, J.L.: An introduction to case-based reasoning. Artificial Intelligence Review 6, 3–34 (1992)
13. Aamodt, A., Plaza, E.: Case-based reasoning: Foundational issues, methodological variations, and system approaches. AI Communications 7(1), 39–59 (1994)
14. Mitchell, T.: Machine Learning. McGraw-Hill (1997)
15. Bozkaya, T., Ozsoyoglu, M.: Distance-based indexing for high-dimensional metric spaces. SIGMOD Rec. 26, 357–368 (1997)
16. Hankerson, D.C., Hoffman, G., Leonard, D.A., Lindner, C.C., Phelps, K.T., Rodger, C.A., Wall, J.R.: Coding Theory and Cryptography: The Essentials, 2nd edn. Marcel Dekker, Inc., New York (2000)
17. Arasu, A., Ganti, V., Kaushik, R.: Efficient exact set-similarity joins. In: Proceedings of the 32nd International Conference on Very Large Data Bases (VLDB), pp. 918–929. VLDB Endowment (September 2006)
18. Bernstein, A., Kaufmann, E., Bürki, C., Klein, M.: How similar is it? towards personalized similarity measures in ontologies. In: Ferstl, O.K., Sinz, E.J., Eckert, S., Isselhorst, T. (eds.) Wirtschaftsinformatik 2005, pp. 1347–1366. Physica-Verlag HD (2005)
19. Anton, A.I., Earp, J.B., Young, J.D.: How internet users' privacy concerns have evolved since 2002. IEEE Security and Privacy 8, 21–27 (2010)
20. Fischer-Hübner, S., Wästlund, E., Zwingelberg, H.: Ui prototypes: Policy administration and presentation version 1. Prime Life, Tech. Rep. D4.3.1 (2009)

Abstract Privacy Policy Framework: Addressing Privacy Problems in SOA

Laurent Bussard and Ulrich Pinsdorf

European Microsoft Innovation Center, Aachen, Germany
{LBussard,Ulrich.Pinsdorf}@microsoft.com

Abstract. This paper argues that privacy policies in SOA needs a life-cycle model. We formalize the lifecycle of personal data and associated privacy policies in Service Oriented Architectures (SOA), thus generalizing privacy-friendly data handling in cross-domain service compositions. First, we summarize our learning in two research projects (PrimeLife and SecPAL for Privacy) by proposing generic patterns to enable privacy policies in SOA. Second, we map existing privacy policy technologies and ongoing research work to the proposed abstraction. This highlights advantages and shortcomings of existing privacy policy technologies when applied to SOA.

1 Motivation

Service Oriented Architectures (SOA) aim at enabling the development and usage of applications that are built by combining autonomous, interoperable, discoverable, and potentially reusable services. These services jointly fulfill a higher-level operation through communication [10]. A common principle is to dynamically bind services hosted in different security domains and by different legal entities. We refer to this as "cross-domain service composition" [7]. In many cases, a distributed system might involve the processing of personal data and thus requires privacy-enhancing technologies [16].

Service composition enables new features but increases risk for the privacy of their users: First, data subjects may no longer be aware of what data relating to them are handled by what entity for what purpose. Data subjects might even not be aware of the involvement of further legal entities at all. Second, the use of standardized data formats and interfaces makes it easy for involved parties to link different sets of personal data and generate profiles on data subjects. Mechanisms to specify data handling are required.

Many individual technologies have been developed to address data handling in distributed systems [24,23,8,6,1,17]. Yet, they typically focus only on specific technical aspects or scenarios. In this paper we take a step back and look at the whole lifecycle of private data and its associated privacy policies in a distributed system, thus generalizing privacy-friendly data handling in cross-domain service compositions. We distill lessons learnt from working on privacy-enhancing technologies for distributed systems in the projects *PrimeLife* [18] and *S4P* [6]. Our

J. Camenisch and D. Kesdogan (Eds.): iNetSec 2011, LNCS 7039, pp. 104–118, 2012.
© IFIP International Federation for Information Processing 2012

result is a *generic framework* that defines the general processing steps to achieve privacy compliance and proper data handling in SOA. We explicitly address downstream data sharing [8] by repeated application of the same principle, i.e. the abstract framework can be "chained". The framework deliberately abstracts from concrete technologies and policy languages. However, we compare existing technologies with the proposed abstract framework in Sect. 5. This validates the feasibility of our approach and makes it possible to compare advantages and shortcomings of existing technical solutions.

The remainder of this paper is structured as follows. Section 2 gives a general overview of involved parties and high-level protocol steps. The subsequent two sections refine the protocol steps for the provider of personal data (Sect. 3) and the consumer of personal data (Sect. 4). Section 5 analyses prior art; the abstract framework is instantiated with existing standards and ongoing research in order to compare their use in SOA. Finally, we conclude with the lessons learnt in Sect. 6.

2 Abstract Privacy Framework

In distributed systems, such as Service Oriented Architectures (SOA), involved parties (users and services) can provide personal data and/or consume personal data. For the sake of readability, we define two roles *PII Provider* and *PII Consumer*. Note that we use PII (personally identifiable information) as a short notation for the broader concept of personal data. A party can have both roles: a service can act as PII Consumer when collecting data and as PII Provider when forwarding collected data; a user can act as PII Provider of her own personal data and as PII Consumer of third parties' data. Figure 1 presents major privacy challenges of SOA: multi-hop data sharing, aggregation of data, privacy-aware discovery and late binding, distributed enforcement, and distributed audit.

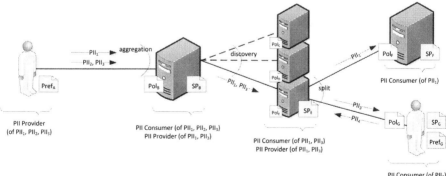

Fig. 1. Privacy Policies in Service Oriented Architecture

2.1   Outline

Figure 2 shows the Abstract Privacy Framework in a visual representation. The figure contains top-level components for the PII Provider and the PII Consumer (dashed boxes). Furthermore it shows the iterative approach by chaining from the PII Consumer to another PII Consumer. Both top-level components contain a best-practice workflow. The combined workflow is an ideal, technology-agnostic, and scenario-independent view on data handling in a composed service. Moreover, the workflows introduce more components that should be part of each role's technical manifestation. The remainder of this section describes all top-level components from Fig. 2. Sections 3 and 4 go into more details for the PII Provider and resp. the PII Consumer.

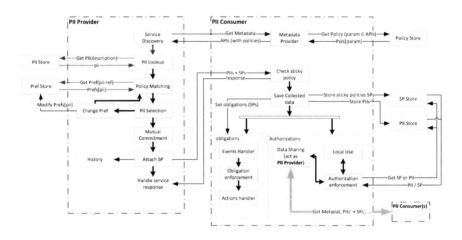

Fig. 2. Overview of abstract privacy policy framework

PII Provider: *PII Provider P* shares personal data with PII Consumers. In most scenarios, the user (or data subject) is acting as PII provider. Sharing personal data with another party is generally restricted by privacy constraints (access control and/or expected data handling). Those privacy constraints can be locally specified (e.g. a data subject can specify privacy constraints on her data), can be external i.e. provided by another party (e.g. a data controller sharing collected data with a third party has to enforce constraints imposed by the data subject), or can be a combination of local and external constraints. The PII Provider's role is essentially about deciding whether it is worth sharing pieces of personal data in order to get services from PII consumers.

PII Consumer: *PII Consumer C* collects personal data provided by PII Providers. In most scenarios, a service (or data controller) is acting as PII Consumer. PII consumers are liable for making sure that collected data are properly handled. Data handling is imposed by the PII Provider and can be refined by the

PII Consumer. The PII Consumer's role is essentially about 1) checking whether actions are authorized before acting on collected personal data and 2) enforcing obligations regarding those data.

PII Store: *PII Store PII_P* is the database containing each piece of personal data $pii \in PII_P$ of PII Provider P. This database can be hosted by the PII Provider (e.g. part of the user agent) or kept remotely (e.g. cloud storage). When personal data are signed credentials, the PII Store can be a local credential store or a remote credential issuer (e.g. Security Token Service).

Preferences Store: *Preferences Store $Prefs_P$* contains all preferences of PII Provider P regarding any of her personal data $pii \in PII_P$. Preferences define how personal data has to be handled by other parties. The PII Provider has preferences for each personal data she is willing to share: $\forall pii \in PII_P \cdot Prefs_P[pii] \neq \emptyset$. No preference would mean that no rights are provided and all possible obligations are expected. *Prefs[pii]* is the subset of preferences in *Prefs* that applies to *pii*. Preference Store can be local (e.g. part of the user agent) or remote (e.g. provided by a trusted third party or by a group). At any time, a PII Provider can create or modify her preferences.

Policy Store: *Policy Store $Pols_C$* contains privacy policies of data controller C regarding collected data. Policies define how collected data are handled. The data controller has a policy for each parameter *param* of each interface *api* collecting personal data: $\forall api \in API_C \cdot \forall param \in api \cdot Pols_C[param] \neq \emptyset$. Policies can be statically defined or derived from a business process. They may depend on the PII Consumer, e.g. when this one is authenticated. Moreover, policies are generally locally defined but often mention external policies (e.g. the policies of downstream data controllers).

The main differences between Policy Store and Preference Store are: 1) Policies and preferences are expressed in different languages (which can be very similar in some technologies). 2) Policies are generally associated to parameters (e.g. any e-mail address collected with this interface) while preferences are associated to types (e.g. all my e-mail addresses) or instances (e.g. alice@contoso.com).

Sticky Policy Store: *Sticky Policy Store SP_C* is very similar to *Preferences Store* (see section 2.1). It contains sticky policies of each collected data pii_C stored in PII_C, i.e. each instantiation of a parameter *param* with a personal data $pii \in PII_P$. Sticky policies are defined for each collected data $\forall pii_C \in PII_C \cdot Prefs_C[pii_C] \neq \emptyset$.

The main differences between sticky policy store and and preference stores are: 1) The data subject (user) can decide to change how her data must be handled and modify her preferences while the PII consumer cannot modify sticky policies associated with collected data (at least cannot make them more permissive). 2) The sticky policies generally define obligations that must be locally enforced (e.g. delete data within one year).

3   A Closer Look at PII Provider Role

This section provides more insight on technical components necessary to fulfill the "PII Provider" role in Figure 2.

Service Discovery: *Service Discovery* is the process of finding potential PII Consumers. Service Discovery takes into account functional properties as well as non-functional properties such as QoS and privacy. This returns a set of discovered interfaces API_{disc} with privacy policies defined for each parameter $param \in api \in API_{disc}$. Note that optional parameters also need a policy. For instance, a PII Consumer asking for $param_1 \vee param_2$ where $param_1 = birth$ $date$ and $param_2 = proof\ of\ majority$, has to provide privacy policy for both parameters even if the PII Provider will send only one of them.

PII Lookup: *PII Lookup* aims at finding all combinations of personal data that satisfy PII Consumers, i.e. all discovered interface API_{disc}. A PII Consumer may accept different types of personal data (e.g. confirmation by e-mail or by SMS), may specify different attributes on personal data (e.g. claim signed by a given third party), and may accept different combinations of personal data. The result of the lookup is a set of possible personal data PII_{param} for each $param$ in each $api \in API_{disc}$. Preferences must exist for each personal data. When personal data is created on the fly (e.g. when filling in HTML Forms), generic preferences are used or new preferences are created.

Policy Matching: *Policy Matching* aims at deciding whether privacy expectations $Prefs_P[pii]$ regarding personal data pii are satisfied by privacy promises $Pols_C[param]$ regarding a parameter $param$ before assignment $param \leftarrow pii$.

Privacy constraint p_2 is a valid enforcement of p_1 (denoted $p_1 \unrhd p_2$) when enforcing p_2 cannot violate p_1. In [6], this notion is expressed in terms of lower- and upper-bounds behaviors. In [8], $\unrhd$ means "more permissive than", i.e. more rights and/or less obligations. We use this operator to implement matching as $Prefs_P[pii] \unrhd Pols_C[param]$. Matching is mainly checking that all privacy constraints defined in preferences and policies can be satisfied.

PII Selection: *PII Selection* aims at selecting (or creating) a suitable piece of personal data pii_{sel} for each parameter $param_{sel}$ that has to be instantiated. $\forall(param_{sel} \leftarrow pii_{sel}) \cdot Prefs_P[pii_{sel}] \unrhd Pols_C[param_{sel}]$.

PII Selection is a complex task that may combine service selection, minimal disclosure (selection and combination of individual pieces of data), identity selection (when personal data are claims), mismatches solving (based on metrics to compare mismatches), impact of released data [2], and history of previously released data. It is not possible to present all aspects to end-users. As a result, "meta-preferences" may be necessary to reduce the number of options.

Change Preferences: In case of mismatch, i.e. $\exists(param_{sel} \leftarrow pii_{sel}) \cdot Prefs_P$ $[pii_{sel}] \not\unrhd Pols_C[param_{sel}]$, the PII Provider may decide to modify her preferences. *Change Preferences* aims at replacing preferences $Prefs_P$ by $Prefs'_P$ so that $\forall(param_{sel} \leftarrow pii_{sel}) \cdot Prefs'_P[pii_{sel}] \unrhd Pols_C[param_{sel}]$.

A usual example is to extend generic preferences (e.g. any bookseller can use my e-mail address to confirm order) with a specific exception (e.g. a specific bookseller can also use my e-mail address for advertisement).

Sticky Policy: Mutual Commitment: The *Sticky Policy* sp expresses the agreement between the PII Provider and PII Consumer. The enforcement of the sticky policy has to be an acceptable enforcement of the PII Provider's preferences, i.e. $Prefs_P \trianglerighteq sp$. Behavior of the PII Consumer has to be a valid enforcement of the sticky policy, i.e. $sp \trianglerighteq Pols_C$. In other words, $\forall (param \leftarrow pii) \cdot Prefs_S[pii] \trianglerighteq sp_{param \leftarrow pii} \trianglerighteq Pols_C[param]$. Generating a sticky policy is about finding an instance that satisfies all privacy constraints defined in preferences and policies.

Depending on the use case, the sticky policy may have to be signed by one or both parties to ensure integrity, authentication of origin, and non-repudiation.

Attach Sticky Policy: The link between the sticky policy and the data it applies to has to be preserved when communicated, when stored in databases, and when the data is shared further (i.e. downstream). Depending on the trust model, different mechanisms can be used. For instance, Enterprise Right Management [14] could bind sticky policies (licenses) to personal data (document).

Domain Specific Languages: Multiple representation of a policy language can be envisioned: XML representation, assertions, predefined options (check boxes), or graphical. Those representations have to be translated to the underlying language. Retrieved policies and results from reasoning (e.g. sticky policy, mismatching information) need a valid translation to the representation chosen by the PII Provider [21].

4   A Closer Look at PII Consumer Role

This section provides more insight on components necessary to fulfill the "PII Consumer" role in Figure 2.

Provide Metadata: Each PII Consumer C must provide metadata about its service. Data are collected as parameters *param* of an interface api_C and associated policy $Pols_C[param]$. The PII Consumer has to enforce its policy, i.e. $Pols_C \trianglerighteq Behavior_C$. In other words, the PII Consumer has to 1) check that its policy is enforceable, e.g. not committing to delete data within one day when some specific execution may require keeping them one week, and 2) enforce (sticky) policies.

Check Sticky Policy: When personal data *pii* is assigned to parameter *param* with sticky policy $sp_{param \leftarrow pii}$, the PII Consumer C has to check that this is a valid sticky policy, i.e. $sp_{param \leftarrow pii} \trianglerighteq Pols_C[param]$. This check ensure that a malicious PII Provider cannot provide sticky policies with insufficient rights or with too strict obligations. This check can be part of a mutual commitment protocol.

Authorization Decision: Checking authorization before using collected personal data is necessary. This step can be skipped in static settings where policies do not evolve and service execution cannot violate the policy. Authorization decision regarding action a on data pii results in checking $sp_{pii} \trianglerighteq Behavior(a, pii)$. There are mainly two types of actions: 1) using collected data locally (within PII Consumer's trust domain) and 2) sharing collected data with a third party.

Local Use: *Local Use* refers to the use of personal data within the trust domain of the PII Consumer for a given purpose. This also covers data controller sharing data with a data processor under its control.

Data Sharing: *Data Sharing* is the action of sharing collected data with a third party (downstream PII Consumer). In this case the data controller C (formerly acting as PII Consumer) acts as a PII Provider and the third party acts as a PII Consumer C'. In other words, most of the components described in Sect. 3 are also part of this component.

The main difference between user P providing her personal data pii to service C and C sharing P's personal data pii with another service C' is that in case of mismatch between P's preferences $Prefs_P[pii]$ and C's policy $Pol_C[param]$, P can modify her preferences while C cannot modify sticky policy $SP_{param \leftarrow pii}$ when there is a mismatch between C and C'.

Composing Sticky Policies: Personal data can be merged and extracted. Computing the policy of resulting personal data is not straightforward and is out of the scope of this paper.

When combining data pii_1 with sticky policy sp_1 and data pii_2 with sticky policy sp_2, we have $pii_{1,2} = f(pii_1, pii_2)$ and corresponding sticky policy $sp_{1,2}$ where $sp_1 \trianglerighteq sp_{1,2}$ and $sp_2 \trianglerighteq sp_{1,2}$. Note that this does not apply when the resulting data $pii_{1,2}$ is structured and makes it possible to refer to initial data (e.g. pii_1) and different sticky policies can thus be applied to different part of $pii_{1,2}$.

When data pii_b (e.g. street name) is extracted from pii_a (e.g. address) with sticky policy sp_a, the sticky policy sp_b to apply to $pii_b = g(pii_a)$ must satisfy $sp_a \trianglerighteq sp_b$. In other words, composing data cannot increase permissiveness.

Obligation Enforcement: A set of well-defined obligations has to be available to let PII Provider and PII Consumer agree on the PII Consumer's obligations. We define an obligation as a pair (a, T), where a is an action and $T = (t_1, t_2, \ldots, t_n)$ is a set of triggers, meaning *"Do action a when triggers $\in (t_1, t_2, \ldots, t_n)$"*. The element "action" defines the action to execute in order to fulfill the obligation and elements "triggers" specify the events and conditions requiring the execution of this action. For instance data retention of one year could be expressed as $(Delete(thisPII), (AtTime(t_0, t_0 + 365d)))$ where t_0 is set to the transaction time. The action can be triggered at any time between t_0 and one year after t_0.

Action Handler: Action Handler is a mechanism to implement the enforcement of actions to execute in order to fulfill obligations. Different actions can result from an obligation: logging, deleting data, notifying data subject, etc. Since it is not possible to define an exhaustive list of actions, domain-specific extensions should be possible.

Event Handler: Event Handler is a mechanism to trigger actions in order to fulfill obligations. Different events can trigger an obligation: scheduler, access decision, action on data, sharing data, request from data subject, violation of an obligation, etc. Since it is not possible to define an exhaustive list of triggers, domain-specific extensions should be possible.

Log and Audit: When each privacy-relevant action is logged, an internal or external auditor can verify that the behavior observable in trace $Behavior_{log}$ is compliant to the policies. In other words $\forall pii \in PII_C \cdot \forall b_{pii} \in Behavior_{log}[pii] \cdot SP_C[pii] \trianglerighteq b_{pii}$ where b_{pii} is a behavior related to data pii. When data are shared with third parties, it is necessary to take their policy into account or to perform a distributed audit.

Trust Model: The abstract framework presented in this paper requires that PII Consumer enforces (sticky) policies. This trust model can be implemented with different mechanisms: 1) PII Provider may know that PII Consumer cannot afford decreasing its reputation, 2) PII Consumer may be audited and certified, and 3) PII Consumer may prove that it is relying on trustworthy hardware (e.g. TPM) and software.

5   Instantiation of the Framework

The *Abstract Privacy Policy Framework* defines an ideal setting to enforce privacy policies in *Service Oriented Architectures* (SOA). In this section, the abstract framework is instantiated with concrete technologies in order to compare them. More precisely, criteria emerging from the abstract framework are used to compare existing privacy policy technologies and to evaluate their relevance to implement privacy policies in SOA.

Several parts of the abstract framework are covered by existing privacy-enhancing technologies. Table 1 summarizes the evaluation of five privacy policy technologies (APPEL + P3P, PrimeLife Policy Language, SecPAL for Privacy, remote configuration of access control, and PRIME data handling policy) with around fifty criteria derived from components of the abstract framework.

5.1   Evaluated Technologies

The first instantiation of the abstract framework is based on a combination of two well-known standards: privacy preferences are expressed with *APPEL* (A P3P Preference Exchange Language) [23] and privacy policies are expressed with *P3P* (the Platform for Privacy Preferences Project) [24]. Enforcement may rely on other technology such as *EPAL* (Enterprise Privacy Authorization Language) [3].

The second instantiation of the abstract framework is based on *PrimeLife Policy Language* (PPL) [18, 19] an extension of XACML [22] with support for data handling. This technology is well aligned with the evaluation criteria since a large part of them were informally taken into account during its design.

The third instantiation of the abstract framework is based on *SecPAL for Privacy* (S4P) [6] an extension of logic-based authorization language SecPAL [4]. Logic foundations makes it possible to reason on the causes of mismatches and furthermore to propose modification of preferences and/or policies thanks to abduction queries [5].

The fourth instantiation refers to *remote management of access control policies* (AC) by the Data Subject at the Data Controller. In this setting, the data subject uploads her data to a data controller and configures the access control policy that must be enforced by this data controller. The evaluation assumes an expressive access control language, i.e. XACML [22]. This approach can be considered as "inadequate" [12] to enforce privacy but is largely used. For instance *OAuth* [11] and *User-Managed Access* (UMA) [13] offer remote management of access control policies.

The fifth instantiation is based on the *PRIME Data Handling Policy* (PDH or PRIME-DHP) [1]. This language is focusing on data handling and access control but lacks important features to enable multi-hop data handling.

In this evaluation, we decided not to address technologies related to *Usage Control* and *Right Expression* such as *eXtensible rights Markup Language* (XrML) [9], *Obligation Specification Language* (OSL) [17], MPEG-21 REL [25], or *Open Digital Rights Language* (ODRL) [15]. Even if those technologies could be used to express and enforce privacy constraints on personal data, the way constraints are agreed upon is fundamentally different than what is required to implement privacy in service oriented architectures. Indeed, in usage control and rights management, constraints are imposed by the author (i.e. the data subject) without preliminary protocol with the party receiving the data. As a result key features such a preferences, policies, and matching algorithm are out of scope.

5.2   Evaluation Results

Each instantiation of the abstract framework has been evaluated with a set of criteria summarizing key concepts of the framework. Results are summarized in Table 1. Details on the choice of the criteria as well as their evaluation can be found in Chapter 6 and Appendix A of a PrimeLife project report [20].

Here are seven criteria related to PII Provider's Preferences. 1) *Simple Syntax*: Privacy preferences are expressed in a human-readable language. Syntax and semantics are well defined and can be processed by machines. 2) *Can Express Access Control*: The language used to express privacy preferences supports access control, i.e. the data subject can specify which (or what kind of) data controllers can get a given type of personal data. 3) *Can Express Expected Data Handling*: The language used to express privacy preferences lets the PII Provider specify how collected data must be handled by the PII Consumer. 4) *Can Express Expected Downstream Access Control*: The preferences can express access control constraints on third parties. In other words, the preferences specify with what kind of third parties the data controller is authorized to share collected data.

Table 1. Instantiations of the abstract framework. Features are rated as completely implemented ●, partially implemented ◐, or not implemented ○. The second column refers to features that could be implemented without breaking changes ●, that could be partially implemented ◐, or that would require important changes ○.

Abstract features / Concrete technologies	A+P	PPL	S4P	AC	PDH
PII Provider's Preferences (Sect. 2.1)					
- Simple Syntax	● ●	◐ ◐	● ●	○ ○	○ ◐
- Can Express Access Control	◐ ◐	● ●	● ●	○ ○	○ ◐
- Can Express Expected Data Handling	◐ ◐	● ●	● ●	○ ○	○ ◐
- Can Express Expected Downstream Access Control	◐ ◐	● ●	● ●	○ ○	○ ◐
- Can Express Expected Downstream Data Handling	◐ ◐	● ●	● ●	○ ○	○ ○
- Can Take Downstream Path into Account	◐ ◐	● ●	● ●	◐ ◐	○ ○
- Can Retrieve Applicable Preferences (Sect. 2.1)	○ ◐	◐ ●	○ ●	○ ○	○ ◐
PII Consumer's Policy (Sect. 2.1)					
- Simple Syntax	◐ ●	◐ ◐	● ●	○ ○	◐ ◐
- Can Express Claims (Credentials)	◐ ◐	● ●	● ●	○ ○	● ●
- Can Express Data Handling	◐ ◐	● ●	● ●	○ ○	● ●
- Can Express Downstream Claims (Credentials)	◐ ◐	◐ ●	● ●	○ ○	● ●
- Can Express Downstream Data Handling	◐ ◐	○ ●	● ●	○ ○	◐ ◐
- Can Retrieve Applicable Policy (Sect. 2.1)	◐ ◐	◐ ●	◐ ●	○ ○	○ ○
PII Store (Sect. 2.1)	○ ◐	◐ ◐	○ ●	● ●	○ ●
Privacy-Aware Service Discovery (Sect. 3)	○ ◐	○ ●	○ ◐	○ ○	○ ○
PII Lookup (Sect. 3)	○ ◐	◐ ●	○ ◐	◐ ●	○ ◐
Policy Matching (Sect. 3)					
- Has Logic Foundations	○ ◐	○ ◐	● ●	○ ○	○ ◐
- Takes Data Handling into Account	◐ ◐	● ●	● ●	○ ○	○ ◐
- Takes Obligations into Account	◐ ◐	● ●	◐ ●	○ ○	○ ◐
- Takes Downstream Properties into Account (One Hop)	◐ ○	◐ ●	● ●	○ ○	○ ○
- Supports Recursive Downstream	○ ○	◐ ●	● ●	○ ○	○ ○
PII Selection (Sect. 3)	○ ○	● ●	○ ●	○ ○	◐ ◐
Change Preferences (Sect. 3)					
- Can Show Mismatches	○ ◐	◐ ◐	○ ●	○ ○	○ ○
- Can Suggest Modifications	○ ◐	◐ ◐	○ ◐	○ ○	○ ○
Sticky Policy (Sect. 3)					
- Optional Sticky Policy	● ●	○ ●	● ●	○ ○	◐ ◐
- Can be Expressive	○ ○	● ●	○ ●	● ●	● ●
- Supports Signature or Commitment	○ ○	○ ●	○ ●	◐ ○	○ ●
- Can Change Sticky Policy	○ ○	◐ ●	○ ◐	● ○	○ ○
- Can Store and Retrieve Sticky Policy (Sect. 2.1)	○ ○	◐ ●	○ ●	● ●	◐ ●
Attach Sticky Policy (Sect. 3)	○ ○	◐ ●	○ ●	◐ ●	◐ ●
High-Level Policy Language (Sect. 3)					
- Same Language for Preferences and Policies	○ ○	● ●	◐ ◐	○ ○	○ ○
- Language Expressiveness	○ ◐	● ●	● ●	● ●	● ●
- Clear Separation of Obligations and Rights	○ ○	● ●	◐ ◐	● ●	● ●
Check Sticky Policy (Sect. 4)	○ ○	○ ●	○ ●	● ●	● ●
Authorization Decision (Sect. 4)					
- Enforces Local Use, e.g. Purpose (Sect. 4)	○ ●	● ●	○ ●	◐ ●	● ●
- Enforces Access Control when Sharing (Sect. 4)	○ ◐	● ●	○ ●	● ●	● ●
- Checks Downstream Data Handling when Sharing	○ ○	● ●	○ ●	○ ○	○ ○
- Attach (New) Sticky Policy when Sharing	○ ○	● ●	○ ●	○ ○	◐ ◐
Composing Sticky Policies (Sect. 4)	○ ◐	○ ◐	○ ◐	◐ ○	○ ○
Obligations (Sect. 4)					
- Supports Enforcement of Obligations	○ ◐	● ●	● ●	◐ ○	◐ ●
- Checks Rights of Enforcing Obligations	○ ○	○ ◐	● ●	○ ○	◐ ◐
- Specifies Action Handler (Sect. 4)	○ ◐	● ●	○ ●	◐ ○	◐ ◐
- Specifies Event Handler (Sect. 4)	○ ◐	● ●	○ ●	◐ ○	◐ ◐
Log and Audit (Sect. 4)	○ ◐	◐ ◐	○ ●	◐ ○	◐ ◐
Trust Model (Sect. 4)	○ ○	○ ◐	◐ ●	◐ ○	○ ◐
Protocol independent (HTTP, WS)	○ ●	● ●	◐ ●	● ○	◐ ●
Policy for Implicit PII (e.g. IP address)	● ●	◐ ●	○ ●	○ ○	○ ●

5) *Can Express Expected Downstream Data Handling*: The preferences can express data handling constraints on third parties. In other words the preferences specify how third parties are expected to handle data they would get from data controllers. 6) *Can Take Downstream Path into Account*: Privacy constraints that apply to data controllers downstream depend on the path. In other words, it is possible to have different privacy constraints for personal data d at service S when S is a data controller directly collecting d, when S acts as downstream data controller and gets d from data controller S_1, or from data controller S_2. 7) *Can Retrieve Applicable Preferences (Sect. 2.1)*: This technology provides a mechanism to get the privacy preferences that apply to a piece of personal data. This mechanism supports different types of personal data: retrieved from a PII Store (e.g. a database), dynamically created by the user (e.g. free text in a HTML Form), or certified (e.g. attributes of credentials).

We define six criteria related to PII Consumer's Policy. 1) *Simple Syntax*: Privacy policies are expressed in a human-readable language. Syntax and semantics are well defined and can be processed by machines. 2) *Can Express Claims (Credentials)*: The policy language can describe trust level and certification of PII Consumers. For instance, it is possible to link Public Key Infrastructure to the policy. 3) *Can Express Data Handling*: Privacy policies can express proposed data handling in terms of purpose, obligations, etc. In other words, PII Consumers express how collected data will be handled. 4) *Can Express Downstream Claims (Credentials)*: The policies can express credentials of third parties. In other words the policy specifies with what kind of third parties the data controller may share collected data. 5) *Can Express Downstream Data Handling*: The policies can express proposed data handling of third parties. In other words the policy specifies how third parties would handle data they may get from the data controllers. 6) *Can Retrieve Applicable Policy (Sect. 2.1)*: There is a mechanism to get or generate the policy applicable to a given parameter, e.g. one "label" of an HTML Form, one parameter of a Web Service, or one claim of a requested credential.

One criterion is related to *PII Store*: Personal data are stored in a database and can be queried according to attributes such as the type of data (e.g. e-mail address) or its certification (e.g. name in identity card).

One criterion focuses on *Privacy-Aware Service Discovery*: This technology provides mechanisms to discover services based on functional properties and on non-functional properties such as privacy.

One criterion compares *PII Lookup*: This technology offers mechanisms to gather pieces of personal data that are required by a given interface of the PII Consumer.

We defined five criteria related to Policy Matching. 1) *Has Logic Foundations*: The evaluation whether privacy policies do fulfill privacy preferences has logic foundations. 2) *Takes Data Handling into Account*: Expected data handling is expressed by the PII Provider and proposed data handling is expressed by the PII Consumer. Both aspects are taken into account during matching phase. 3) *Takes Obligations into Account*: Expected obligations are expressed by the PII

Provider and proposed obligations are expressed by the PII Consumer. Both aspects are taken into account while matching. 4) *Takes Downstream Properties into Account (One Hop)*: Not only the privacy policy of the data controller is taken into account while matching but also the policy of third parties, which may get subsequently access to the personal data. 5) *Supports Recursive Downstream*: Complex chains of downstream data sharing can be expressed in privacy policies and preferences and can be taken into account during matching phase.

One criterion is related to *PII Selection*: Privacy-aware identity selection is supported by the protocol (i.e. privacy policies are specified for all expected claims and privacy preferences are associated with all issued claims) and by the user interface (i.e. the selection of claims takes privacy into account).

Two criteria focus on mechanisms to Change Preferences. 1) *Can Show Mismatches*: In case of mismatch, the root causes of the mismatch can be identified and highlighted. 2) *Can Suggest Modifications*: Privacy preferences can be automatically updated to get a match next time a similar case occurs. Previous changes, and similarity of preferences can be taken into account.

Here are five criteria related to Sticky Policy. 1) *Optional Sticky Policy*: Instead of creating a sticky policy describing agreed privacy constraints on personal data, a Boolean response can be used to state that the privacy policy is acceptable and must be enforced. The Boolean response can be implicit, e.g. agree by sending personal data. 2) *Can be Expressive*: The sticky policy can express complex constraints with conditions. 3) *Supports Signature or Commitment*: The sticky policy can be signed by one or more parties to ensure non-repudiation of agreed privacy constraints. 4) *Can Change Sticky Policy*: There is a mechanism to let data subjects modify sticky policies associated with their own personal data when such an action is authorized. 5) *Can Store and Retrieve Sticky Policy (Sect. 2.1)*: There is a mechanism to store sticky policies and to query the sticky policy associated with a given piece of personal data.

One criterion focuses on mechanisms to Attach Sticky Policy: Mechanism to attach the sticky policy to data on the wire and in databases. Mechanisms such as Enterprise Rights Management (e.g. [14]) would be an example where personal data cannot be decrypted without acknowledging the sticky policy (i.e. licenses).

We define three criteria for High-Level Policy Language. 1) *Same Language for Preferences and Policies*: Privacy preferences, policies, and sticky policies are expressed in a common language that avoid semantics mismatches. 2) *Language Expressiveness*: The common language is expressive and allows the specification of conditions, nested or recursive policies, and variables. 3) *Clear Separation of Obligations and Rights*: Obligations and rights are clearly expressed to handle, for instance, the right to store personal data for 3 months, the obligation of storing data for 3 months, and the obligation of deleting data within 3 months.

One criterion focuses on mechanisms to *Check Sticky Policy*: When a sticky policy is pushed to a PII Consumer, this one can check whether the sticky policy is acceptable, i.e. more permissive than the related policy. See details in Appendix.

We define four criteria for Authorization Decision. 1) *Enforces Local Use, e.g. Purpose (Sect. 4)*: Before using collected data, the PII Consumer can verify that actions are authorized according to sticky policies. 2) *Enforces Access Control when Sharing (Sect. 4)*: Authorization of sharing data with a third party takes into account the sticky policy and attributes (e.g. certificates) of the third party. 3) *Checks Downstream Data Handling when Sharing*: Authorization of sharing data with a third party takes into account the sticky policy of the personal data and the privacy policy of the third party. 4) *Attach (New) Sticky Policy when Sharing*: A new sticky policy is created when the personal data is shared with a third party. The rights and obligations of a third party may be different than the rights and authorizations of the initial data controller.

We define one criterion for *Composing Sticky Policies*: Possibility of computing the resulting sticky policy $sp_{1,2}$ of personal data $pii_{1,2}$ resulting from the combination of multiple personal data. In other words, defining each $sp_{1,2} = F(sp_1, sp_2)$ for each way of combining $pii_{1,2} = f(pii_1, pii_2)$.

Four criteria focus on Obligations. 1) *Supports Enforcement of Obligations*: There are mechanisms to automatically enforce obligations that can be specified in (sticky) policies. 2) *Checks Rights of Enforcing Obligations*: Mechanisms to define lower bound and upper bound of behavior. 3) *Specifies Action Handler (Sect. 4)*: There are mechanisms to parse and execute actions associated with obligations. It is possible to extend the set of actions that are handled. 4) *Specifies Event Handler (Sect. 4)*: There are mechanisms to parse triggers and react to specific events (time, event) leading to the execution of an action. It is possible to extend the set of triggers that are handled.

We define one criterion for *Log and Audit*: There are mechanisms to log privacy-relevant events such as: use of personal data, authorization decisions, obligation enforcement, etc. Audit can be based on those traces.

Here is one criterion for *Trust Model*: Support for different trust models such as certification, audit, reputation, and/or trusted hardware. This makes the link between the committed behavior and the actual behavior.

We define one criterion for *Protocol independent (HTTP, WS)*: It is possible to use the evaluated language and associated mechanisms with different communication protocols (Web Services, HTTP, etc.) and to define separately protocol-specific aspects (e.g. cookies).

We define one criterion for *Policy for Implicit PII*: It is possible to specify how PII Consumer handles personal data that are implicitly collected (e.g. IP address).

6   Conclusions

The Abstract Privacy Policy Framework defines key features required to enforce privacy policies in Service Oriented Architecture (SOA). Future work will extend the framework and refine each component.

In this paper, the abstract framework has been instantiated with different technologies in order to compare their suitability in SOA:

It appears that using P3P [24], APPEL [23], and EPAL [3] together is not suitable to tackle complex scenarios. First those technologies do not support multi-hop data handling, which is quite common in SOA. This is mainly due to the fact that those technologies are mainly targeting Web 1.0 scenarios. Second the use of three different languages for expressing privacy preferences, privacy policies, and enforcement leads to semantics mismatches and difficulty to use them recursively.

Letting data subjects specify access control on their data (e.g. OAuth [11], UMA [13]) is not sufficient even when obligations can be specified (e.g. XACML [22]). The main limitation is due to the fact that remote setting of access control only covers a small subset of data handling. One advantage of this approach is to limit the number of copies of personal data and to centralize their management.

PRIME-DHP [1] provides more features than P3P but does not address the preference side and complex downstream cases.

S4P [6] offers promising features but only the core functionality (evaluation of queries) has been implemented. Tools tools for creating sticky policies, for enforcing policies, and for auditing execution traces need to be developped.

Finally PPL [18] supports a large part of the abstract privacy policy framework. This is not surprising since PrimeLife's work packages on SOA and on Policies are strongly connected. PPL mainly lacks homogeneity and logic foundations to enable reasoning on the policies.

Future work will add columns to Table 1 by evaluating the use of Usage Control and Right Expression Languages to instantiate the abstract framework. Moreover, the number of rows will increase by refining evaluation criteria. This work will also impact the evolution of policy languages we are contributing to.

Acknowledgements. We would like to thank Claudio Agostino Ardagna (Uni Milano), Gregory Neven (IBM), Franz-Stefan Preiss (IBM), Slim Trabelsi (SAP), Mario Verdicchio (Uni Bergamo), and Rigo Wenning (W3C), for their feedback on the different instantiations of the abstract framework.

The research leading to these results has received funding from the European Community's Seventh Framework Programme (FP7/2007-2013) under grant agreement no. 216483 for the project PrimeLife.

References

1. Ardagna, C.A., Cremonini, M., De Capitani di Vimercati, S., Samarati, P.: A privacy-aware access control system. J. Comput. Secur. 16(4), 369–397 (2008)
2. Ardagna, C., De Capitani di Vimercati, S., Foresti, S., Paraboschi, S., Samarati, P.: Minimizing disclosure of private information in credential-based interactions: A graph-based approach. In: Proc. of the 2nd IEEE International Conference on Information Privacy, Security, Risk and Trust (PASSAT 2010), Minneapolis, Minnesota, USA (August 2010)
3. Ashley, P., Hada, S., Karjoth, G., Powers, C., Schunter, M.: Enterprise privacy authorization language, EPAL 1.2 (2003)
4. Becker, M.Y., Fournet, C., Gordon, A.D.: SecPAL: Design and semantics of a decentralized authorization language. Journal of Computer Security (2009)

5. Becker, M.Y., Mackay, J.F., Dillaway, B.: Abductive authorization credential gathering. In: IEEE International Symposium on Policies for Distributed Systems and Networks (POLICY) (July 2009)
6. Becker, M.Y., Malkis, A., Bussard, L.: A Practical Generic Privacy Language. In: Jha, S., Mathuria, A. (eds.) ICISS 2010. LNCS, vol. 6503, pp. 125–139. Springer, Heidelberg (2010)
7. Bussard, L., Nano, A., Pinsdorf, U.: Delegation of access rights in multi-domain service compositions. Identity in the Information Society 2(2), 137–154 (2009), http://www.springerlink.com/content/020524p066765742/
8. Bussard, L., Neven, G., Preiss, F.S.: Downstream usage control. In: IEEE Policy 2010 (July 2010)
9. ContentGuard: XrML 2.0 Technical Overview (2002), http://www.xrml.org/reference/XrMLTechnicalOverviewV1.pdf
10. Coulouris, G., Dollimore, J., Kindberg, T.: Distributed Systems. Concepts and Design, 4th edn. Addison Wesley (2005)
11. Hammer-Lahav, E.: RFC 5849: The OAuth 1.0 Protocol (2010), http://tools.ietf.org/html/rfc5849
12. Kagal, L., Abelson, H.: Access control is an inadequate framework for privacy protection. In: W3C Workshop on Privacy for Advanced Web APIs (July 2010)
13. Kantara Initiative: User managed initiative, http://kantarainitiative.org/confluence/display/uma/
14. Microsoft: Rights Management Services (2009), http://www.microsoft.com/windowsserver2008/en/us/ad-rms-overview.aspx
15. ODRL: Open Digital Rights Language (ODRL), version 1.1 (2002), http://www.odrl.net/1.1/ODRL-11.pdf
16. Pinsdorf, U., Bussard, L., Meissner, S., Schallaböck, J., Short, S.: Privacy in Service Oriented Architectures. In: Camenisch, J., Fischer-Huebner, S., Rannenberg, K. (eds.) Privacy and Identity Management for Life, pp. 383–411. Springer, Heidelberg (2011)
17. Pretschner, A., Schütz, F., Schaefer, C., Walter, T.: Policy evolution in distributed usage control. In: 4th Intl. Workshop on Security and Trust Management. Elsevier (June 2008)
18. PrimeLife Consortium: Draft 2nd design for policy languages and protocols (heartbeat: H5.3.2). Tech. rep. (July 2009)
19. PrimeLife Consortium: Second Release of the Policy Engine (D5.3.2). Tech. rep. (September 2010)
20. PrimeLife Consortium: Infrastructure for Privacy for Life (D6.3.2). Tech. rep (January 2011), http://www.primelife.eu/images/stories/deliverables/d6.3.2-infrastructure_for_privacy_for_life-public.pdf
21. Rahman, S.T.: Analyzing Causes of Privacy Mismatches in Service Oriented Architecture. Master's thesis, RWTH (2010)
22. Rissanen, E.: OASIS eXtensible Access Control Markup Language (XACML) Version 3.0. OASIS committee specification 01, OASIS (August 2010)
23. W3C: A P3P preference exchange language 1.0, APPEL1.0 (2002)
24. W3C: The platform for privacy preferences 1.1 (P3P1.1) specification (2006)
25. Wang, X.: MPEG-21 Rights Expression Language: Enabling Interoperable Digital Rights Management. IEEE MultiMedia 11(4), 84–87 (2004)

Flexible and Dynamic Consent-Capturing

Muhammad Rizwan Asghar[1,2] and Giovanni Russello[1]

[1] Create-Net, Italy
{asghar,russello}@create-net.org
[2] University of Trento, Italy

Abstract. Data usage is of great concern for a user owning the data. Users want assurance that their personal data will be fairly used for the purposes for which they have provided their consent. Moreover, they should be able to withdraw their consent once they want. Actually, consent is captured as a matter of legal record that can be used as legal evidence. It restricts the use and dissemination of information. The separation of consent capturing from the access control enforcement mechanism may help a user to autonomously define the consent evaluation functionality, necessary for the automation of consent decision. In this paper, we present a solution that addresses how to capture, store, evaluate and withdraw consent. The proposed solution preserves integrity of consent, essential to provide a digital evidence for legal proceedings. Furthermore, it accommodates emergency situations when users cannot provide their consent.

Keywords: Consent Management, Consent Evaluation, Consent Automation, Consent-Capturing, Consent-Based Access Control.

1 Introduction

Data usage is of great concern for a user owning the data. Users want assurance that their personal data will be fairly used for the purposes for which they have provided their consent. Moreover, they should be able to withdraw their consent once they want. Actually, consent is captured as a matter of legal record that can be used as legal evidence. It restricts the use and dissemination of information which is controlled by the user owning the data. For the usage of personal data, organisations need to obtain user consent, strictly regulated by the legislation. This forces organisations to implement not only the organisational compliance rules but also the legislation rules to access the user data. Currently, the law enforcement agencies are forcing organisations to collect users consent every time their data is accessed where users can decide not to provide consent or they may withdraw their consent any time they want[1]. In the electronic environment, consent can be determined by the automatic process without the explicit involvement of the user owning the data, also known as a *data subject*. This enables enormous amount of data to be processed in a automated and faster manner where consent is captured at the runtime.

---

[1] http://www.bloomberg.com/news/2011-03-16/facebook-google-must-obey-eu-data-protection-law-reding-says.html

J. Camenisch and D. Kesdogan (Eds.): iNetSec 2011, LNCS 7039, pp. 119–131, 2012.
© IFIP International Federation for Information Processing 2012

1.1 Motivation

The motivation behind consent-capturing is from the real-world, where a user inter-vention is reduced as much as possible. Let us consider the healthcare scenario where a patient provides his/her written consent to the hospital. Later on, the hospital staff refers to this written consent in order to provide access to patient's records. For instance, if a nurse needs to access patient's record, she needs first to make it sure that she has access and patient has provided his/her consent for a nurse. In the healthcare scenario, we can realise access controls at two different levels. At the first level, the access controls are enforced by the care/service provider while at the second level, it is enforced by the patient, where a patient provides his/her consent to the first level in order her data to be accessed. In short, consent is a mean to control the access on the personal data. There are two obvious questions which needs to be addressed when we capture the notion of consent in an automated manner. First, how to capture and store the consent. Second, how to evaluate consent from the written consent.

Unfortunately, traditional access control techniques, such as Role-Based Access Con-trol (RBAC) [12], fail to capture consent. However, there are only a few access control techniques [1, 7] that can capture consent but they tightly couple the access control en-forcement mechanism with the consent-capturing. The separation of consent-capturing from the enforcement mechanism may help a user to autonomously define the consent evaluation functionality, necessary for regulating the automation of consent decision. The main drawback of state-of-the-art consent-capturing schemes [4, 9, 10, 14] is that consent-capturing mechanism is too rigid as they consider the consent with a predefined set of attributes and it is not possible to take the contextual information into account in order to provide consent. This contextual information may include time, location or other information about the requester, who makes an access request. In short, the exist-ing consent-capturing mechanisms are not expressive enough to handle the real-world situations. Moreover, the existing access control techniques do not address how to en-sure transparent auditing while capturing the consent. The transparent auditing could be required for providing digital evidence in the court.

1.2 Research Contributions

In this paper, we present how to capture, store and evaluate consent from the written consent. We consider the written consent as a consent-policy where a data subject indi-cates who is permitted to access his/her data. In the proposed solution, the consent eval-uation functionality can be delegated to a third party. The advantage of this delegation is to separate the access control enforcement mechanism from the consent-capturing. This research is a step towards the automation of the consent-capturing. The automation do not only captures consent dynamically but also increases efficiency as compared to providing consent requiring data subject's intervention. Moreover, the proposed solu-tion enables a data subject to withdraw his/her consent. Moreover, it treats emergency situations when a data subject cannot provide his/her consent. Last but not least, the integrity of consent is preserved and a log is maintained by system entities to provide a digital evidence for legal proceedings.

1.3 Organisation

The rest of this paper is organised as follows: Section 2 describes the legal requirements in order to capture consent. Section 3 reviews the related work. Section 4 presents the proposed solution. Section 5 focuses on the solution details. We follow with a discussion about availability, confidentiality and increased usability in Section 6. Finally, Section 7 concludes this paper and gives directions for the future work.

2 Legal Requirements to Capture Consent

Consent is an individual's right. In fact, consent can be regarded one's wish to provide access on one's personal information. Legally, a data subject should be able to provide, modify or withhold statements expressing consent. The given consent should be retained for the digital evidence. Generally, the paper-based consent is considered valid once signed by the data subject. In some countries, specific legislation may require the digital consent to be signed using the digital signature. In other words, an electronically signed consent can be considered equivalent to the manually signed paper-based consent.

According to article 2(h) of the EU Data Protection Directive (DPD) [5], consent is defined as: *"'the data subject's consent' shall mean any freely given specific and informed indication of his wishes by which the data subject signifies his agreement to personal data relating to him being processed."* This definition clearly indicates three conditions, i.e., the consent must be *freely given*, *specific* and *informed*.

- **Freely given:** A consent can be considered free if captured/provided in the absence of any coercion. In other words, it is a voluntary decision of a data subject.
- **Specific:** A consent can be considered specific when it is captured/provided for a dedicated purpose. Moreover, one consent is for one action which is specified to the data subject. Therefore, one consent cannot be used for any other purposes.
- **Informed:** The consent is not considered valid until a data subject is provided with the necessary information. The data subject must be provided with information to understand all benefits and drawbacks of giving and not giving consent. This information must be accurate and given in a transparent, clear and understandable manner.

In legal terms, consent is often a positive response. However, a data subject can express a negative response as it can be regarded as the right of a data subject to express his/her desire for not sharing a certain piece of data.

3 Related Work

In RBAC [12], each system user is assigned a role and a set of permissions are granted to that role. A user can get access on data based on his/her role. RBAC is motivated by the fact that users in the real-world make the decisions based on their job functions within an organisation. The major drawback of RBAC is that it does not take into considerations the user consent for providing the access.

In the British Medical Association (BMA) policy model [1], access privileges for each medical record are defined in the form of Access Control Lists (ACLs) that are managed and updated by a clinician. The main goal of the BMA model is to capture consent, preventing multiple people in obtaining access to large databases of identifiable records. The shortcoming is that the ACLs are not flexible and expressive enough for defining the access. Moreover, the consent structure is not discussed. In Provision-Based Access Control (PBAC) [7], access decisions are expressed as a sequence of provisional actions instead of simple permit or deny statements. The user consent can be captured if stated within the access policy. In both techniques [1] and [7], the consent-capturing mechanism is tightly coupled with the access control enforcement. This restricts the possibility of consent-capturing in an automated manner.

Cassandra [3], a role-based trust management language and system for expressing authorisation policy in healthcare systems, captures the notion of consent as a special role to inform the user that his/her data is being accessed. Cassandra has been used for enforcing the policies of the UK national Electronic Heath Record (EHR) system. The requirement of consent-capturing notion as a special role adds an extra workload because in most of the situations, the consent can be implicitly derived if a user has allowed the system to do so.

Usage-based access control [16] aims to provide dynamic and fine-grained access control. In the usage-based access control, a policy is defined. This policy is based on attributes of the subject, target and environment. The attributes are continuously monitored and updated. If needed, a policy can be enforced repeatedly during a usage session. Attributes can be used for capturing information related to the consent while the access session is still active. If the information changes, such as the user revokes the consent, the access session is terminated. Russello et al. [11] propose a framework for capturing the context in which data is being accessed. Both approaches [16] and [11] have major limitation of tightly coupling the access control enforcement mechanism with the consent capturing.

Ruan and Varadharajan [10] present an authorisation model for handling e-consent in healthcare applications. Their model supports consent delegation, denial and consent inheritance. However, it is not possible to capture the contextual information in order to provide the consent. In e-Consent [4], the consent can be identified in four different forms including, *general consent, general consent with specific denial, general denial with specific consent* and *general denials*. They provide some basics of consent and associated security services. They suggest to store consent in the database. However, it is not clear how they can express the consent rules and evaluate the request against those rules in order to provide the consent. O'Keefe, Greenfield and Goodchild [9] propose an e-Consent system that captures, grants and withholds consent for access to manage electronic health information. Unfortunately, the consent-capturing mechanism is static, restricting the possibility of expressive consent rules.

Jin et al. [6] proposes an authorisation framework for sharing EHR, enabling a patient to control his/her medical data. They consider three types of consents, i.e., *break-glass consent, patient consent* and *default consent*. The *break-glass consent* has the highest priority, representing emergency situations, while the *default consent* has the lowest one. The *patient consent* is captured if no *default consent* is provided. They store consent in the database. Unfortunately, the consent-capturing mechanism is not expressive enough to define the real-world consent rules.

Verhenneman [13] provides a discussion about the legal theory on consent and describes the lifecycle of consent. The author provides a legal analysis in order to capture consent. However, the work is theoretical without any concrete solution. Wuyts *et al.* [14] propose an architecture to integrate patient consent in e-health access control. They capture consent as Policy Information Point (PIP), where consent is stored in the database. The shortcoming of storing consent in the database is that it limits the data subject to rely on only pre-defined of attributes with a very limit expressivity to define the consent rules. While in our proposed solution, we do not consider a fix set of pre-defined attributes, instead we dynamically capture the attributes in the form of contextual information.

The existing research on access control lacks in providing a user to autonomously define the consent evaluation functionality, necessary for regulating the automatic collection of consent. That is, it requires investigation how to capture consent independent of the access control enforcement mechanism. Moreover, it is not clear how to provide transparent auditing while giving (or obtaining) the consent so that later on a forensic analysis can be performed by an investigating auditor.

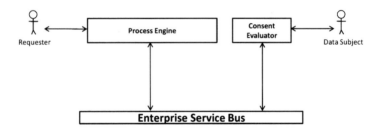

Fig. 1. System architecture of the proposed solution

4   The Proposed Approach

Before presenting the details of the proposed solution, it is necessary to discuss the system model which is described as follows:

4.1   System Model

In this section, we identify the following system entities:

- **Data Subject:** Data Subject is the user whose consent is being captured. A Data Subject interacts with the Consent Evaluator to manage consent-policy corresponding to a resource. Furthermore, a Data Subject interacts with the Requester using the enterprise service bus to collect the contextual information.

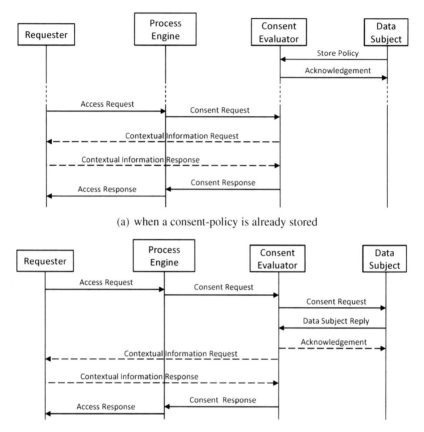

(a) when a consent-policy is already stored

(b) when a data subject replies dynamically

Fig. 2. Capturing consent in the proposed solution

- **Requester:** A Requester is a user that sends access request to the Process Engine. If required, a Requester sends contextual information to the Data Subject. This information may include, but not limited to, Requester's role, Requester's name, Requester's location, time, etc.
- **Process Engine:** It is the data controller who is responsible to enforce access controls. It works as a bridge between a Requester and a Data Subject. Once required, it sends consent request to the Consent Evaluator and receives back the consent.
- **Consent Evaluator:** The Consent Evaluator is an entity responsible to manage and evaluate consent-policy. When requested, it provides consent back to the Process Engine. This is an additional entity that is not present in the traditional access control systems.

The main idea is to have two levels of access controls. The first level of access controls to define access control policies which could be defined by the Data Subject, the data controller or both. While, the second level of access controls are defined by the Data

Subject in order to authorise someone to get his/her consent in an automated manner. The first level of access controls express either consent is required or not. The second level of access controls are managed by the Data Subject. In other words, each Data Subject defines consent-policies in order to indicate who is authorised to get his/her consent. Moreover, a Data Subject may withdraw his/her consent by deleting the corresponding consent-policy. In this paper, our main focus is to elaborate the second level of access controls.

Figure 1 shows the abstract architecture of the proposed solution. The Process Engine is responsible to handle the first level of access controls defining who can access the resource while the Consent Evaluator is responsible to capture and store the consent of a Data Subject. The Consent Evaluator is maintained for each Data Subject. Once the Process Engine identifies that consent is required, it interacts with the Consent Evaluator via the enterprise service bus.

Figure 2 illustrates how system entities interact with each other. We can distinguish between two cases for capturing consent. The first case is when consent can be stored statically while the second case is when consent is captured dynamically.

In the first case, shown in Figure 2(a), a Data Subject stores the consent-policy and gets back an acknowledgment. Once a Requester sends an access request, the Process Engine identifies if the access control policy corresponding to the requested resource requires any consent. If the Data Subject consent is required, the Process Engine generates and sends the consent request to the Consent Evaluator. Since the consent-policy is already stored, the Consent Evaluator does not need to interact with the Data Subject. However, the Consent Evaluator may collect contextual information from the Requester in order to evaluate the consent-policy. After the consent-policy has been evaluated, consent is sent from the Consent Evaluator to the Process Engine. Finally, the Process Engine evaluates the access policy and sends the access response back to the Requester.

In the second case, shown in Figure 2(b), we assume that the consent-policy is not already stored as we considered in the above case. Once a Requester makes an access request, the Process Engine identifies if the access control policy corresponding to the requested resource requires any consent. If the Data Subject consent is required, the Process Engine generates and sends the consent request to the Consent Evaluator. Since the consent-policy is not stored, the Consent Evaluator needs to interact with the Data Subject. For this purpose, the Consent Evaluator forwards the consent request to the Data Subject. The Data Subject may reply with consent, consent-policy or both. In case if the Data Subject reply includes the consent-policy, the Consent Evaluator sends an acknowledgment back to the Data Subject; moreover, the Consent Evaluator may collect contextual information from the Requester in order to evaluate the consent-policy. After the consent-policy has been evaluated, consent is sent from the Consent Evaluator to the Process Engine. However, if the Data Subject reply includes consent, then the Consent Evaluator does on to do evaluation. Once the Process Engine receives consent, it evaluates the access control policy and sends the access response back to the Requester.

In the proposed solution, it is possible to provide a Data Subject with a tool for the consent management; this not only enables the administration of the consent-policy but also supports the inspection service to check who has obtained consent automatically.

In other words, the system maintains a log at the Consent Evaluator side to facilitate a Data Subject with both the administration of consent-policies and inspection of consent log. The consent log may be provided as digital evidence.

4.2 Consent-Policy Types

The consent-policy in the proposed solution refers to the written consent. When a Requester needs to verify whether he or she has consent in order to access the data, he or she refers to the written consent, which is consent-policy in the proposed solution. The purpose of the Consent Evaluator is to store the consent-policy and evaluate the consent decision, whenever requested.

The consent-policy may require a set of attributes in order to evaluate consent. The consent-policy attributes include, but not limited to, the following:

- Request date
- Request time
- Requester name
- Requester role
- Requester location
- Requester age
- Access reason
- Access specification

There are two types of consent-policy.

Open Policy. The open policy can be categorised further into two types. One is *black-list* while the other is *white-list*. The black-list associated with an attribute limits access to a resource for Requesters holding that attribute with values in the list. For instance, in Table 1, a black-list of Requesters (i.e., Requester name attribute) is maintained to limit the access on resource R_1. On the other hand, the white-list associated with an attribute permits access to a resource only for Requesters holding that attribute with values in the list. For instance, in Table 1, a white-list of Requesters (i.e., requester role attribute) is maintained to permit access to resource R_2.

Complex Policy. The complex policy is the one that may involve conditional expressions in order to provide consent. Typically, a conditional expression is evaluated against the Requester attributes. These conditional expressions are evaluated by the Consent Evaluator. If the Requester attributes satisfy all the conditional expressions in the consent-policy, the consent is *Yes* and *No* otherwise. For instance, in Table 1, a Requester can access to resource R_5 if the time of request is between 8:00 hrs and 17:00 hrs, and the Requester is located in HR-ward.

5   Solution Details

For each of the resource, requiring consent of the Data Subject, the Consent Evaluator stores the corresponding consent-policy. Table 1 illustrates how consent-policies are

Table 1. Consent-policy storage at the consent evaluator side

Resource ID	Consent-Policy Type	Contextual Information	Policy Description
R_1	Open	Requester-name	Black-list: {Alice, Bob, Charlie}
R_2	Open	Requester-role	White-list: {Nurse, Doctor}
R_3	Complex	Request-time	Condition: 8:00 hrs $\leq$ Time $\leq$ 17:00 hrs
R_4	Complex	Requester-location	Condition: Location=HR-Ward
R_5	Complex	Request-time, Requester-location	Condition: 8:00 hrs $\leq$ Time $\leq$ 17:00 hrs AND Location=HR-Ward
$\vdots$	$\vdots$	$\vdots$	$\vdots$

stored at the Consent Evaluator. Each row in Table 1 corresponds to the consent-policy per resource. For each resource, the Consent Evaluator stores the consent-policy type (that is, open or complex), parameters (that is, contextual information) required in order to evaluate the consent-policy and the description providing further details of the consent-policy. In case of the open type, the policy description provides the information about the type of access list, either black-list or white-list. While in case of the complex type, the policy description expresses the conditional expressions required to be fulfilled in order to provide consent as *Yes*.

5.1   Communication Messages

For both static and dynamic consent-capturing, the detail of each message, shown in Figure 2, is described as follows:

Store Policy. When a Data Subject desires to store his/her consent, he/she sends *Store Policy* message to the Consent Evaluator. Each Data Subject has his/her own Consent Evaluator. This message includes resource ID, consent-policy type, a list of attributes used in the consent-policy and the consent-policy. Upon receiving this message, a Consent Evaluator stores this information, as shown in Table 1.

Acknowledgment. We can distinguish between two different cases which are based on how the consent-policy is stored. If the consent-policy is stored statically, then after the *Store Policy* message, the *Acknowledgment* message is sent back to th Data Subject. In case if the consent-policy is stored dynamically then it is sent after the *Data Subject Reply*. In both cases, if the consent-policy is stored successfully then the *Acknowledgment* will include *OK*. Otherwise, it will include the error message with the error details.

Access Request. A Requester sends the *Access Request* to the Process Engine in order to request access to the resource. The *Access Request* includes Requester's URI, target resource ID, the access operation, date and time.

Consent Request. Whenever the Process Engine identifies in the access control policy that the Data Subject consent is required, it sends the *Consent Request* to the Consent Evaluator. The *Consent Request* contains the Requester's URI, target resource ID, the access operation, date and time. Here, we can see that both the *Access Request* and the *Consent Request* contain the same information, since the consent-policy is managed by the Data Subject while the access control policy does not necessarily need to be managed by the Data Subject.

Data Subject Reply. In case of dynamic consent capturing, this message is sent from the Data Subject to the Consent Evaluator in response to the Consent Request. It may contain the consent response, the consent-policy or both. The Consent Evaluator takes actions based on this message. That is, the Consent Evaluator either forwards the consent response or evaluates the consent-policy. In case if it contains both the consent response and the consent-policy then the evaluation can be skipped. In case if a Data Subject replies with consent then it may be accomplished synchronously or asynchronously using a handheld device such as PDA or mobile device. Alternatively, consent can also be provided by email.

Contextual Information Request. After the consent-policy has been found against the requested resource, the Consent Evaluator needs to collect the contextual information by sending the *Contextual Information Request* to the Requester that is identified by his/her URI. The *Contextual Information Request* contains all the parameters required for the consent-policy corresponding to the requested resource.

Contextual Information Response. The Requester replies the *Contextual Information Request* with the *Contextual Information Response*. The *Contextual Information Response* contains all the parameters requested in the *Contextual Information Request*. The contextual information may be collected in multiple round trips of request and response.

Consent Response. After the Consent Evaluator has evaluated the consent-policy against the contextual information, the *Consent Response* is sent back to the Process Engine. In case if the contextual information of the Requester satisfies the consent-policy corresponding to the requested resource, the *Consent Response* contains the consent. Otherwise, it contains an error message.

Access Response. Finally, the Process Engine sends the *Access Response* to the Requester. For the successful access response, it is necessary that the Consent Evaluator replies with the required consent.

5.2   Consent Withdrawal

In the proposed architecture, a Data Subject may withdraw his/her consent any time he/she wants. This can be accomplished by deleting the consent-policy stored on the Consent Evaluator. In other words, the resource entry will be deleted from Table 1 by the Data Subject. This maps well to the real-world situations. Consider the healthcare scenario where a patient has provided his/her consent in order to provide access on his/her medical data for the research purpose. Every time the access is made, the consent will be checked. Let suppose that the patient calls the care-provider to withdraw his/her consent. After the withdrawal, the patient medical data cannot be accessed anymore. The same is the situation in the proposed solution. After a Data Subject has defined the consent-policy, consent can be provided by the Consent Evaluator. However, once the Data Subject wants to withdraw, the consent-policy is deleted by the Consent Evaluator. After the consent-policy has been deleted, no consent can be provided until the Data Subject provides the new consent or the consent-policy.

5.3   Integrity of Consent

Let us assume that the PKI is already in place, where each entity, including the Requesters and Data Subjects, has a private-public key pair. For providing the integrity, the consent-policy can be signed with the signing (or private) key of the Data Subject while the contextual information is signed with the signing key of the Requester. Once a Requester provides the contextual information, first an integrity check is performed to verify if the information is not altered or forged by an adversary. In case if a dispute occurs, the log of entities can be inspected in order to investigate the matter. Technically, the signature will be checked on the transmitted data. The digital signature not only guarantees integrity but also ensures non-repudiation and unforgeability of consent.

5.4   Emergency Situations

In case of emergency, the *Emergency Response Team* may provide consent on the behalf of the Data Subject. Let us consider the healthcare scenario where a patient is in emergency condition, such as heart-attack or some similar situation. In this situation, if a doctor needs any consent for which the patient has not defined any consent-policy then the *Emergency Response Team* or a legal guardian may provide consent on the behalf of the patient. Moreover, just like the paper-based consent, the consent-policy of minors or one who is mentally incapable can be provided by a legal guardian.

5.5   Digital Evidence

Once consent is requested by a Process Engine, the request should be logged. Not only this but also the Consent Evaluation should log once the consent is provided to the Process Engine. Since the contextual information is provided by a Requester to the Consent Evaluator, a Requester should also log the information requested by a Consent Evaluator. This would prevent repudiation of all the involved entities. These logs can be provided to the court as digital evidence.

5.6   Data Subject Tool

The proposed solution may provide a Data Subject with a tool to manage the consent-policies. Furthermore, a Data Subject may be provided with an inspection tool for observing who has obtained consent in an automated manner.

5.7   Implementation Overview

For evaluating the consent-policy against the Requester's attributes, we may consider the widely accepted policy-based framework proposed by IETF [15], where the Consent Evaluator manages the Policy Enforcement Point (PEP) (only the for the second level of access controls defined in the consent-policy) in order to provide the consent.

The Consent Evaluator also manages Policy Decision Point (PDP) for making decision about the consent either *Yes* or *No*. The consent-policy store can be realised as the Policy Administration Point (PAP). In the proposed solution, the request is sent by the Process Engine while the Requester can be treated as a PIP. For representing the consent-policy, we may consider XACML policy language proposed by OASIS [8].

5.8 Performance Overhead

The performance overhead of the proposed solution is $O(m+n)$, where m number of conditional predicates in the consent-policy while n is the number contextual attributes required to evaluate the consent-policy in order to provide consent.

6 Discussion

This section provides a discussion about how the proposed solution may provide security properties including availability and confidentiality. Moreover, this section also gives a brief overview about how to increase the usability for a Data Subject.

6.1 Availability and Confidentiality

For providing availability, the Consent Evaluator can be considered in the outsourced environment, such as the cloud service provider. If the Consent Evaluator is managed by a third party service provider, then there is a threat of information leakage about the consent-policy or the contextual information. In order to provide confidentiality to the consent-capturing in outsourced environments, we may consider ESPOON (Encrypted Security Policies in Outsourced Environments) proposed in [2].

6.2 Increased Usability

In order to increase usability for defining a consent-policy, a Data Subject can be provided with a drag-and-drop policy definition tool for a pre-defined set of parameters of the contextual information. Moreover, a full-fledged pre-defined set of consent-policies can also be provided to the Data Subject.

7 Conclusions and Future Work

In this paper, we have proposed an architecture capture and manage consent. The proposed architecture enables the data controller to capture the consent in an automated manner. Furthermore, consent can be withdrawn any time a Data Subject wishes to do so. In the future, we are planning to implement and evaluate the performance overhead incurred by the proposed solution. In case if a Data Subject associates multiple consent-policies with a resource, then consent resolution strategies needs to investigated.

Acknowledgment. This work is supported by the EU FP7 programme, Research Grant 257063 (project Endorse).

References

1. Anderson, R.J.: A security policy model for clinical information systems. In: Proceedings of 1996 IEEE Symposium on Security and Privacy, pp. 30–43 (May 1996)

2. Asghar, M.R., Ion, M., Russello, G., Crispo, B.: ESPOON: Enforcing encrypted security policies in outsourced environments. In: The Sixth International Conference on Availability, Reliability and Security, ARES 2011 (2011)
3. Becker, M.Y., Sewell, P.: Cassandra: distributed access control policies with tunable expressiveness. In: Proceedings of Fifth IEEE International Workshop on Policies for Distributed Systems and Networks, POLICY 2004, pp. 159–168 (2004)
4. Coiera, E., Clarke, R.: e-Consent: The design and implementation of consumer consent mechanisms in an electronic environment. Journal of the American Medical Informatics Association: JAMIA 11(2), 129–140 (2004)
5. European Communities. Directive 95/46/ec of the european parliament and of the council of 24 October 1995 on the protection of individuals with regard to the processing of personal data and on the free movement of such data (November 1995), http://eur-lex.europa.eu/LexUriServ/
LexUriServ.do?uri=OJ:L:2001:008:0001:0022:EN:PDF
6. Jin, J., Ahn, G.-J., Hu, H., Covington, M.J., Zhang, X.: Patient-centric authorization framework for sharing electronic health records. In: Proceedings of the 14th ACM Symposium on Access Control Models and Technologies, SACMAT 2009, pp. 125–134. ACM, New York (2009)
7. Kudo, M.: Pbac: Provision-based access control model. International Journal of Information Security 1, 116–130 (2002), doi:10.1007/s102070100010
8. OASIS. extensible access control markup language (xacml) version 2.0 (February 2005), http://docs.oasis-open.org/xacml/2.0/
access_control-xacml-2.0-core-spec-os.pdf
9. O'Keefe, C.M., Greenfield, P., Goodchild, A.: A decentralised approach to electronic consent and health information access control. Journal of Research and Practice in Information Technology 37(2) (2005)
10. Ruan, C., Varadharajan, V.: An Authorization Model for E-consent Requirement in a Health Care Application. In: Zhou, J., Yung, M., Han, Y. (eds.) ACNS 2003. LNCS, vol. 2846, pp. 191–205. Springer, Heidelberg (2003)
11. Russello, G., Dong, C., Dulay, N.: Consent-based workflows for healthcare management. In: IEEE Workshop on Policies for Distributed Systems and Networks, POLICY 2008, pp. 153–161 (2008)
12. Sandhu, R.S., Coyne, E.J., Feinstein, H.L., Youman, C.E.: Role-based access control models. Computer 29(2), 38–47 (1996)
13. Verhenneman, G.: Consent, an instrument for patient empowerment? In: Proceedings of the 49th FITCE Congress (2010)
14. Wuyts, K., Scandariato, R., Verhenneman, G., Joosen, W.: Integrating patient consent in e-health access control. IJSSE 2(2), 1–24 (2011)
15. Yavatkar, R., Pendarakis, D., Guerin, R.: A Framework for Policy-based Admission Control. RFC 2753 (Informational) (January 2000), http://www.ietf.org/rfc/rfc2753.txt
16. Zhang, X., Nakae, M., Covington, M.J., Sandhu, R.: A usage-based authorization framework for collaborative computing systems. In: Proceedings of the Eleventh ACM Symposium on Access Control Models and Technologies, SACMAT 2006, pp. 180–189. ACM, New York (2006)

Towards User Centric
Data Governance and Control in the Cloud

Stephan Groß and Alexander Schill

Technische Universität Dresden
Fakultät Informatik
D-01062 Dresden, Germany
{Stephan.Gross,Alexander.Schill}@tu-dresden.de

Abstract. Cloud Computing, i. e. providing on-demand access to virtu-
alised computing resources over the Internet, is one of the current mega-
trends in IT. Today, there are already several providers offering cloud
computing infrastructure (IaaS), platform (PaaS) and software (SaaS)
services. Although the cloud computing paradigm promises both economical as well as technological advantages, many potential users still
have reservations about using cloud services as this would mean to trust
a cloud provider to correctly handle their data according to previously
negotiated rules. Furthermore, the virtualisation causes a location inde-
pendence of offered services which could interfere with domain specific
legislative regulations. In this paper, we present an approach of putting
the cloud user back into power when migrating data and services into and
within the cloud. We outline our work in progress, that aims at providing
a platform for developing flexible service architectures for cloud computing with special consideration of security and non-functional properties.

1 Motivation

The recent progress in virtualising storage and computing resources combined
with service oriented architectures (SOA) and broadband Internet access has led
to a renaissance of already known concepts developed in research fields like grid,
utility and autonomic computing. Today, the term cloud computing describes
different ways of providing on-demand and pay-per-use access to elastic virtu-
alised computing resource pools [15]. These resources are abstracted to services
so that cloud computing resources can be retrieved as infrastructure (IaaS), platform (PaaS) and software (SaaS) services respectively. The pay-per-use model
of such service oriented architectures includes Service Level Agreements (SLA)
negotiated between service provider and user to establish guarantees for required
non-functional properties including mandatory security requirements. The (economical) advantages of this approach are fairly obvious: One saves costly invest-
ments for procuring and maintaining probably underused hardware and at the
same time gains new flexibility to react on temporal higher demands.

Nevertheless, there are reasonable reservations about the deployment of cloud
computing services, e.g. concerning data security and compliance. Most of these

J. Camenisch and D. Kesdogan (Eds.): iNetSec 2011, LNCS 7039, pp. 132–144, 2012.
© IFIP International Federation for Information Processing 2012

concerns result from the fact, that cloud computing describes complex socio-technical systems with a high number of different kinds of stakeholders following different and possibly contradicting objectives. From a user's perspective, one has to hand over the control over his data and services when entering the cloud, i.e. the user has to trust that the cloud provider behaves in compliance with the established SLA. However, to actually agree on a specific SLA a user first has to assess his organizational risks related to security and resilience [5].

Current solutions that restrict the provision of sensible services to dedicated private, hybrid or so-called national clouds[1] do not go far enough as they reduce the user's flexibility when scaling in or out and still force him to trust the cloud provider. Furthermore, private clouds intensify the vendor lock-in problem. Last but not least, there is no support for deciding which services and data could be safely migrated to which cloud. Instead we demand new methods and technical support to put the user in a position to benefit from the advantages of cloud computing without giving up the sovereignty over his data and applications. In our current work, we follow a system oriented approach focussing on technical means to achieve this goal.

The remainder of this paper is structured as follows. We first refine our problem statement in section 2. Then, in section 3, we sketch our approach of developing a secure platform for easy and flexible cloud service architectures. Our solution is based on the idea of a personal secure cloud (Π-Cloud), i.e. the conglomerate of a user's resources and devices, that can be controlled by a specialized gateway, the so-called Π-Box. We elaborate on its basic components in section 3 and further exemplify how the Π-Box supports the controlled storage of a user's data in the cloud in section 4. We conclude with a discussion of our approach and compare it with related work in section 5. Finally, section 6 provides an outlook on future work.

2   Problem Statement

We identified security as a major obstacle that prevents someone to transfer his resources into the cloud. In order to make sound business decisions and to maintain or obtain security certifications, cloud customers need assurance that providers are following sound security practices and behave according to agreed SLAs [4]. Thus, our overall goal is the development of a flexible open source cloud platform that integrates all necessary components for the development of user-controlled and -monitored secure cloud environments. This platform should provide the following functionality:

---

[1] The mentioned cloud types define different deployment models of cloud computing systems. In contrast to public clouds that make services available to the general public, private clouds are operated solely for an organization although the resources used might be outsourced to some service company. Hybrid clouds describe a mixture of public and private cloud, i.e. when users complement their internal IT resources with public ones. The term national clouds describes a scenario, where the location of the cloud resource pool is restricted to one country or legislative eco-system like the EU.

1. Mechanisms to enable a *user-controlled migration of resources and data into the cloud*. These mechanisms should support (semi-)automatic configuration of cryptographic algorithms to simplify the enforcement of a user's security requirements as well as the dynamic selection of cloud providers that best fit the user's requirements and trust assumptions. Thus, we need a formalised way to acquire a user's requirements. Furthermore, we need to integrate the user's private resources and different cloud providers in our cloud platform, e.g. by using wrapper mechanisms or standardised interfaces.
2. A sound and *trustworthy monitoring system for cloud services* that is able to gather all relevant information to detect or even predict SLA violations without manipulations by the cloud provider under control. To support the configuration of the monitoring system, there should be some mechanism that derives relevant monitoring objectives from negotiated SLAs. Thus, we need a formalised language for machine-readable SLA focussing on the technical details of a cloud computing environment.
3. *Adaptation mechanisms optimizing the cloud* utilization according to user-defined constraints like cost, energy consumption as well as to react on SLA violations detected by the monitoring system in order to mitigate the resulting negative effects. This includes migration support to transparently transfer resources between different cloud providers as well as adaptation tools that leaves the resources at the chosen provider but transforms them to further meet the user's non-functional and security requirements.

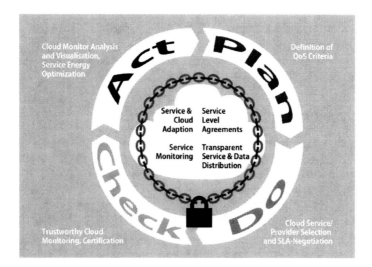

Fig. 1. Support for major cloud computing quality management objectives

In other words, we demand the implementation of an iterative quality management process to establish a secure cloud computing lifecyle that enables the user to constantly supervise and control his cloud computing services. By applying the well-established PDCA model [13] the major objectives of such a cloud computing management process can be summarized as depicted in figure 1.

3   Introducing FlexCloud

Within the FlexCloud project we aim at developing methods and mechanisms to support the development of flexible and secure service architectures for cloud computing. Our major objective is to put the user in a position to externalize his IT infrastructure without losing control. For this, we have first refined the definition of cloud deployment models by introducing the concept of a personal secure cloud.

We define a *personal secure cloud* or Π-*Cloud* as a hybrid cloud that covers all ressources, services and data under complete control of a user. The user is able to dynamically adjust the Π-Cloud's shape according to his actual demands, i.e. to securely include foreign services and ressources as well as to securely share parts of his Π-Cloud with others.

Thus, we need to control the data-flow as well as the service distribution and execution. The technical means to control the Π-Cloud when sharing ressources or exchanging data are provided by the so-called Π-*Gateway*. The Π-Gateway provides all mechanisms to manage and optimize a user's policies concerning security and other non-functional properties, e.g. performance, energy-efficiency or costs. Furthermore, it provides the necessary means to enforce these policies such as adaptation and migration mechanisms for services and data.

To bridge the gap between a Π-Cloud's raw ressources, i.e. a user's devices, and the actually used services, we rely on a *service platform*. Its primary task is to dynamically allocate a user's software service to the available infrastructure services.

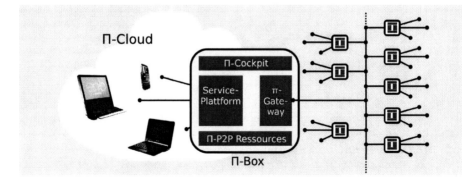

Fig. 2. Controlling the cloud with the Π-Box

Figure 2 shows our vision of a secure cloud computing setup. On the left hand side we have a user's personal devices building his Π-Cloud. It is controlled by his Π-Box (rectangle in the middle) that combines service platform and Π-Gateway. Depending on the Π-Cloud's size, the Π-Box can be realized physically (either as a separate hardware appliance or as a part of an existing device such as a router). It can also be virtualized, thus it can be migrated within the Π-Cloud or to some trustworthy cloud provider.

The following subsections give more details on the differnt parts of our approach.

3.1   Service Platform

A major foundation of our work is represented by our service platform SPACE. SPACE is an open source platform for the Internet of services which provides basic tools for contract-bound adaptive service execution and acts as a hosting and brokering environment for services. It already integrates techniques for trading Internet services and their surveillance during execution by the user as well as the service provider.

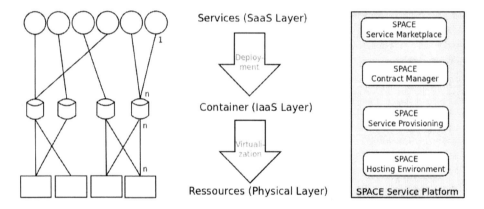

Fig. 3. Functionality of the SPACE service platform

Figure 3 summarizes the functionality implemented by SPACE. In general, SPACE provides a platform for building marketplaces for contract-bound adaptive service execution. The service marketplace and contract manager components comprise mechanisms for trading services, i.e. offering, searching, configuring, using and rating them. The service hosting enviroment binds heterogenous implementation technologies to a unified interface for service deployment, execution and monitoring. Overall, SPACE provides all necessary functions for the deployment of arbitrary software services on virtualized physical ressources provided as IaaS containers.

Being designed as a stand-alone server in the beginning, we are now working on bringing SPACE into the cloud, making it a fully distributed platform. Its latest extension already integrates Amazon EC2-compatible cloud environments as target environment for complex services delivered as virtual machines [20]. However, adding and removing new ressources and infrastructure services is still a rather static process.

3.2 Π-P2P Ressources

Π-P2P Ressources The Π-P2P Ressource component aims at improving the functionality to dynamically adjust the ressource and infrastructure pool available within a Π-Cloud. This includes the different devices in the Π-Cloud under the user's control as well as external cloud ressources (right part in figure 2). The on-going work on this topic are twofold.

On the one hand, we are further extending the SPACE by specific protocols to organize the physical ressource pool in a peer-to-peer network. This includes adaption algorithms to reorganize the container setup at the IaaS layer.

On the other hand, the Π-P2P Ressources component gets integrated with the Π-Gateway to implement a control flow that guarantees the combination of services and ressources according to a user's given policies.

For further details the interested reader is refered to [16].

3.3 Π-Gateway

We illustrate the Π-Gateway's functionality by an example: confidential cloud storage. Although there already exist first cloud storage solutions providing client-side encryption (e.g. [10]), it is cumbersome to integrate these systems into a company's existing IT infrastructure. For example, they introduce new potential for human errors as they ignore available access control systems and must be manually configured, e.g. by (re)defining the encryption keys for authorised users. It is also difficult to control if they comply with given regulations.

Figure 4 sketches how the Π-Gateway incorporates different tools, such as existing access control and user management systems, face recognition or information retrieval tools to determine the users authorised to access a specific file. For example, it could search a text file for a specific confidentiality note, analyse the people displayed on a foto, or simply check the file system's access rights in combination with the operating systems user database to determine the user identities to be granted access. By using these identities it is able to retrieve the necessary public keys from a public key infrastructure and to encrypt the data accordingly before storing it into the cloud.

Thus, the Π-Gateway consolidates all functionality to control and coordinate a user's cloud. This includes

– the management and enforcement of user policies concerning security and other non-functional properties;

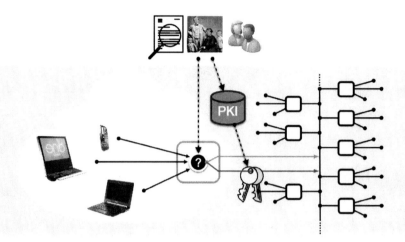

Fig. 4. Automized confidentiality for cloud storage

- the aggregation and analyzation of monitoring data retrieved by sensors implemented in the service platform as well as in the Π-P2P Ressources component;
- mechanisms to react on monitoring events and to optimize the ressource utilization of the Π-Cloud;
- technical foundations to improve the Π-Box's joy of use.

In other words, whereas the Π-Gateway represents the Π-Box's brain the service platform and the Π-P2P Ressources forms its body and extremeties respectively.

3.4   Π-Cockpit

Although we are aiming to include as much intelligence in our Π-Box to disburden the user from cumbersome administration tasks, it would be impudent to claim that our Π-Cloud is able to maintain itself. As we call for user-control, we need the necessary means to put him into this position even if he is not an expert. In short, we need a Π-Cockpit, i.e. adequate user interfaces to supervise and adjust the Π-Box. These user interfaces must be able to adjust to the user's skills and preferences as well as to the device's capabilities it is currently used on. The foundations for our work in this area are two-fold:

On the one hand, we aim at following up recent research in the area of usable security and privacy technologies that proposes an interdisciplinary approach to support a user in meeting his security demands independent of his skills and expertise. For an overview on related work in this field we refer to [6, 8, 9].

On the other hand, we are in line with recent developments in the human-computer interaction community that started to discuss the impact of cloud computing on the design of the user experience [7].

4   A First Use Case: Enterprise Cloud Storage

As a first evaluation scenario for our approach we have chosen the cloud storage use case already mentioned in the previous section. Thus, our pool of physical ressources consists of disk storage space that is provided by different cloud storage providers as an infrastructure service.

4.1   Problems of Current Cloud Storage Solutions

Current cloud storage offers suffer from different issues. First of all, off-site data storage raises several security and privacy concerns. Due to the nature of cloud computing the user can usually be not be sure about the geographical placement of his data. This leads to a possible mismatch of legislative rules in the cloud user's and provider's country respectively. Recent media reports document that even geographic restrictions for used ressources and services as assured by some cloud providers cannot guarantee a user's security compliance [22].

As a solution to ensure confidentiality, several cloud storage providers therefor rely on cryptography. However, for sake of simplicity and usability, most of them retain full control of the key management. Thus, the user's data stored at a trustworthy provider might be safe from intruders but can still subject to internal attacks or governmental desires. Even more, this increases the user's dependability on a specific storage provider leading to the point of a complete vendor-lockin and a possible loss of availability.

With respect to the functionality stated in section 2 we claim the following requirements for an ideal cloud storage solution:

User-controlled migration: The user should always be in the position to decide which data shall be migrated to which cloud storage provider. Furthermore, he should be assisted in applying cryptographic tools to enforce his security policies. To ensure best possible trustworthiness these security tools must be applied at the user's premises or at least by a fully trusted third party.

Trustworthy monitoring: After having transfered his data to the cloud the user should be able to control the reliability and trustworthiness of the chosen cloud storage providers. This includes audit mechanisms for the preservation of evidence to support subsequent legal enforcement.

Adaptation mechanisms: Finally, the user should be supported when recovering from detected malfunctions or inadequateness, e.g. securely restoring data stored at a provider or migrating it to another more trusted one.

4.2   Proposed Solution

We have developed a first prototype of a cloud storage integrator that aims at providing the stated functionality. Our prototype called SecCSIE (Secure Storage Integrator for Enterprises) implements a Linux based proxy server to be placed in a company's intranet. It mediates the data flow to arbitrary cloud storage providers and provides a SMB/CIFS file based access to them for the average users. SecCSIE consists of five major components (for more details please refer to [19]):

Cloud Storage Protocol Adapter: To integrate and homogenize multiple cloud storage services we have implemented several protocol adapters. This includes adapters for common protocols like NFS, SMB/CIFS, WebDav and (S)FTP to access files over an IP network. Furthermore we provide access to Amazon S3, Dropbox and GMail storage by using existing FUSE (Filesystem in Userspace) models.

Data Dispersion Unit: Besides the cloud storage protocol adapter our data dispersion unit contributes to overcoming the vendor-lockin. By utilizing recent information dispersal algorithms [17] it distributes the user's data over different storage providers with higher efficiency than simple redundant copies. This also increases the overall availability and performance.

Data Encryption Unit: The encryption unit encapsulates different encryption algorithms to ensure confidentiality of the data stored. It also takes measures to preserver the stored data's integrity, e.g. by using AES-CMAC. The necessary key management can be handled by SecCSIE itself or delegated to an existing public key infrastructure.

Metadata Database: Within the metadata database all relevant information are collected to reconstruct and access the data stored in the cloud. Overall, this includes configuration parameters for data dispersion and encryption unit. Thus, the metadata database is absolutely irreplaceable for the correct functioning of our storage integrator.

Management Console: The management console implements a very straightforward web-based user interface to control SecCSIE's main functions. It provides rudimentary methods with which an enterprise's system administrator can check and restore the vitality of his storage cloud. Figure 5 gives an overview of the management console. Specific monitoring or configuration tasks can be accessed via the menu bar at the top or by clicking the respective component in the architecture overview.

The cloud storage protocol adapter together with the data dispersion and encryption units contribute to our overall objective of user-controlled migration. The trustworthy monitoring is accomplished by the storage proxy itself using the integrity checks provided by the data encryption unit as well as frequent checks of the network accessability of each storage provider. The management console provides an easy to use interface for this process so that one can estimate the reliability of the configured storage providers. Adaptation can be manually triggered in the management console. Furthermore, if an integrity check fails

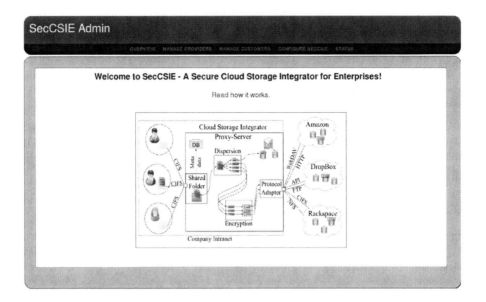

Fig. 5. Preliminary management console showing system architecture and data flow

when accessing a file, it can be automatically restored by switching to another storage provider and data chunk. The number of tolerable faults depends on the configuration of the dispersion unit, thus, it can be adjusted to the user's preferences.

5   Discussion and Related Work

In contrast to a common hybrid cloud, a Π-Cloud provides the following advantages:

- The user of a Π-Cloud retains full control over his data and services respectively.
- The user gains improved scalability as the Π-Gateway provides dedicated mechanisms to securely externalize data and services according to his security policies.
- The user no longer suffers from a vendor-lockin as the Π-Gateway integrates arbitrary service provider into a homogeneous view.

Thus, we achieve our goal of user-controlled migration into the cloud. The Π-Gateway together with the Π-Cockpit also provide a framework for implementing a sound monitoring system. Together with the Π-P2P Ressources framework it provides broad support for adaption and optimization scenarios.

Being more or less a topic only for industry in the beginning, cloud computing has seen more and more interest by academia over the last 3 years. Thus, there exist several work with similar approaches to FlexCloud. The recently initiated Cloud@Home project [2] for example also aims at clients sharing their ressources with the cloud. Although the project also addresses SLAs and QoS it only sets a minor focus on security. The same applies for Intel's recent cloud initiative [12].

A major part of current research work on cloud computing is about cloud storage. Most theoretical publications in this area like [11, 21] apply existing algorithms from cryptography, peer-to-peer networking and coding theory to improve the integrity and availability of cloud storage. More sophisticated approaches lik [14] argue for a virtual private storage service that provides confidentiality, integrity and non-repudiation while retaining the main benefits of public cloud storage, i.e. availability, reliability, efficient retrieval and data sharing. However, although promising these approaches are still impractical to use. Other work tries to predict the required storage space to optimize the ressource allocation [3] or aims at the better integration with existing IT infrastructures [23]. However, to our best knowledge none of these work has presented a usable prototype implementation. On the practical side of the spectrum there are works like [1] or [18]. Both provide a similar approach to ours but only provide web-service based access to the storage gateway that complicates an integration with existing environments.

6   Conclusion

We have presented the overall objectives and first results of the FlexCloud project. In general, we are trying to keep the cloud user in control when using cloud services. We aim at providing a platform, the Π-Box, that provides all functionality to span a so-called Π-Cloud for flexible and secure cloud computing applications. As a first evaluation scenario we have chosen the use case of enterprise cloud storage for which we have implemented an initial prototype of the Π-Box called SecCSIE.

Concerning future work, our short-term objectives aim at consolidating the results achieved with SecCSIE. This includes further testing and optimization especially with respect to performance evaluation. We also plan to improve our monitoring and optimize our data dispersion mechanisms with respect to the user's requirements. Long-term objectives include the generalization of the storage scenario to other service types. We are especially interested in dynamic ressource allocation, e.g. by means of peer-to-peer mechanisms. Furthermore we plan to investige the implementation and evaluation of user interfaces with respect to his role and skills to improve the surveillance and management of the Π-Cloud.

Acknowledgement. The authors would like to express their gratitude to all members of the FlexCloud research group, especially its former member Gerald Hübsch, for many fruitful discussions that contributed to the development of the ideas presented in this paper.

This work has received funding under project number 080949277 by means of the European Regional Development Fund (ERDF), the European Social Fund

(ESF) and the German Free State of Saxony. The information in this document is provided as is, and no guarantee or warranty is given that the information is for any particular purpose.

References

1. Abu-Libdeh, H., Princehouse, L., Weatherspoon, H.: RACS: a case for cloud storage diversity. In: Proceedings of the 1st ACM Symposium on Cloud Computing, SoCC 2010, pp. 229–240. ACM, New York (2010), http://doi.acm.org/10.1145/1807128.1807165
2. Aversa, R., Avvenuti, M., Cuomo, A., Di Martino, B., Di Modica, G., Distefano, S., Puliafito, A., Rak, M., Tomarchio, O., Vecchio, A., Venticinque, S., Villano, U.: The Cloud@Home Project: Towards a New Enhanced Computing Paradigm. In: Guarracino, M.R., Vivien, F., Träff, J.L., Cannataro, M., Danelutto, M., Hast, A., Perla, F., Knüpfer, A., Di Martino, B., Alexander, M. (eds.) Euro-Par-Workshop 2010. LNCS, vol. 6586, pp. 555–562. Springer, Heidelberg (2011)
3. Bonvin, N., Papaioannou, T.G., Aberer, K.: A self-organized, fault-tolerant and scalable replication scheme for cloud storage. In: Proceedings of the 1st ACM Symposium on Cloud computing (SoCC 2010), pp. 205–216. ACM, New York (2010)
4. Catteddu, D.: Cloud Computing – Benefits, risks and recommendations for information security. ENISA Report, ENISA (November 2009)
5. Catteddu, D.: Security & Resilience in Governmental Clouds – Making an informed decision. ENISA Report, ENISA (January 2011)
6. Cranor, L.F., Garfinkel, S.L.: Designing Secure Systems That People Can Use. O'Reilly (September 2005) ISBN 978-0-596-00827-7
7. England, D., Randles, M., Taleb-Bendiab, A.: Designing interaction for the cloud. In: Proceedings of the 2011 Annual Conference Extended Abstracts on Human Factors in Computing Systems, CHI EA 2011, pp. 2453–2456. ACM, New York (2011), http://doi.acm.org/10.1145/1979742.1979582
8. Fischer-Hübner, S., Iacono, L.L., Möller, S.: Usable Security und Privacy. Datenschutz und Datensicherheit (DuD) (11), 773 (2010)
9. Garfinkel, S.L.: Design principles and patterns for computer systems that are simultaneously secure and usable. Ph.D. thesis, Massachusetts Institute of Technology (2005), http://simson.net/thesis/
10. Grolimund, D., Meisser, L., Schmid, S., Wattenhofer, R.: Cryptree: A folder tree structure for cryptographic file systems. Technical report, Purdue University, Department of Computer Science, West Lafayette, IN, USA (2006)
11. He, Q., Li, Z., Zhang, X.: Study on Cloud Storage System Based on Distributed Storage Systems. In: 2010 International Conference on Computational and Information Sciences, ICCIS (December 2010)
12. Intel Corporation: Benefits of a Client-aware Cloud. White Paper Client-aware Cloud Computing (2011),
http://partnerzones.i41.nbsp.de/_misc/download.cfm?filepath=/4/0/0/4/
Benefitsofclientawarecloud.pdf&filename=Benefitsofclientawarecloud
&filetype=pdf&filename=Benefitsofclientawarecloud&filetype=pdf&fid=624
13. Information technology – Security techniques – Information security management systems – Requirements. No. 27001 in ISO/IEC Standard, International Organization for Standardization (2005)

14. Kamara, S., Lauter, K.: Cryptographic Cloud Storage. Tech. rep., Microsoft Research Cryptography Group (2011)
15. Mell, P., Grance, T.: The NIST Definition of Cloud Computing. Recommendations of the National Institute of Standards and Technology (NIST), Special Publication 800–145 (January 2011),
http://csrc.nist.gov/publications/drafts/800-145/
Draft-SP-800-145_cloud-definition.pdf
16. Mosch, M.: User-controlled data sovereignty in the Cloud. In: Proceedings of the PhD Symposium at the 9th IEEE European Conference on Web Services (ECOWS 2011), Lugano, Switzerland (September 2011)
17. Resch, J.K., Plank, J.S.: AONT-RS: blending security and performance in dispersed storage systems. In: 9th Usenix Conference on File and Storage Technologies FAST 2011 (February 2011)
18. Schnjakin, M., Meinel, C.: Plattform zur Bereitstellung sicherer und hochverfügbarer Speicherressourcen in der Cloud. In: Sicher in die digitale Welt von morgen – 12. Deutscher IT-Sicherheitskongress des BSI. SecuMedia Verlag, Bonn (2011)
19. Seiger, R., Groß, S., Schill, A.: SecCSIE: A Secure Cloud Storage Integrator for Enterprises. In: International Workshop on Clouds for Enterprises (C4E). Luxemburg (September 2011)
20. Spillner, J.: Spaceflight – A versatile live demonstrator and teaching system for advanced service-oriented technologies. In: Crimean Conference on Microwave and Telecommunication Technology (CriMiCo), Sewastopol, Ukraine (September 2011) (accepted for publication)
21. Wang, C., Wang, Q., Ren, K., Lou, W.: Ensuring data storage security in Cloud Computing. In: Proceedings of the 17th International Workshop on Quality of Service, Charleston, SC, USA (2009)
22. Whittaker, Z.: Microsoft admits patriot act can access EU-based cloud data. ZDNet iGeneration Blog (June 2011),
http://www.zdnet.com/blog/igeneration/
microsoft-admits-patriot-act-canb-access-eu-based-cloud-data/11225
23. Xu, P., Zheng, W., Wu, Y., Huang, X., Xu, C.: Enabling Cloud Storage to Support Traditional Applications. In: 5th Annual ChinaGrid Conference (2010)

Securing Data Provenance in the Cloud

Muhammad Rizwan Asghar[1,2], Mihaela Ion[1,2],
Giovanni Russello[1], and Bruno Crispo[2]

[1] Create-Net, Italy
{asghar,ion,russello}@create-net.org
[2] University of Trento, Italy
crispo@disi.unitn.it

Abstract. Cloud storage offers the flexibility of accessing data from anywhere at any time while providing economical benefits and scalability. However, cloud stores lack the ability to manage data provenance. Data provenance describes how a particular piece of data has been produced. It is vital for a post-incident investigation, widely used in healthcare, scientific collaboration, forensic analysis and legal proceedings. Data provenance needs to be secured since it may reveal private information about the sensitive data while the cloud service provider does not guarantee confidentiality of the data stored in dispersed geographical locations. This paper proposes a scheme to secure data provenance in the cloud while offering the encrypted search.

Keywords: Secure Data Provenance, Encrypted Cloud Storage, Security, Privacy.

1 Introduction

Cloud storage has recently received great attention from the IT industry ranging from small-scale to large-scale enterprises. It offers flexibility of accessing data at any time from anywhere and any terminal, such as computers, laptops or hand-held devices. It not only provides scalability but also reduces IT infrastructure and management costs. The cloud raises security challenge of protecting data confidentiality. Thus, users may not trust the cloud provider for storing their data securely in dispersed geographical locations. Data security, which is of great concern for the users, is a strong obstacle in widespread adoption of the cloud for a number of applications involving sensitive data of the healthcare and banking domains.

Unfortunately, today's clouds are missing to manage data provenance. Data provenance describes how a particular piece of data has been produced. It is generated once the data is processed. An auditor can obtain it by querying the store where it is recorded. Data provenance plays a vital role in forensic analysis, enabling the collection of digital evidence by a post-incident investigation. It is widely used not only for forensics analysis but also for scientific collaborations and in legal proceedings. Generally, data provenance may include, but not limited to, what action was taken, who took it, where it was taken, why it was taken, how it was taken, when it was taken, in which environment it was taken and what the sequence of those actions is [18].

J. Camenisch and D. Kesdogan (Eds.): iNetSec 2011, LNCS 7039, pp. 145–160, 2012.
© IFIP International Federation for Information Processing 2012

Consider a healthcare scenario where a patient visits the general physician, Dr. Alice, assigned to her. Dr. Alice performs a medical checkup and prepares a preliminary medical report based on her observations. Next, Dr. Alice recommends the patient to go for some medical tests in any medical lab. The patient goes to a medical lab where a lab assistant Bob conducts the medical tests recommended in the medical report. After conducting the medical tests, Bob adds the details of results in the medical report and gives it to the patient. The patient comes back to Dr. Alice with the medical report. Dr. Alice reviews the medical report and forwards the patient to the cardiologist, Dr. Charlie. Dr. Charlie reads the medical report and starts diagnosing the disease. In this scenario, data provenance describes how the medical report has been generated and who has worked on it and what the sequence of processing is. Since, each action taken on the medical report is recorded, the data provenance may answer the queries like *who took action on the medical report?*, *what actions are taken by Alice today?*, *did Bob and Charlie work on the medical report?*, etc. In other words, the data provenance may be obtained as a result of the query.

1.1 Motivation

The provenance of sensitive data may reveal some private information. For instance, in the above scenario, we can notice that even if the medical report is protected from unauthorised access, the data provenance still may reveal some information about a patient's sensitive data. That is, an adversary may deduce from the data provenance that the patient might have heart problems considering the fact that a cardiologist has processed patient's medical report. Therefore, in addition to provide protection to the sensitive data, it is vital to make the data provenance secure.

Another motivation to secure data provenance is for providing the unforgeability and non-repudiation. For instance, in the aforementioned healthcare scenario, assume that carelessness in reporting has resulted in the mis-diagnosis. In order to escape the investigation of mis-diagnosis, a victim would try to either forge the medical report with the fake data provenance or repudiate his/her involvement in generating the medical report. Moreover, the query to data provenance and the response should be encrypted, otherwise, a victim may threaten the auditor by eavesdropping the communication channel to check if his/her case is being investigated. The data, such as the medical report, may be critical; therefore, it should be subject to the availability at any time from anywhere.

A significant amount of research has been conducted on securing data provenance. For instance, secure data provenance schemes proposed in [10, 9] ensures confidentiality by employing state-of-the-art encryption techniques. However, this scheme does not address how an authorised auditor can perform search on data provenance. The scheme proposed in [12] provides anonymous access in the cloud environment for sharing data among multiple users. The scheme can track the real user if any dispute occurs. However, there is no detail about how the scheme manages data provenance in the cloud. Both [11] and [7] assume a trusted infrastructure, restricting the possibility of managing data provenance in cloud environments. Unfortunately, the existing research lacks in securing data provenance while offering search on data provenance stored in the cloud.

1.2   Research Contribution

This paper investigates the problem of securing data provenance in the cloud and proposes a scheme that supports encrypted search while protecting confidentiality of data provenance stored in the cloud. One of the main advantages of the proposed approach is that neither an adversary nor a cloud service provider learns about the data provenance or the query. Summarising, the research contributions of our approach are threefold. First of all, the proposed scheme ensures secure data provenance by providing confidentiality, integrity, non-repudiation, unforgeability and availability in the cloud environment. Second, proposed solution is capable of handling complex queries involving non-monotonic boolean expressions and range queries. Third, the system entities do not share any keys and the system is still able to operate without requiring re-encryption even if a compromised user (or auditor) is revoked.

1.3   Organistaion

The rest of this report is organised as follows: Section 2 lists down the security properties that a secure data provenance scheme should guarantee. Section 3 provides a discussion of existing data provenance schemes based on the security properties listed in Section 2. Section 4 describes the threat model. The proposed approach is described in Section 5. Section 6 focuses on the solution details. Section 7 provides a discussion about how to optimise performance overheads incurred by the proposed scheme. Finally, Section 8 concludes this paper and gives directions for the future work.

2   Security Properties of a Data Provenance Scheme

A data provenance scheme must fulfil the general data security properties in order to guarantee the trustworthiness. In the context of data provenance, the security properties are described as follows:

- **Confidentiality:** Data provenance of a sensitive piece of data (that is, the source data) may reveal some private information. Therefore, it is necessary to encrypt not only the source data but also the data provenance. Moreover, a query to and/or a response from the data provenance store may reveal some sensitive information. Thus, both the query and its response must be encrypted in order to guarantee confidentiality on the communication channel. Last but not least, if data provenance is stored in the outsourced environment such as the cloud then the data provenance scheme must guarantee that neither the stored information nor the query and response mechanism must reveal any sensitive information while storing data provenance or performing search operations.
- **Integrity:** The data provenance is immutable. Therefore, the integrity must be ensured by preventing any kind of unauthorised modifications in order to get the trustworthy data provenance. The integrity guarantees that data provenance cannot be modified during the transmission or on the storage server without being detected.

- **Unforgeability:** An adversary may forge data provenance of the existing source data with the fake data. The unforgeability refers that the source data is tightly coupled with its data provenance. In other words, an adversary cannot forge the fake data with existing data provenance (or vice versa) without being detected.
- **Non-Repudiation:** Once a user takes an action, as a consequence, the data provenance is generated. A user must not be able to deny once data provenance has been recorded. The non-repudiation ensures that the user cannot deny if he/she has taken any actions.
- **Availability:** The data provenance and its corresponding source data might be critical; therefore, it must available at any time from anywhere. For instance, the life-critical data of a patient is subject to high availability, considering emergency situations that can occur at any time. The availability of the data can be ensured by a public storage service such as provided by the cloud service provider.

3 Related Work

In the following subsections, we describe state-of-the-art data provenance schemes which can be categorised as the **general data provenance schemes** and the **secure data provenance schemes**. The schemes in the former category are designed without taking into consideration the security properties while the schemes in the latter category explicitly aim at providing the certain security properties.

3.1 General Data Provenance Schemes

Several systems have been proposed for managing data provenance. Provenance-Aware Storage Systems (PASS) [15] is a first storage system towards the automatic collection and maintenance of data provenance. PASS collects information flow and workflow details at the operating system level by intercepting system calls. However, PASS does not focus on security of data provenance. Open Provenance Model (OPM) [14] is a model that has been designed as a standard. In OPM version 1.1 [13], data provenance can be exchanged between systems. Moreover, it defines how to represent data provenance at very abstract level. The focus of OPM is standardisation, however, it does not take into account the security and privacy issues related to data provenance. Muniswamy-Reddy et al. [17, 16] explain how to introduce data provenance to a cloud storage server. They define a protocol to prevent forgeability between the data provenance and the source data. However, they leave the data provenance security as an open issue. Sar and Cao [19] propose *Lineage File System* that keeps record of data provenance of each file at the file system level. Unfortunately, they do not address the security and privacy aspects of the file system.

Buneman et al. [5][1] use the term *data provenance* to refer to the process of tracing and recording the origin of data and its movements between databases. Data provenance, as defined by [4], broadly refers to a description of the origins of a piece of data and the process by which it arrived in the database. They explain *why-provenance*, who

---

[1] This is only the scheme that follows data-oriented approach while rest of the schemes in this paper are based on process-oriented approach.

Table 1. Summary of data provenance schemes

Scheme	Year	Application Domain	Confidentiality				Integrity	Unforgeability	Non-Repudiation	Availability
			Provenance	Query	Response	Source Data				
Buneman et al. [5]	2001	Database System	-	-	-	-	-	-	-	-
Lineage File System [19]	2005	File System	No	No	No	No	No	No	No	-
PASS [15]	2006	Operating System	No	No	No	No	No	No	No	-
Tan et al. [20]	2006	SOA	Yes	-	-	-	Yes	Yes	Yes	-
OPM [14]	2008	-	-	-	-	-	-	-	-	-
Braun et al. [3]	2008	-	-	-	-	-	-	-	-	-
SPROV [10, 9]	2009	Operating System	Yes	-	-	No	Yes	Yes	Yes	-
Zhou et al. [21]	2009	Networks	No	-	-	-	Yes	-	Yes	-
ExSPAN [22]	2010	Networks	No	No	No	-	No	No	No	Yes
Muniswamy-Reddy and Seltzer [17]	2010	Cloud Storage	-	-	-	-	-	-	-	Yes
Muniswamy-Reddy et al. [16]	2010	Cloud Storage	No	No	No	No	No	Yes	No	Yes
Aldeco-Perez and Moreau [1]	2010	-	No	No	No	No	Yes	-	Yes	-
Lu et al. [12]	2010	Cloud Computing	Yes	-	-	Yes	Yes	Yes	Yes	Yes
PSecON [11]	2010	E-Science	Yes	-	-	Yes	Yes	Yes	Yes	Yes
Davidson et al. [6, 7]	2010 - 2011	-	-	-	-	-	-	-	-	-

'-' means not applicable

contributed to or why a tuple is in the output, and *where-provenance*, where does the a piece of data comes from. Unfortunately, they do not focus on the security of data provenance.

Zhou *et al.* [21] use the notion of data provenance to explain the existence of a network state. However, they do not address the security of data provenance. In EXtenSible Provenance Aware Networked systems (ExSPAN) [22], Zhou *et al.* extend [21] and propose ExSPAN which provides the support for queries and maintenance of the network provenance in a distributed environment. However, they leave the issue of protecting the confidentiality and authenticity of provenance information as open.

3.2   Secure Data Provenance Schemes

The Secure Provenance (SPROV) scheme [10,9] automatically collects data provenance at the application layer. It provides security assurances of confidentiality and integrity of the data provenance. In this scheme, confidentiality is ensured by employing state-of-the-art encryption techniques while integrity is preserved using the digital signature of the user who takes any actions. Each record in the data provenance includes the signed checksum of previous record in the chain. For speeding up the auditing, they have introduced the spiral chain where the auditors can skip verification of records wrote by the users they already trust. However, the SPROV scheme has some limitations. First, it does not provide confidentiality to the source data whose data provenance is being recorded. Second, it does not provide any mechanisms to query data provenance. Third, it assumes that secret keys are never revoked or compromised. Last but not least, it cannot be employed in the cloud as it assumes a trusted infrastructure in order to store data provenance.

Jung and Yeom [11] propose the Provenance Security from Origin up to Now (PSecOn) scheme for e-science, a cyber laboratory to collaborate and share scientific resources. In an e-science grid, researchers can ensure integrity of the scientific results and corresponding data provenance through the PSecOn scheme. The PSecOn scheme ensures e-science grid availability from anywhere at any time. When an object is created, updated or transferred from one grid to another then the corresponding data provenance is prepared automatically. Each e-science grid has its own public history pool that manages the signature on data provenance, signed with the private key of an e-science grid. The public history pool prevents repudiation of both the data sender and the data receiver. The PSecOn scheme encrypts the source data. It revokes the secret key of a user who is compromised. However, it does not provide any query-response mechanisms to search data provenance. The main drawback of PSecOn is its strong assumption of relying on a trusted infrastructure, restricting the possibility of managing data provenance in the cloud.

Lu *et al.* [12] introduce a scheme to manage data provenance in the cloud where data is shared among multiple users. Their scheme provides users access to the online data. To guarantee confidentiality and integrity, a user encrypts and signs the data while a cloud service provider receives and verifies the signature before storing that data. Once the data is in dispute, a cloud service provider can provide the anonymous access information to a trusting authority who uses the master secret key of the system to trace the real user. The shortcoming of this approach is that it only traces the user while it does not provide any details about how the data provenance is managed by the cloud service provider.

Aldeco-Perez and Moreau [1] ensure integrity of data provenance by providing concrete cryptographic constructs. They describe the information flow of an auditable provenance system which consists of four stages including recording provenance, storing provenance, querying provenance and analysing provenance graph in order to answer questions regarding execution of the entities within the system. They ensure integrity at two levels. The first level is when data provenance is recorded and stored while the second level is at the analysis stage. Unfortunately, they do not provide any details about how to provide confidentiality to data provenance.

Braun *et al.* [3] focus on security model of data provenance at the abstract level. They consider data provenance as a causality graph with annotations. They argue that the security of data provenance is different from the source data it describes. Therefore, each of these need different access controls. However, they do not address how to define and enforce these access controls. Tan *et al.* [20] discuss security issues related to a Service Oriented Architecture (SOA) based provenance system. They address the problem of accessing data provenance for auditors with different access privileges. As a possible solution, they suggest to restrain auditors by limiting the access to the results of a query using cryptographic techniques. However, there is no concrete solution. Davidson *et al.* [7] consider the privacy issue while accessing and searching data provenance. In [6], Davidson *et al.* formalise the notion of privacy and focus on a mathematical model for solving privacy-preserving view as a result of query by an auditor. However, their approach is theoretic and there is no concrete construction for addressing security.

Table 1 summarises existing data provenance schemes based on the security properties listed in Section 2. Currently, there is not a single data provenance scheme that could guarantee all the security properties listed in Section 2.

4 Threat Model

This section describes the system entities involved, potential adversaries and possible attacks. The proposed system may include following entities:

- **User:** A User is an individual who takes action on the source data and generates data provenance. It is managed in the trusted environment. In the healthcare scenario, medical staff members, such as doctor and lab assistant, are Users.
- **Auditor:** An Auditor is the one who audits actions taken by a User. An Auditor also verifies data provenance up to the origin and identifies who took what action on the source data. An auditor may be an investigator or a regular quality assurance checker to check processes within an organisation. It is managed in the trusted environment.
- **Cloud Service Provider (CSP):** A CSP is responsible for managing the source data and its corresponding data provenance in the cloud environment. It is assumed that a CSP is honest-but-curious, means it is honest to follow the protocol for performing required actions but curious to deduce stored or exchanged data provenance and the source data. The CSP guarantees the availability of data provenance store from anywhere at any time.

– **Trusted Key Management Authority (KMA):** The KMA is fully trusted and responsible for generating and revoking the cryptographic keys involved. For each authorised entity described above, the KMA generates and transmits the keys securely. The KMA requires less resource and less management efforts. Since a very limited amount of data needs to be protected, securing the KMA is much easier and it can be kept offline most of the time.

The proposed scheme assumes that a CSP will not mount active attacks such as modifying the exchanged messages, message flow and the stored data without being detected. The main goals of an adversary is to gain information from the data provenance record about the actions performed, the provenance chain, and modifying existing data provenance entries.

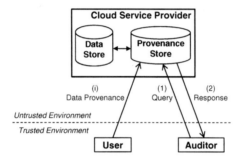

Fig. 1. An abstract architecture of the proposed scheme

5   The Proposed Approach

The proposed scheme provides the support for storing and searching data provenance in the cloud environment. The proposed scheme aims at providing the security properties listed in Section 2. In the proposed scheme, a CSP manages a Provenance Store to store data provenance. Moreover, the proposed scheme provides the support for storing the source data corresponding to the data provenance. The source data is stored in the Data Store which is also managed by a CSP. The CSP is in the untrusted environment while both the User and the Auditor are in the trusted environment. Figure 1 shows an abstract architecture of the proposed scheme. In the proposed scheme, after a User has taken an action on the source data, he/she (i) sends the corresponding data provenance to the Provenance Store. An Auditor may (1) send a query to the Provenance Store and as a result he/she (2) obtains the Response.

5.1   Structure of a Data Provenance Entry

This subsection describes how data provenance may look like. Typically, a provenance record may include, but not limited to, the following fields:

Table 2. Representation of data provenance

Revision	Date	Time	User ID	Action				Previous Revision	Hash	Signature
				Name	Reason	Description	Location			
1	01-01-08	14:40:30	Alice	Create	Clinic Visit	Medical Report	Trento	0	X-bits	Y-bits
2	02-01-08	09:30:00	Bob	Append	Lab Visit	Blood Test	Rovereto	1	X-bits	Y-bits
⋮	⋮	⋮	⋮	⋮	⋮	⋮	⋮	⋮	⋮	⋮

Typically, X and Y may be of size 128, 512 or more.

– *Revision:* indicates the version number.
– *Date and time:* indicating when the action was taken.
– *User ID:* who took the action.
– *Action:* provides the details of action taken on the source data. It is divided into four parts: *Name, Reason, Description* and *Location. Name* describes what action was taken. *Reason* states why the action was taken. *Description* gives the additional information that may include how the action was taken. *Location* indicates where the action was taken.
– *Previous Revision:* indicates the version number of the previous action taken on the same source data.
– *Hash:* of the current source data after the action has been taken. This guarantees the unforgeability.
– *Signature:* is obtained after signing the hash of the all above fields with the private key of the User who took the action. This ensures the integrity and non-repudiation.

Once a User takes an action, the corresponding data provenance entry is sent to the Provenance Store. Table 2 illustrate how a typical data provenance entry looks like. The first entry in Table 2 has revision 1 with date 01-01-08 and time 14:40:30 hrs where action was taken by Alice who created a medical report when a patient visited her clinic located in Trento. The previous revision of this data provenance is 0 since it is the first entry. Bob adds the details of the blood test after that patient has visited his lab in Rovereto on 02-01-08 at 09:30:00 hrs. The previous revision corresponds to 1 as Bob is appending the existing medical report. Each entry includes the hash of the corresponding source data and signatures of Alice and Bob on entry 1 and 2, respectively.

In order to support the search, for an Auditor, on the encrypted data provenance stored in the Provenance Store, each field of the data provenance entry is transformed in to string or numerical attributes. One string attribute represents a single element while a numerical attribute of size n bits represents n elements. In the proposed scheme, we consider that the maximum revision number possible is represented by a numerical attribute of size m. For the ease of understanding, let us assume that the value of m is 4. The first entry in Table 2 contains the revision with value 1, which is 0001 in a 4-bit representation. This can be transformed in to 4 elements, i.e., $0***$, $*0**$, $**0*$ and $***1$. The date can be considered as 3 numerical attributes, the first numerical attribute to represent day in 5 bits, the second numerical attribute to represent month in 4 bits and the third numerical attribute to represent year in 7 bits. Similarly, the time can be considered as 3 numerical attributes, the first numerical attribute to represent hour in 5 bits, the second numerical attribute to represent minute in 6 bits and the third numerical attribute to represent second in 6 bits. The user ID is a string attribute. Each sub-field of action can be treated as a string attribute. The previous revision is again a numerical attribute of size m. In the proposed scheme, we omit the search support for the hash and the signature fields as we assume that an Auditor cannot query based on these fields as these are just large numbers of size X and Y bits, respectively. Typically, one can have both the User and the Auditor roles simultaneously.

The source data is stored in the Data Store managed by the CSP. For each revision in the Provenance Store, there is a corresponding data item in the Data Store. In other words, the Data Store maintains a table containing two columns: one column to keep the revision while the other to store the source data item after the action has been taken.

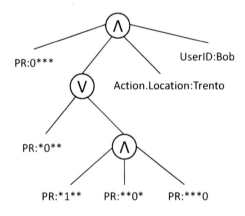

Fig. 2. Query representation

5.2 Query Representation

This section provides an informal description of the query representation used in the proposed scheme. To represent the query, we use the tree structure similar to one used in [2]. The tree structure of the query allows an Auditor to express conjunctions and disjunctions of equalities and inequalities. Internal nodes of the tree represent AND and OR gates while leaf nodes represent the values of conditional predicates. The tree employs the representation of *bag of bits* in order to support comparison between numerical values. Let us consider that an Auditor sends the following query: search all actions taken by Bob in Trento with previous revision (PR) between 1 to 4. Alternatively, this query can be written as follows: $UserID = Bob$ AND $Action.Location = Trento$ AND $PR \geq 1$ AND $PR \leq 4$. The query is illustrated in Figure 2.

6 Solution Details

The main idea is to perform encryption for providing confidentiality to the data provenance both on the communication channel and in the cloud. In order to search the data provenance, an Auditor sends a query that is also encrypted. In fact, the search is performed in an encrypted manner, which is based on the Searchable Data Encryption (SDE) proposed by Dong *et al.* [8]. The SDE scheme allows an untrusted server to perform search on the encrypted data without revealing information about the data provenance or the query. The advantage of this scheme is the multi-user support without requiring any key sharing between Auditors/Users. In other words, each Auditor or User has a unique set of keys. The data provenance encrypted by a User can be searched and decrypted by an authorised Auditor. However, the SDE scheme in [8] only allows an Auditor to perform query containing comparison based on equalities. For supporting complex queries, we extend the SDE scheme to handle complex boolean expressions such as non-conjunctive and range queries in the multi-user settings.

In addition to providing support for search on the encrypted data provenance, each entry of the data provenance is encrypted using Proxy Encryption (PE) scheme proposed in [8]. In other words, an Auditor performs search on the encrypted data provenance using the extended version of the SDE scheme while the searched data corresponding to the query is accessed by the PE scheme. Furthermore, the source data corresponding to the data provenance is also encrypted using the PE scheme. The proposed solution guarantees all the security properties listed in Table 1 that the existing research on data provenance lacks.

In general, there are three main phases in the data provenance life cycle: the first phase is the **storing data provenance** in to the Provenance Store; the second phase is the **searching data provenance** when an Auditor sends a query; and the third phase is the **accessing data provenance**. In the following, we provide the details of algorithms involved in each phase, where the SDE and the PE schemes are used in each phase.

6.1 Intialisation

In this phase, the proposed scheme is intialised for generating the required keying material for all involved entities in the system.

- $Init(1^k)$: The Trusted KMA takes as input the security parameter 1^k and outputs two prime numbers p, q such that q divides $p - 1$, a cyclic group $\mathbb{G}$ with a generator g such that $\mathbb{G}$ is the unique order q subgroup of $\mathbb{Z}_p^*$. It chooses $x \xleftarrow{R} \mathbb{Z}_q^*$ and computes $h = g^x$. Next, it chooses a collision-resistant hash function H, a pseudorandom function f and a random key s for f. Finally it publicises the public parameters $Params = (\mathbb{G}, g, q, h, H, f)$ and keeps securely the master secret key $MSK = (x, s)$.
- $KeyGen(MSK, i)$: For each User (or Auditor) i, the Trusted KMA chooses $x_{i1} \xleftarrow{R} \mathbb{Z}_q^*$ and computes $x_{i2} = x - x_{i1}$. It securely transmits $K_{u_i} = (x_{i1}, s)$ to the User (or Auditor) i and $K_{s_i} = (i, x_{i2})$ to the CSP which inserts K_{s_i} in the Key Store, that is, $K_S = K_S \cup K_{s_i}$.[2]

6.2 Storing Data Provenance

During this phase, a User takes an action and creates a data provenance entry and the source data which are encrypted using the SDE and PE schemes. For both the SDE and

---

[2] The Key Store is initialised as $K_S = \Phi$.

PE schemes, the first round of encryption is performed by the User while the Second round of encryption is performed by the CSP. After this phase, the data provenance entry is stored in the Provenance Store while the source data is stored in the Data Store.

- $Hash(D)$: The User calculates hash over the source data D and populates the hash field of the data provenance entry with the calculated value.
- $Signature(e, K_{u_i})$: The User i calculates a hash $H(e)$ over the all fields (except the signature) in a data provenance entry e. Then, the User populates the signature field of the data provenance entry with the value calculated as follows: $g^{-x_{i1}} H(e)$.
- $User\text{-}SDE(m, K_{u_i})$: The User encrypts each element m of the fields (except the hash and the signature) of the data provenance entry in order to support encrypted search. The User chooses $r \xleftarrow{R} \mathbb{Z}_q^*$ and computes $c_i^*(m) = (\hat{c}_1, \hat{c}_2, \hat{c}_3)$ where $\hat{c}_1 = g^{r+\sigma}, \sigma = f_s(m), \hat{c}_2 = \hat{c}_1^{x_{i1}}, \hat{c}_3 = H(h^r)$. The User transmits $c_i^*(m)$ to the CSP.
- $User\text{-}PE(m, D, K_{u_i})$: The User encrypts each element m of the fields (except the hash and the signature) of the data provenance entry and the source data D. The User chooses $r \xleftarrow{R} \mathbb{Z}_q^*$ and outputs the ciphertexts $PE_i^*(m) = (g^r, g^{rx_{i1}} m)$ and $PE_i^*(D) = (g^r, g^{rx_{i1}} D)$, which are sent to the CSP.
- $Server\text{-}SDE(i, c_i^*(m), K_{s_i})$: The CSP retrieves the key K_{s_i} corresponding to the User i from the Key Store. Each User encrypted element $c_i^*(m)$ is re-encrypted to $c(m) = (c_1, c_2)$, where $c_1 = (\hat{c}_1)^{x_{i2}} \cdot \hat{c}_2 = \hat{c}_1^{x_{i1}+x_{i2}} = (g^{r+\sigma})^x = h^{r+\sigma}$ and $c_2 = \hat{c}_3 = H(h^r)$. The re-encrypted entry $c(e)$ (where each $c(m) \in c(e)$) of data provenance is stored in the Provenance Store.
- $Server\text{-}PE(i, PE_i^*(m), PE_i^*(D), K_{s_i})$: The CSP retrieves the key K_{s_i} corresponding to the User i from the Key Store. Each User encrypted element $PE_i^*(m)$ is re-encrypted to $PE(m) = (p_1, p_2)$, where $p_1 = g^r$ and $p_2 = (g^r)^{x_{i2}} g^{rx_{i1}} m = g^{r(x_{i1}+x_{i2})} m = g^{rx} m$. Similarly, the $PE_i^*(D)$ is re-encrypted to $PE(D)$. Finally, the ciphertexts $PE(e)$ (where $PE(m) \in PE(e)$) and $PE(D)$ are sent to and stored[3] in the Provenance Store and the Data Store, respectively.

6.3 Searching Data Provenance

During this phase, an Auditor encrypts the search query and then sends the search query to the CSP. The CSP performs the encrypted matching against data provenance entires in the Provenance Store.

- $Auditor\text{-}Query\text{-}Enc(Q, K_{u_j})$: An Auditor transforms the query in to a tree structure Q, as shown in Figure 2. The tree structure Q denotes a set of string and numerical comparisons. Each non-leaf node a' in Q represents a threshold gate with the threshold value $k_{a'}$ denoting the number of its children subtrees that must be satisfied where a' has total $c_{a'}$ children subtrees, i.e. $1 \leq k_{a'} \leq c_{a'}$. If $k_{a'} = 1$, the threshold gate is an OR and if $k_{a'} = c_{a'}$, the threshold gate is an AND. Each leaf node a represents either a string comparison or subpart of a numerical comparison (because one numerical comparison of size n bits is represented by n leaf

---

[3] In the CSP, each entry $c(e)$ of the data provenance corresponds with the ciphertexts $PE(e)$ and $PE(D)$.

nodes at the most) with a threshold value $k_a = 1$. For every leaf node $a \in Q$, the Auditor chooses $r \xleftarrow{R} \mathbb{Z}_q^*$ and computes trapdoor $T_j(a) = (t_1, t_2)$ where $t_1 = g^{-r} g^{\sigma}$ and $t_2 = h^r g^{-x_{j1}r} g^{x_{j1}\sigma} = g^{x_{j2}r} g^{x_{j1}\sigma}$, where $\sigma = f_s(a)$. The Auditor encrypts all leaf nodes in Q and sends the encrypted tree structure $T_j^*(Q)$ to the CSP.

- *Server-Search*$(j, T_j^*(Q), K_{s_j}, c(e))$: The CSP receives the encrypted tree structure $T_j^*(Q)$. Next, it it retrieves the key K_{s_j} corresponding to the Auditor j and the data provenance entries. For each encrypted entry $c(e)$, the CSP runs a recursive algorithm starting from the root node of $T_j^*(Q)$. For each non-leaf node, it checks if the number of children that are satisfied is greater than or equal to the threshold value of the node. If so, the node is marked as satisfied. For each encrypted leaf node $T_j^*(a) \in T_j^*(Q)$, there may exist a corresponding encrypted element $c(m) \in c(e)$. In order to perform this check, it computes $T = t_1^{x_{j2}} \cdot t_2 = g^{x\sigma}$ and tests if $c_2 \overset{?}{=} H(c_1.T^{-1})$. If so, the leaf node is marked as satisfied. After running the recursive algorithm, if the root node of the encrypted tree structure $T_j^*(Q)$ is marked as satisfied then the entry $c(e)$ is marked as matched. This algorithm is performed for each encrypted entry $c(e)$ in the Provenance Store and it finds sets of ciphertexts $PE(e)$ and $PE(D)$ corresponding to the matched entries.

6.4   Accessing Data Provenance

During this phase, the data provenance entries can be accessed and then ultimately be verified by the Auditor. First, the CSP performs one round of decryption for sets of ciphertexts found during the search. The Auditor performs the second round of decryption to access data provenance and its corresponding source data. Furthermore, an Auditor gets the verification key from the CSP in order to verify the signature on the data provenance entries.

- *Server-Pre-Dec*$(j, PE(e), PE(D), K_{s_j})$: The CSP retrieves the key K_{s_j} corresponding to the Auditor j from the Key Store. Each encrypted element $PE(m) \in PE(e)$ is pre-decrypted by the CSP as $PE_j(m) = (\hat{p}_1, \hat{p}_2)$, where $\hat{p}_1 = g^r$ and $\hat{p}_2 = g^{rx}m$ $\cdot (g^r)^{-x_{j2}} = g^{r(x-x_{j2})}m = g^{rx_{j1}}m$. Similarly, $PE(D)$ is pre-decrypted by the CSP as $PE_j(D)$. Finally, the ciphertexts $PE_j(e)$ and $PE_j(D)$ are sent to the Auditor.
- *Auditor-Dec*$(PE_j(e)), PE_j(D)), K_{u_j})$: Finally, the Auditor decrypts the ciphertext $PE_j(m) \in PE_j(e)$ as follows: $\hat{p}_2 \cdot \hat{p}_1^{-x_{j1}} = g^{rx_{j1}}m \cdot g^{-rx_{j1}} = m$. Similarly, the source data D is retrieved from $PE_j(D)$).
- *Get-Verification-Key*(i) : In the proposed solution, an Auditor may verify the signature by first obtaining the verification key of the User who took the action. This algorithm is run by the CSP. It takes an input the User ID i. For calculating the verification key, the CSP first obtains the key $K_{s_i} = (i, x_{i2})$ corresponding to the User i and then calculates the verification key as follows: $h \cdot g^{-x_{i2}} = g^x \cdot g^{-x_{i2}} = g^{x-x_{i2}} = g^{x_{i1}}$.
- *Verify-Signature-Key*$(e, g^{-x_{i1}} H(e'), g^{x_{i1}})$: Given the signature $g^{-x_{i1}} H(e')$ over the data provenance entry e and the verification key $g^{x_{i1}}$, an Auditor can verify the signature first by calculating $g^{-x_{i1}} H(e') g^{x_{i1}} = H(e')$. Next, an Auditor calculates the hash over the data provenance entry e as $H(e)$. Finally, an Auditor checks if

$H(e) \stackrel{?}{=} H(e')$. If so, the signature verification is successful and this algorithm returns *true* and *false* otherwise.

6.5   Revocation

In the proposed solution, it is possible to revoke a compromised User (or Auditor). This is accomplished by the CSP.

- *Revoke*(*i*) Given the User (or Auditor) *i*, the CSP removes the corresponding key K_{S_i} from the Key Store as $K_S = K_S \setminus K_{S_i}$. Therefore, the CSP needs to check the revocation of a User or an Auditor before invoking any actions including storing, searching and accessing the data provenance.

7   Discussion

This section provides a discussion about how to optimise the storage and performance overheads incurred by the proposed scheme.

7.1   Storage Optimisation

The storage can be optimised if the source data changes are stored as difference (as is done in any subversion system) instead of managing a complete source data item against each revision. In other words, the complete source data item is stored against the first revision while for the subsequent revisions, only the changes are stored.

7.2   Performance Optimisation

In order to improve the search performance, the indexing and partitioning of the data provenance can be done. However, this is subject to the future work. Moreover, the performance at the Auditor level can be improved by maintaining a list of verification keys of the Users who are taking actions very frequently instead of interacting each time with the CSP.

8   Conclusion and Future Directions

This paper has investigated the problem of securing provenance and presented a proposed scheme that supports encrypted search while protecting confidentiality of data provenance stored in the cloud, given the assumption that the CSP is honest-but-curious. The main advantage of our proposed scheme is that neither an adversary nor a cloud service provider learns about the data provenance or the query. The proposed solution is capable of handling complex queries involving non-monotonic boolean expressions and range queries. Finally, the system entities do not share any keys and even if a compromised User (or Auditor) is revoked, the system is still able to perform its operations without requiring re-encryption.

As future research directions, the proposed solution will be formalised in more rigorous terms to prove its security features. Moreover, a prototype would be developed for estimating the overhead incurred by the cryptographic operations of the proposed scheme. Other long-term research goals are 1) how to apply the scheme in the distributed settings 2) to investigate how to make such architecture more efficient in terms of query-response time without compromising the security properties.

Acknowledgment. The work of the first and third authors is supported by the EU FP7 programme, Research Grant 257063 (project Endorse).

References

1. Aldeco-Pérez, R., Moreau, L.: Securing Provenance-Based Audits. In: McGuinness, D.L., Michaelis, J.R., Moreau, L. (eds.) IPAW 2010. LNCS, vol. 6378, pp. 148–164. Springer, Heidelberg (2010)
2. Bethencourt, J., Sahai, A., Waters, B.: Ciphertext-policy attribute-based encryption. In: IEEE Symposium on Security and Privacy, pp. 321–334. IEEE Computer Society (2007)
3. Braun, U., Shinnar, A., Seltzer, M.: Securing provenance. In: Proceedings of the 3rd Conference on Hot Topics in Security, pp. 4:1–4:5. USENIX Association, Berkeley (2008)
4. Buneman, P., Khanna, S., Tan, W.-C.: Data Provenance: Some Basic Issues. In: Kapoor, S., Prasad, S. (eds.) FST TCS 2000. LNCS, vol. 1974, pp. 87–93. Springer, Heidelberg (2000)
5. Buneman, P., Khanna, S., Tan, W.-C.: Why and Where: A Characterization of Data Provenance. In: Van den Bussche, J., Vianu, V. (eds.) ICDT 2001. LNCS, vol. 1973, pp. 316–330. Springer, Heidelberg (2000)
6. Davidson, S.B., Khanna, S., Roy, S., Boulakia, S.C.: Privacy issues in scientific workflow provenance. In: Proceedings of the 1st International Workshop on Workflow Approaches to New Data-centric Science, Wands 2010, pp. 3:1–3:6. ACM, New York (2010)
7. Davidson, S.B., Khanna, S., Roy, S., Stoyanovich, J., Tannen, V., Chen, Y.: On provenance and privacy. In: Proceedings of the 14th International Conference on Database Theory, ICDT 2011, pp. 3–10. ACM, New York (2011)
8. Dong, C., Russello, G., Dulay, N.: Shared and searchable encrypted data for untrusted servers. J. Comput. Secur. 19, 367–397 (2011)
9. Hasan, R., Sion, R., Winslett, M.: The case of the fake picasso: preventing history forgery with secure provenance. In: Proccedings of the 7th Conference on File and Storage Technologies, pp. 1–14. USENIX Association, Berkeley (2009)
10. Hasan, R., Sion, R., Winslett, M.: Preventing history forgery with secure provenance. Trans. Storage 5, 12:1–12:43 (2009)
11. Jung, I.Y., Yeom, H.Y.: Provenance security guarantee from origin up to now in the e-science environment. Journal of Systems Architecture (2010) (in press, corrected proof)
12. Lu, R., Lin, X., Liang, X., Shen, X.: Secure provenance: the essential of bread and butter of data forensics in cloud computing. In: Proceedings of the 5th ACM Symposium on Information, Computer and Communications Security, ASIACCS 2010, pp. 282–292. ACM, New York (2010)
13. Moreau, L., Clifford, B., Freire, J., Futrelle, J., Gil, Y., Groth, P., Kwasnikowska, N., Miles, S., Missier, P., Myers, J., Plale, B., Simmhan, Y., Stephan, E., Van den Bussche, J.: The open provenance model core specification (v1.1). In: Future Generation Computer Systems (2010) (in press)

14. Moreau, L., Freire, J., Futrelle, J., McGrath, R.E., Myers, J., Paulson, P.: The Open Provenance Model: An Overview. In: Freire, J., Koop, D., Moreau, L. (eds.) IPAW 2008. LNCS, vol. 5272, pp. 323–326. Springer, Heidelberg (2008)
15. Muniswamy-Reddy, K.-K., Holland, D.A., Braun, U., Seltzer, M.: Provenance-aware storage systems. In: Proceedings of the Annual Conference on USENIX 2006 Annual Technical Conference, pp. 4–4. USENIX Association, Berkeley (2006)
16. Muniswamy-Reddy, K.-K., Macko, P., Seltzer, M.: Provenance for the cloud. In: Proceedings of the 8th USENIX Conference on File and Storage Technologies, pp. 14–15. USENIX Association, Berkeley (2010)
17. Muniswamy-Reddy, K.-K., Seltzer, M.: Provenance as first class cloud data. SIGOPS Oper. Syst. Rev. 43, 11–16 (2010)
18. Ram, S., Liu, J.: Understanding the Semantics of Data Provenance to Support Active Conceptual Modeling. In: Chen, P.P., Wong, L.Y. (eds.) ACM-L 2006. LNCS, vol. 4512, pp. 17–29. Springer, Heidelberg (2007)
19. Sar, C., Cao, P.: Lineage file system (2005),
    http://theory.stanford.edu/~cao/lineage
20. Tan, V., Groth, P., Miles, S., Jiang, S., Munroe, S., Tsasakou, S., Moreau, L.: Security Issues in a SOA-Based Provenance System. In: Moreau, L., Foster, I. (eds.) IPAW 2006. LNCS, vol. 4145, pp. 203–211. Springer, Heidelberg (2006)
21. Zhou, W., Mao, Y., Loo, B.T., Abadi, M.: Unified declarative platform for secure netwoked information systems. In: Proceedings of the 2009 IEEE International Conference on Data Engineering, pp. 150–161. IEEE Computer Society, Washington, DC (2009)
22. Zhou, W., Sherr, M., Tao, T., Li, X., Loo, B.T., Mao, Y.: Efficient querying and maintenance of network provenance at internet-scale. In: Proceedings of the 2010 International Conference on Management of Data, SIGMOD 2010, pp. 615–626. ACM, New York (2010)

Author Index